Globale Politische Ökonomie

Ralf J. Leiteritz

National Economic Identity and Capital Mobility

State-Business Relations in Latin America

Springer VS

Ralf J. Leiteritz
Universidad del Rosario,
Bogotá, Colombia

Gedruckt mit freundlicher Unterstützung der Universidad del Rosario, Bogotá, Colombia.

UNIVERSIDAD DEL ROSARIO

ISBN 978-3-531-18528-6 ISBN 978-3-531-19094-5 (eBook)
DOI 10.1007/978-3-531-19094-5

The Deutsche Nationalbibliothek lists this publication in the Deutsche Nationalbibliografie; detailed bibliographic data are available in the Internet at http://dnb.d-nb.de.

Springer VS

Cover design: KünkelLopka GmbH, Heidelberg

Printed on acid-free paper

Springer VS is a brand of Springer DE. Springer DE is part of Springer Science+Business Media
www.springer-vs.de

Table of Content

List of Figures and Tables

Figures

Tables

Abstract

Financial liberalization programs have been adopted by many countries in Latin America during the past twenty years. Opening the economy to inflows and outflows of capital – 'opening the capital account' – has been a key part of these programs. While some governments have sustained the opening of their capital account over decades, others have reversed course after only a short time. The existing literature has focused on the adoption of capital account liberalization, but has neglected to consider the reasons for its durability or fragility. This book addresses the question of why different countries have sustained their opening of the capital account to different degrees and for different periods.

The central argument of the book is that the *sustainability* of capital account openness is inextricably linked to national economic identity. National economy identity encompasses (i) domestic informal institutions and (ii) a concomitant set of state-business relations. By informal institutions I refer to the shared understandings or rules among a country's policymaking and business elites about legitimate economic policies. Whether capital account openness is sustained over time depends on the extent of domestic agreement as to whether capital controls continue to be perceived as effective and legitimate, or whether they have lost their effectiveness and legitimacy as instruments of macroeconomic policymaking.

Informal institutions legitimizing or delegitimizing controls on international capital movements are closely related to specific state-business relations. Capital account openness is unlikely to be sustained over time if small- and medium-sized actors within the export-oriented sector of the economy – concerned about a stable and competitive exchange rate – preserve their leverage over national policymaking. Conversely, capital account openness tends to become a durable policy if 'big business' actors such as multinational corporations and domestic conglomerates benefitting from unfettered capital mobility and largely unaffected by exchange-rate fluctuation dominate state-business relations.

I utilize my theoretical framework to explain capital account policy in two Latin American countries during the last two decades where openness has either been sustained (Peru), or partially reversed after the initial opening (Colombia). I show that the different trajectory of both countries in terms of capital account policy is based on a different nature of national economic identity.

Scholars interested in explaining the sustainability of neoliberal economic reforms ignore the role of national economic identity at their peril. Paying heed to the change and continuity of shared understandings about legitimate economic policies, in conjunction with the configuration of state-business relations, is key to understanding the durability or fragility of economic reforms. In order to become institutionalized in the domestic political economy, free-market policies must encounter a social *and* material context in which alternative development strategies have lost their legitimacy.

Acknowledgements

This book had a long way coming into fruition. It is based on my PhD dissertation which I submitted in 2010 to the Department of International Relations at the London School of Economics and Political Science. Various people and institutions deserve credit for helping me to get through the extended process of researching and writing the dissertation. First of all, even though I am not allowed to label her a co-author, my wife Eulalia Sanín for all practical purposes has had a highly substantial input. Not only did she read and – with the trained eyes of an economist and management consultant – comment on innumerable drafts of each chapter, but perhaps even more importantly has been an infallible source of emotional support and encouragement. I therefore wish to dedicate this book to her. It is as much mine as hers.

The following people have helped me with specific comments and suggestions in order to sharpen my argument and strive towards a clearer, somewhat less Teutonic writing style: my dissertation supervisors, Robert Wade and Ken Shadlen, my dissertation examiners, Timothy Sinclair and Lauren Phillips, Edward Davey, Markus Lederer and Axel Hülsemeyer for very useful and detailed comments, Liliana Galvis for excellent research assistance, the two anonymous reviewers of the initial manuscript based on my PhD dissertation, and my former colleagues at the Department of Political Science at the Universidad de los Andes in Bogotá. Finally, my thanks go to the members of the "Constructivist Political Economy" group, especially Rawi Abdelal, Mark Blyth, and Craig Parsons, who convened for a workshop at Harvard University in February 2005. Despite their best efforts, I have not fully converted to their church, though.

In addition, I wish to thank the following institutions for financial support: my current employer, the Universidad del Rosario in Bogotá for enabling the publication of this book, the Crisis States Research Programme at the LSE for supporting my fieldwork in Washington, DC in 2003, and the Central Research Fund of the University of London and the Society for Latin American Studies in the UK for supporting my fieldwork in Latin America in 2004–5. Many thanks to you all!

Ralf J. Leiteritz
Bogotá, December 2011

Chapter 1: Introduction

1.1 The Research Question: The Sustainability of Open Capital Accounts

Economic globalization, it is often said, moves all countries in the same policy direction, towards free markets. But if so, why do we still observe so much national variation in economic institutions and policies? If developing countries are the weakest players in the game, why do some of them – not necessarily the biggest – resist the trend towards global convergence, whether by not instituting free-market reforms in the first place or by pulling back after having put them in place? *Why are neoliberal economic policy choices durable in certain countries but not in others?*

I seek to answer these general questions with respect to one specific public policy: government intervention in the international flow of capital. National governments traditionally possess a variety of legal instruments to limit the entry and departure of financial flows across their borders. International capital flows are affected by the administrative restrictions recorded on the capital account of the balance of payments. Measuring the openness or closedness of the capital account provides an important indicator for government priorities vis-à-vis macroeconomic policymaking. Capital account openness signals outward-oriented economic objectives and an explicit commitment to achieve integration into global capital markets as the basis for domestic investment and growth. In contrast, capital account closedness signals inward-oriented economic objectives, giving priority to domestic sources of finance, and preserving government autonomy over monetary policy. As a result, exploring the evolution of capital account policy provides important insights into the political priorities for macroeconomic policymaking in an age of economic globalization.

Despite national prerogatives over capital account policy, some general trends at the international level can be discerned over time. Stringent limits on capital mobility were the rule in the history of the international monetary system during the twentieth century. Most often, short-lived episodes of capital freedom were succeeded by longer periods of restrictions in the aftermath of financial crashes (Frieden 2006; Eichengreen 2008). Historically, free capital mobility has had several comings and an at least equal number of reversals. Hence, there is no in-built guarantee that the current era of capital mobility is bound to last (Flandreau et al. 2003).

The political ascent of Keynesian economic thinking after the Great Depression provided the intellectual background for one of the pillars of the Post-World War II monetary system: extensive controls on short-term capital flows in the context of the Bretton Woods regime (Ruggie 1983; Eichengreen 1996). However, at the beginning of the 1990s, it seemed as if the pendulum had turned decidedly in favor of capital freedom. An increasing number of developing countries followed the example of the industrial world and abolished administrative restrictions on international capital flows. Global finance was the poster-child for demonstrating the unifying force of economic globalization, especially for developing countries. Once the floodgates for international capital flows opened, there was, supposedly, no turning back. The removal of all remaining legal restrictions on international capital movements was merely a matter of time. Powerful structural forces and political coalitions at the national and international level had formed to see to their end. Capital account openness appeared to be here to stay.

Latin America has been the favorite laboratory for such predictions. Having learned the 'hard lessons' from the 1980s debt crisis, countries embraced the blessings of free trade and free capital in the 1990s. The end of the Cold War and the concomitant change of the development model towards neoliberalism provided the overall context for capital account liberalization. Despite its exclusion from the original list of policy commandments contained in the 'Washington Consensus' (Williamson 2003), the opening of the capital account was an integral part of virtually all economic reform programs in Latin America during the late 1980s and early 1990s.[1]

Yet after two decades of neoliberal economic reforms, capital account policy has reflected a surprising degree of variation. Even though the overall level of capital account openness has increased in virtually all regions of the developing world during the past twenty years, capital account liberalization has not proved sustainable everywhere. Some countries still follow the free-market teachings to the letter and have maintained or even increased their capital account openness during the past twenty years. In contrast, other countries have developed second thoughts about the neoliberal reform agenda, retracting or abolishing altogether at least some of the economic policies they had embraced earlier. This book explores the variation of national capital account policy amidst the global trend towards greater capital account openness. It focuses on the Latin American region, which together with Eastern Europe was the leading capital account liberalizer in the developing world during the 1990s. It analyzes the different paths of capital account policy that Latin American countries have pursued after the initial adoption of open capital accounts.

Rather than focusing on the well-known 'globalization rebels' condemning the underlying ideology and the malignant consequences of the 'Washington Consensus' (think of Venezuela under President Hugo Chávez), I am interested in the contrast between countries which belong to the group of 'capital mobility enthusiasts' and those which belong to the group of 'capital mobility laggards'. What factors determine to which group a country belongs in the medium and long run? Applied to capital account policy, the puzzle motivating my research agenda is *why certain countries have pursued a consistently open capital account policy, whereas other countries have been more reluctant to embrace capital mobility.*

Possible explanations in the political science literature point to international forces that shape domestic policymaking – so-called 'outside-in' explanations. One strand argues that pressure from international financial organizations such as the International Monetary Fund (IMF), using coercive and persuasive instruments in order to spread and embed the emerging norm of capital account openness, lies behind domestic capital account policy.

1 In his path-breaking article from 1990 Williamson wrote that "there is relatively little support for the notion that liberalization of international capital flows is a priority objective for a country that should be a capital importer and ought to be retaining its own savings for domestic investment" (Williamson 1990: 14).

Another approach emphasizes the importance of the epistemic community of neoliberal economists that has come to dominate economic policymaking in Latin America.

On the other hand, 'inside-out' explanations of capital account policy highlight the role of domestic political and economic institutions such as the partisanship of the executive, the fragmentation of the legislative, the exchange-rate regime, or the independence of the Central Bank as crucial variables. Complementing these approaches, I point to the role of *national economic identity* as a crucial factor underlying capital account policy. First, national economic identity encompasses *informal institutions* which I define as socially shared understandings or rules among a country's policymaking and economic elites[2] about legitimate economic policies. I argue that the transformation of pre-liberalization informal institutions during the process of economic opening is a key element behind the durability of capital account openness in Latin America. Second, national economic identity is inextricably linked to a specific set of *state-business relations* in which economic actors benefitting from unfettered capital mobility and who are largely unaffected by exchange-rate fluctuations dominate the interactions between the private sector and the national government.

This introductory chapter describes the overall context for the global trend towards greater capital account openness starting at the end of the twentieth century. At the same time, it highlights the variation of capital account policies between countries, with a particular focus on the Latin American region, amidst the global convergence around higher capital account openness. The chapter briefly reviews the state of the literature explaining capital account policy from distinct analytical perspectives. It suggests that domestic informal institutions constitute a crucial factor which determines the durability or fragility of open capital accounts. The chapter illustrates the explanatory power of domestic informal institutions and the nature of state-business relations with regard to the different trajectories of capital account policy in Peru and Colombia after 1990. The chapter also justifies the chosen qualitative methodology based on a comparative case study design in conjunction with process-tracing against the limits of large-N, quantitative studies. Finally, it provides an overview of the organization of the book.

1.2 The International Campaign for Open Capital Accounts

Despite its arcane technical character allegedly only accessible to economists, capital account policy has genuine political salience. Indeed, the history of the international monetary system during the twentieth century reflects the 'battle of ideas' between the supporters of capital freedom and its critics (Abdelal 2007). The openness or closedness of the capital account became a bone of contention well beyond academic discussions among economists. Whether a country was open or closed to international capital flows was seen as an important element of its model of economic development and its priorities for macroeconomic

2 I distinguish between political and economic elites. The former refers to high-ranking policymakers without a direct or material interest in capital account policy. The latter refer to members of the business community directly affected in terms of their income by regulations of international capital movements. I posit that socially shared understandings about legitimate economic policies permeate both types of elite.

policymaking. In other words, capital account policy is inextricably linked with political decisions on the general path of economic development that countries pursue. Similar to the perennial academic and political debates over free trade, national capital account policy has been subjected to changing international conditions, trends, and incentives.

Capital account liberalization is a subset of macroeconomic reforms that represent the opening of the national to the international economy. Similar to current account liberalization, the relaxation of national rules and standards for multinational companies, and the move towards central bank independence, opening the capital account is a signifier of a changing model of economic development. Instead of privileging national economic sovereignty and autonomy, capital account freedom squarely associates economic growth and welfare with the international economy and a liberalized national economy.

In the last decades of the twentieth century, the inward-oriented development model used by many developing countries after the end of World War II came under attack from various fronts. Severe legal limits on the free flow of international capital were an essential element of this model, known as import-substituting industrialization (ISI) and applied in virtually all Latin American countries. Combining Keynesian economics with the heterodox, structuralist tradition of the so-called "ECLA school"[3] personified by Raúl Prebisch (Love 2005; Rodríguez 2006; Dosman 2008), almost all Latin American countries pursued a policy of closed capital accounts. Apart from a short-lived episode of capital account liberalization during the late 1970s in the Southern Cone countries (Argentina, Chile, and Uruguay), the level of capital account openness in Latin America was rather low, although slightly higher than in other regions of the developing world until the early 1980s due to Latin America's traditional dependence on foreign capital. In the course of the 1980s, the ISI model became a victim of its internal faults and a sustained campaign at the national and international level facilitated by the rise of its principal competitor – neoclassical economics (Palma 2009).

Neoclassical economics and its political off-spring in the form of neoliberalism propagate an outward-oriented model of economic development focused on the liberalization of markets. The end of the Cold War and the disappearance of its principal ideological contender provided free-market enthusiasts with the political and intellectual basis for their campaign to relegate the ISI model to the history books. The liberalization of trade and finance became the battle cry for a new generation of economists and policymakers in Latin America. In many countries, they succeeded in replacing the ISI model with a new strategy or ideology for economic development based on neoclassical economics and epitomized by the 'Washington Consensus'. Associated with this overall intellectual and political change was a negative perspective on capital controls as an integral part of the old, now defunct economic paradigm. An international campaign was launched during the 1980s – following the trend in industrial countries – to rid the developing world generally, and Latin America specifically, of closed capital accounts. This campaign possessed intellectual protagonists within the international academic discourse and determined political actors united by their

3 Named after the Economic Commission for Latin America and the Caribbean (ECLA) of the United Nations based in Santiago de Chile.

shared commitment to neoclassical economics and their declared intention to make the developing world safe for global finance.

In turn, many orthodox economists and policymakers have heralded the opening of the national economy to inflows and outflows of capital as a 'fast track' to economic growth and efficiency, especially in developing countries (for particularly outspoken examples, see Guitián 1995, Fischer 1997, and Summers 1998). Obstfeld succinctly summarizes the benefits of international capital mobility according to conventional wisdom among neoclassical economists:

> International financial markets allow residents of different countries to pool various risks, achieving more effective insurance than purely domestic arrangements would allow. Furthermore, a country suffering a temporary recession or natural disaster can borrow abroad. Developing countries with little capital can borrow to finance investment, thereby promoting economic growth without sharp increases in saving rates. At the global level, the international capital market channels world savings to its most productive uses, irrespective of location. (...) The other main potential positive role of international capital markets is to discipline policymakers who might be tempted to exploit a captive domestic capital market. Unsound policies – for example, excessive government borrowing or inadequate bank regulation – would spark speculative capital outflows and higher domestic interest rates. In theory, a government's fear of these effects should make rash behavior less attractive (Obstfeld 1998: 10).

In contrast, heterodox economists, harking back to the warnings of John Maynard Keynes and Hyman Minsky about unfettered international financial markets, emphasize the resulting constraints on government autonomy in several economic policy domains, the substantial risks of capital account liberalization for macroeconomic stability, especially its close relationship with the occurrence of financial crises, and the lack of compelling evidence for the growth-enhancing effects of open capital accounts (Díaz-Alejandro 1985, Ffrench-Davis and Griffith-Jones 1995, Bhagwati 1998, Rodrik 1998, Stiglitz 2000, Eatwell and Taylor 2001, Grabel 2003, Rodrik and Subramanian 2009). For these scholars, the rather tangible costs of capital account openness outweigh the benefits as described by Obstfeld. They argue that capital controls maintain important macroeconomic functions for developing countries in today's globalized, complex international financial system: they can be used to stabilize short-term volatile capital flows; they can give policymakers additional policy instruments that allow them more effective and less costly macroeconomic stabilization measures; they can promote growth and increase economic efficiency by reducing the volatility of financing and of real macroeconomic performance; and they can discourage long-term capital outflows (Ocampo et al. 2008).

Leaving behind the debate in the narrow circles of academic discourse, the supporters of capital account freedom counted with powerful political allies, too. Having established capital account freedom in their own economies during the 1970s and 1980s, industrial country governments now sought to promote its adoption in the developing world. In line with neoclassical economics, they prescribed capital account liberalization as a panacea for integrated global markets promising faster economic growth everywhere. A prominent and forceful spokesperson for this campaign – crossing intellectual and political boundaries –

was Harvard economics professor, former US Treasury Secretary, and currently Director of the White House's National Economic Council for President Obama, Lawrence Summers. He outlined a world free of restrictions on trade and finance in prosaic terms:

> Imagine a country whose harbors are filled with rocks, a special kind of rock that blocks any ship carrying products from coming in. And imagine a proposal to remove the rocks from the harbors. Would it be a good thing? Many people would say yes. They would say that citizens would have a wider choice of goods at lower prices. They would say that producers would have a wider choice of inputs at lower costs, making them more competitive and able to pay higher wages. They would say that greater competition would spur productivity, would expand capacity, would reduce inflation, and would reduce capital costs. To be sure, the removal of these rocks would bring about changes in the economy. But every day, in every way, our market economy, through changes in technology, communications, and transportation, is removing natural barriers and making communication and trade much easier (Summers 2000: 3–4).

What had been a successful strategy for industrial countries, i. e., the free flow of international capital, must be a good thing for developing countries, too. Capital account freedom was meant to lift all boats with the tide.[4]

The fact that dissimilar countries in the developing world arrived at similar conclusions in terms of 'appropriate' economic policies at around the same time indicates the importance of international factors in explaining domestic choices on capital account policy. An international norm advocating the liberalization of the capital account emerged during the 1980s and 1990s and found its intellectual host and key political advocate in the International Monetary Fund (Leiteritz 2005; Moschella 2009, 2010, 2012; Chwieroth 2010a).

Largely independent from outside pressure, the IMF signed up to the neoclassical imperative of capital account freedom during the 1980s and subsequently promoted the adoption of capital account liberalization in developing countries. The IMF acted as a "norm entrepreneur" (Finnemore and Sikkink 1999) for the cause of financial openness and tried to change its Articles of Agreement in 1997 in order to provide the organization with legal jurisdiction over national capital account policies.

Up until the Asian financial crisis during the late 1990s, the IMF was an active supporter and key advocate of the emerging norm of capital account openness in the international monetary system. While the organization stopped promoting the rapid, unconditional liberalization of the capital account in the aftermath of the Asian crisis and the failure of the amendment to change its legal charter, the Fund nonetheless continues to support the goal of international capital mobility until the present day (IMF 2007: chap. 3, 9–12 and 2009; Chwieroth 2010a: 226–254).

However, ascertaining the IMF's actual impact on capital account policy outcomes requires detailed country-level studies because domestic actors also respond to quite dif-

4 In the context of the current financial crisis, Summers has become somewhat more skeptical that economic globalization will automatically bring benefits for all countries – including workers in his own country – and has called for international regulatory measures to promote "healthy globalization" (*Financial Times*, May 5, 2008).

ferent incentives than those of the IMF – incentives rooted in the domestic polity. The domestic social context is the cognitive filter through which emerging international norms are refracted. Understanding the national variation of capital account policy after the initial adoption of liberalization thus requires a closer look inside the 'black box' of domestic politics. Whereas international factors might explain the simultaneous adoption of similar economic policies in developing countries, a purely structural perspective fails to account for the variation of capital account policy despite powerful universal forces in favor of its homogenization.[5]

1.3 The Variation of Capital Account Policy Amidst Global Convergence

This book is concerned with the explanation of capital account policy *after* the initial adoption of liberalization. Why has capital account liberalization been sustainable only in some countries given comparable external and internal challenges for all countries? Before discussing the relevant academic literature and my focus on national economic identity, a few words on the national variation amidst global and regional convergence in capital account policy are in order.

The global trend of capital account policy over the last four decades is straightforward: the world as a whole has been moving steadily towards greater openness (see Figure 1.1 below). The process of dismantling capital controls after the breakdown of the Bretton Woods monetary system usually started with restrictions on capital outflows and quickly spilled over to all types of administrative controls. During the late 1970s and early 1980s, industrial countries generally, and Western European ones specifically, took the lead in the gradual relaxation of capital account restrictions (Reisen and Fischer 1993; Helleiner 1994). Especially in the context of formal agreements under auspices of the OECD and the European Union, virtually all industrial countries established high levels of capital account openness by the end of the 1980s and have maintained them until the present time.[6] By 1993, the threshold of zero, i. e., the mean, in the Chinn-Ito index of financial openness (see Appendix 1) was passed. As a result, from that point onwards capital accounts at the global level have been more open than closed.

The developing world jumped on the liberalization bandwagon 10 to 15 years after the industrial countries. But once they did, their pace towards greater capital account openness was impressive. According to the Chinn-Ito index, financial openness across 130 developing countries more than doubled between 1975 and 2002 (see Figure 1.2 below).

5 Structural accounts of international norm diffusion have come under attack in other policy areas, too. For example, Risse et al. (1999) open the "black box" of domestic politics in order to account for the variation of human rights policies, or differing degrees of adaption of international human rights standards, in developing countries. Beyond political-institutional factors, their study also takes social or informal conditions into account.

6 There may indeed be reversals of this trend in developed countries in the aftermath of the current financial crisis but the relevant cross-country data are not available yet. The last available year in the relevant dataset refers to 2007.

Figure 1.1 Capital account openness worldwide, 1970–2007

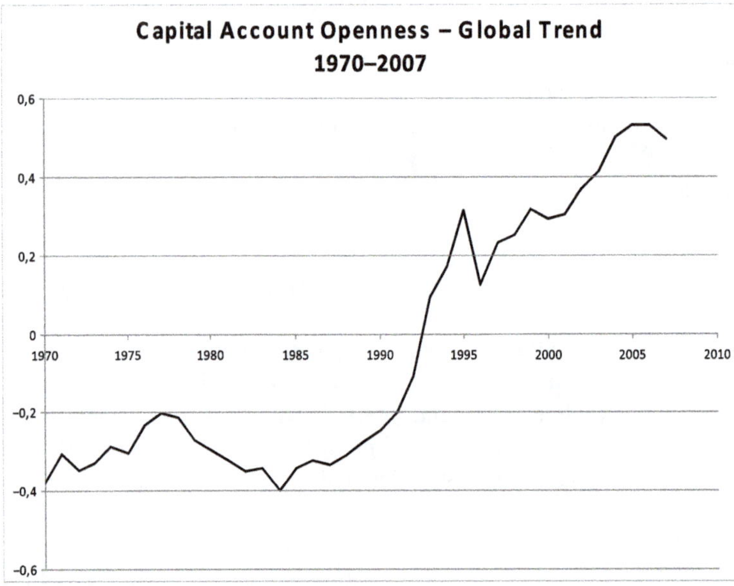

Source: Chinn and Ito 2008. In this index, "0" is constructed as the mean of the series.

Figure 1.2 Capital account openness in developed and developing countries, 1970–2007

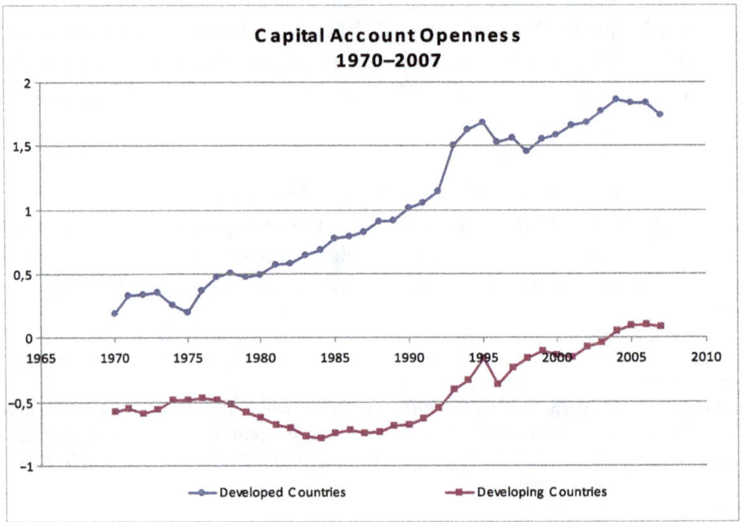

Source: Chinn and Ito 2008.

Despite the striking growth of capital account freedom in the developing world, notable differences persist in terms of the level of openness and the pace and pattern of opening between industrial and developing countries. The widespread expectation that developing countries would simply follow the lead of their industrial counterparts and quickly and steadily move towards higher levels of capital account openness has not been matched by reality (see Figure 1.3 below).

In fact, significant regional variation of capital account policy has been a defining feature of the post-Bretton Woods monetary era (see Figure 1.4 below). While some regions such as the Middle East and North Africa registered stagnation in capital account liberalization after an initial leap in the early 1970s, others such as East and Southeast Asia showed a moderate reversal after the experience with the financial crisis in the late 1990s. Besides Eastern and Central Europe, Latin America experienced the most dramatic decline in capital account restrictions in the early 1990s. Starting in the mid-1990s, Latin America has had the highest degree of capital account openness among all developing regions, while still trailing behind the industrial world by around 40 %.

In the context of changing their development model from import-substituting industrialization to neoliberalism, many Latin American countries lifted their often multifaceted restrictions on international capital movements, primarily by abolishing longstanding restrictions on capital outflows. Controls on capital outflows had actually been tightened in many countries in the context of the debt crisis at the beginning and during the middle of the 1980s. As a result, capital account openness in Latin America hit a historic low point at around 1984. By using controls on outflows, governments had hoped to stem the avalanche of capital flight during the debt crisis, yet with very limited success. The downward trend reversed rather quickly – the early 1990s saw a dramatic jump in liberalization, returning capital account openness in Latin America as a whole to the level of the early 1970s. The upward trend steadily continued after a slight reversal in the mid-1990s and in recent years has reached a historically high plateau (see Figure 1.5 below).

Figure 1.3 Percentage of developing countries opening or closing a capital control, 1971–2004

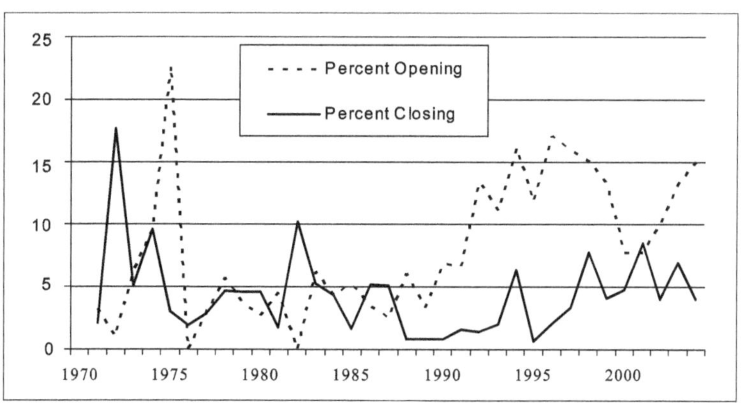

Source: Brune and Gibbons Guisinger 2009.

Figure 1.4 Financial openness in different regions of the world, 1965–2003

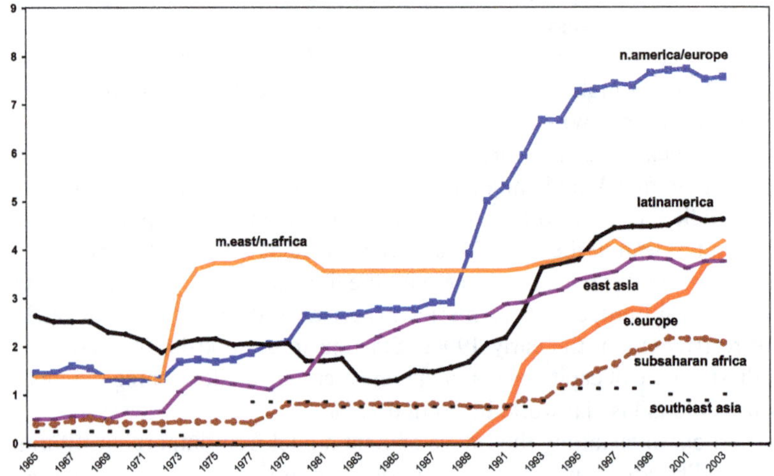

Source: Brune 2006.

In the context of changing their development model from import-substituting industrialization to neoliberalism, many Latin American countries lifted their often multifaceted restrictions on international capital movements, primarily by abolishing longstanding restrictions on capital outflows. Controls on capital outflows had actually been tightened in many countries in the context of the debt crisis at the beginning and during the middle of the 1980s. As a result, capital account openness in Latin America hit a historic low point at around 1984. By using controls on outflows, governments had hoped to stem the avalanche of capital flight during the debt crisis, yet with very limited success. The downward trend reversed rather quickly – the early 1990s saw a dramatic jump in liberalization, returning capital account openness in Latin America as a whole to the level of the early 1970s. The upward trend steadily continued after a slight reversal in the mid-1990s and in recent years has reached a historically high plateau (see Figure 1.5 below).

However, the overall regional trend somewhat obscures the national variation of capital account policies in the aftermath of liberalization. Although the regional trend clearly points towards greater financial openness, national capital account policies after 1990 did not follow a uniform pattern. Most Latin American countries liberalized administrative restrictions on capital outflows *and* inflows in the early 1990s. As a result, the regional trend towards greater capital account openness during the 1990s reflects the experience of the majority of countries with the *simultaneous* liberalization of both capital outflows and inflows. Only after experiencing the negative effects of drastically increased capital inflows did some, but by no means all, governments reintroduce inflow controls or invent them from scratch.

Figure 1.5 Capital account openness in Latin America, 1970–2007

Source: Chinn and Ito 2008.

On the other hand, as they relaxed controls on outflows, some Latin American governments moved more reluctantly to remove restrictions on capital inflows fearing that increased capital flows could bring more volatility. In particular, large inflows and sudden outflows of capital, including short-term flows or 'hot money' could lead to macroeconomic instability, the loss of monetary autonomy, and to the undermining of export growth through real exchange-rate appreciation (Magud and Reinhart 2007). At the same time, once liberalized, capital outflows have been left largely unrestricted.[7]

Let me briefly illustrate the different paths of capital account policy in Latin America with reference to the cases of Argentina, Brazil, and Chile. While their policies before 1990 showed a relative homogeneity at a low level of capital account openness, their post-1990 policy trajectories have substantially diverged from each other. Even though the overall trend is towards greater capital account openness, somewhat erratic changes and frequent reversals have characterized the capital account policies of the three leading Latin American economies. As a result, the capital account openness indicator locates them at rather different levels by 2007 (see Figure 1.6 below).

7 The strategy to simultaneously introduce controls on capital inflows and liberalize capital outflows was justified as corresponding measures to dampen the appreciation of domestic currencies (Larraín 2000). For example, Colombia liberalized outflows in 1992 following a surge of inflows during the previous year. The government did so by extending the liberalization of export-surrender requirements to all exporters, by allowing local agents to hold offshore stocks (up to a limit), and by easing restrictions on the provision of foreign loans (Labán and Larraín 2000: 22–23).

Figure 1.6 Capital account openness in Argentina, Brazil, and Chile, 1970–2007

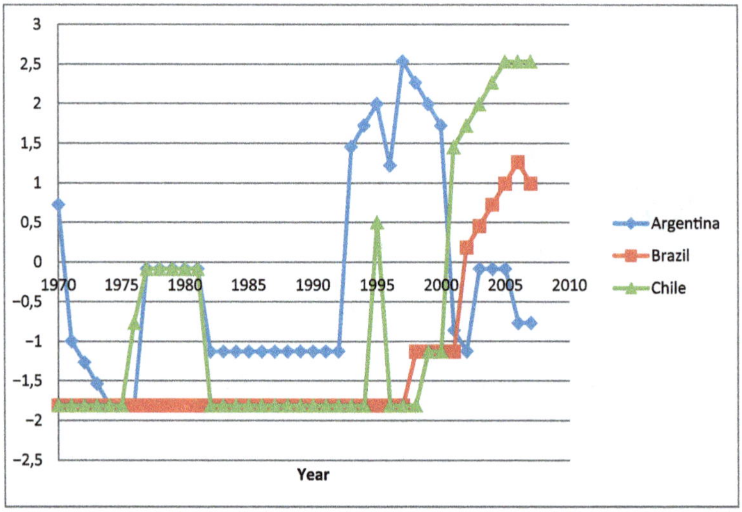

Source: Chinn and Ito 2008.

Argentina embarked on a full-scale financial liberalization program during the Menem administration. The country was portrayed as the poster-child of 'Washington Consensus' policies in its most radical version (Blustein 2005). The capital account openness indicator went up exponentially during the early 1990s and experienced relatively few changes, least of all in the backward direction. Yet the financial crisis of 2001–2002 changed the picture dramatically. Within record time, Argentina's capital account openness indicator went from being one of the highest to one of the lowest in Latin America. The three Kirchner governments have maintained a relatively low level of capital account openness until the present time (Dominguez and Tesar 2007; Frenkel and Rapetti 2007).

Brazil's capital account policy has traditionally been characterized by a cautious approach. The government did not subscribe to the free-market enthusiasm that befell the Latin American region during the early 1990s. While it did open its economy consistent with the regional trend, it did so much slower and in a more gradual fashion compared to its neighbors. This approach is also reflected in the longitudinal trend of its capital account policy. Brazil has never been a vanguard for either radical capital account openness or closedness. It has consistently maintained its steady, 'middle-of-the-road' policy – including the preservation of some controls on capital outflows during the neoliberal era (Gottschalk 2000; Goldfajn and Minella 2007).

Finally, the Chilean government is credited with innovative approaches to managing capital inflows, including the unremunerated reserve requirement (URR), introduced in 1991. In the context of an overall financial liberalization program that started earlier than in most other Latin American countries, during the 1990s and 2000s Chile consistently moved to higher levels of capital account openness, making it today one of the most open countries to international capital flows in Latin America. At the same time, the government has maintained its traditional instruments for the regulation of capital inflows within its macroeconomic policy toolkit, applying them selectively throughout the recent past (Cowan and De Gregorio 2007).[8]

The variation of capital account policies in Latin America amidst the general trend towards greater openness is surprising. The enthusiasm for liberalization during the early 1990s was replaced by frequent policy reversals indicating the fragility of open capital accounts. As a result, the exponential increase in capital account openness in the early 1990s came to a halt, giving rise to policy changes, most dramatically in Argentina. The neoliberal fever for open capital accounts quickly dissipated in some countries (Argentina), never really blossomed in others (Brazil), and took hold in a few countries, albeit with some important limitations (Chile). Given similar macroeconomic challenges as well as formal political and economic institutions during the liberalization period, one would have expected broadly similar policies – moving quickly and steadily towards the level of capital account openness reached by industrial countries. In sum, the observed variation of capital account policies in Latin America in an age of financial globalization – purportedly leading to uniform economic policies – needs explanation.

International factors constitute the structural context for national capital account policy. To what extent international actors such as the IMF are able to shape domestic decisions on capital account management is an important issue for empirical research. Based on the analysis of the Peruvian and Colombian cases during the 1990s and 2000s, I argue that national policy decisions on the flow of international capital are not determined by outside actors such as the IMF. Although the Fund was the principal disseminator and key 'intellectual cheerleader' for capital account liberalization in the early and mid-1990s, it did not dictate the content of the adopted policies in the two countries. Instead, domestic-level factors are responsible for the variation of capital account policy in Latin America, turning countries into capital mobility enthusiasts or laggards, respectively.

1.4 Capital Mobility Enthusiasts Vs. Laggards: Comparing Peru and Colombia

Explanations of capital account policy have become somewhat of a cottage industry in political science. An area usually reserved for economists, the remarkable increase in capital account openness during the past four decades has sparked the interest and attention of a wide range of political scientists. Scholars have primarily focused on the question of why capital account liberalization became a policy outcome in several countries at around the same time. Their theoretical and empirical analyses initially focused on industrial or OECD countries where capital account liberalization started earlier than in the rest of the world.

In addition, the existing approaches overwhelmingly focus on the *adoption* of capital account liberalization, but are less able to account for the variation of capital account policy *after* the initial opening. In this book I seek to rectify this analytic shortcoming.

8 However, the Chile-United States Free Trade Agreement signed in 2004 significantly limits the application of these instruments (Bhagwati and Tarullo 2003).

In the following, I briefly describe the trajectory of capital account policy in Peru and Colombia after 1990 in order to highlight the principal causal mechanisms, drawn on a variety of theoretical perspectives, at work. Despite similar macroeconomic challenges and comparable formal institutions, both countries pursued different paths after the initial adoption of capital account liberalization. I posit that the different nature of national economic identity in both countries accounts for the sustainability (Peru) vs. fragility (Colombia) of capital account openness after 1990. National economic identity, in turn, encompasses (i) socially shared rules and understandings about legitimate economic policies, and (ii) a specific set of state-business relations.

The change in social rules and understandings in the context of the initial adoption of capital account liberalization during the early 1990s constitutes the ideational foundation for the durability of capital account openness in Peru. In contrast, the survival and continued relevance of pre-liberalization collective beliefs and social practices, specifically the tradition of pragmatism and consensus-orientation among the political and economic elites, account for the fragility of capital account openness in Colombia.

Peru and Colombia illustrate the different paths that countries have taken in response to the dilemma between maintaining real exchange-rate stability in order to preserve the external competitiveness of the domestic economy, or giving priority to capital inflows as a source of domestic growth. Although both countries arrived at the initial decision to open the capital account for different reasons, they faced similar macroeconomic challenges in its aftermath. Both had to deal with exchange-rate appreciation and its negative consequences for the domestic economy. Their choices in response to this situation reflected different priorities – based on a different national economic identity – in terms of macroeconomic policymaking. While both countries adopted floating exchange-rate regimes during the 1990s, Peruvian policymakers privileged inflation control and stable or increasing capital inflows over other macroeconomic objectives, whereas their Colombian counterparts tried to reconcile a low inflation policy with the preservation of external competitiveness for the national economy. Both strategies, in turn, led to different capital account policies. Capital controls were virtually outlawed in Peru after 1990. In contrast, Colombia's capital account policy reflected frequent changes between opening and closing, mainly in reaction to drastic movements of capital inflows and the exchange rate.

The different priorities for capital account management are informed by specific informal institutions governing economic policymaking and specific state-business relations in both countries, or what I consider to be the elements of a national economic identity. In fact, socially shared understandings governing economic policymaking, including capital account policy, are closely linked to the structure of state-business relations. Legitimizing sustained capital account openness requires a supporting coalition within the domestic business community that is able to dominate the interactions between the private sector and the government. In particular, the pro-capital mobility coalition must become the preferred interlocutor for the government within the business community. Taken together, embedding capital account openness in the national economic identity in Latin America and leaving behind the previous model of macroeconomic management inspired by import-substituting industrialization, require a change in state-business relations towards the political dominance of a coalition of economic groups for whom the free access to or entry of foreign capital take precedence over exchange-rate stability.

In addition, socially shared understandings about legitimate capital account policy change if an external event such as a profound economic crisis undermines the collective belief in the effectiveness and legitimacy of capital controls. As a result, the specific political and economic context in which capital account openness is adopted plays a critical role for its endurance over time. An economic crisis per se is not a necessary condition for the initial adoption of capital account liberalization. However, the long-term political and social effects of an economic crisis help explain when and why capital account openness becomes a durable policy. Conversely, the absence of an economic crisis during the initial adoption of capital account liberalization undermines its viability over the medium and long run.

Peru

The deep economic crisis that engulfed Peru in the second half of the 1980s provided the launching pad for the initial liberalization of the capital account. The crisis enabled the rapid adoption of several components of capital account openness. First, due to the legacy of the (first) García administration, the country was trapped in an untenable macroeconomic situation in 1990, having become a pariah of the international financial community because of hyperinflation and the moratorium on debt payments. Capital inflows had virtually dried up, and capital flight was rampant. The incoming Fujimori administration quickly realized that its room for maneuver in economic policy was close to zero. This, in turn, shaped the risk perception on part of the political leadership, driving the government to accept high risks in economic policy. In other words, the risks of capital account liberalization for macroeconomic stability were systematically discarded, hoping that the short-term gains in form of low inflation and increased capital inflows would materialize just in time before the risks of radical free-market reforms became apparent.

Second, the crisis undermined the legitimacy of any form of heterodox economic thinking and their associated policies, as practiced by the García administration during the 1980s. It also enabled the rise and integration into the Fujimori government of a new epistemic community: neoliberal economists. Representatives of this group were appointed to high-ranking positions during the first years of the Fujimori administration, from where they could implement their economic agenda without much interference from society.

Third, the economic crisis gave international financial institutions, and the IMF in particular, an important role vis-à-vis the Peruvian government. In exchange for providing fresh financial resources, it could dictate the terms of the required economic reforms. However, outside pressure for the adoption of neoliberal reforms was not necessary. In fact, the Fujimori administration became a model student in its interactions with the IMF, liberalizing the economy well beyond what it was asked to do by the IMF and other international financial institutions. The government's eagerness for liberalization also included capital account policy.

However, the factors that explain the initial adoption of capital account openness do not necessarily guarantee its maintenance over time. Two domestic-level processes have accompanied the sustainability of capital account liberalization in Peru. First, a structural shift in the balance of power among domestic business groups and the subsequent reconfiguration of state-business relations.

After introducing radical economic reforms in the early 1990s, several leading protagonists of the neoliberal epistemic community lost their positions in the government and were replaced by business sector representatives. These new actors represented the interests of a specific group within the business community, namely the financial and mining sectors, now mostly in the hands of foreign investors. In contrast, industrialists and non-traditional exporters lost political influence during the 1990s. As a result, the longevity of capital account openness in Peru is linked to the political leverage of a specific alliance of business sectors that profit from free capital mobility but are less affected by its negative consequences in terms of exchange-rate volatility. This pro-capital mobility coalition gained the upper hand influencing government policy over the non-mining export-oriented sectors of the economy during the Fujimori administration. This coalition has been able to maintain its veto-player position in terms of capital controls until the present time.

However, the control of a specific business alliance over policy decisions is not a sufficient condition to explain why capital account openness has enjoyed widespread support in the Peruvian society at large. Second, I argue that one of the long-term effects of the late 1980s economic crisis has been a national taboo regarding the use of capital controls. Restrictions on the free flow of international capital lost their justification as a legitimate tool of economic policymaking in Peru based on the widely shared association between capital controls and economic chaos in the collective memory of the late 1980s. Thus, the social agreement around capital mobility extends beyond the neoliberal epistemic community of economists and specific members of the domestic business community. Capital account freedom has become part and parcel of the national economic identity in Peru.

Colombia

In contrast to Peru, the factors explaining the initial adoption of capital account liberalization in Colombia during the early 1990s do not have an economic origin. In fact, compared with its regional neighbors, Colombia was in a rather privileged macroeconomic position at the end of the 1980s. Neoliberal economic reforms were not a response to a desperate state of the national economy. Instead, they were the result of a comprehensive attempt to "modernize" the country initiated by the Gaviria administration in 1990. Parts of its economic modernization agenda was capital account liberalization. The Gaviria administration – mainly composed of members of the neoliberal epistemic community represented by the youngish president himself – was able to convince the political and economic elites of the country that liberalization was the only viable path to maintain the competitiveness of the Colombian economy in the long run.

However, the political and discursive dominance of the neoliberal epistemic community was relatively short-lived. Most importantly, it was not able to do away with an important element of the national economic identity: *pragmatism*.[9] Described as an economic policy stance "based on selective but firm government intervention, that neither fully choked the private sector with overregulation, nor allowed it to flourish" (Edwards 2001: 28), pragmatism tries to correct the negative effects of free-market economic policies with corresponding state interventions. In other words, it tries to establish a balance between the reign of market forces and the need to ensure macroeconomic stability. Faced with one of the negative side-effects of free-market reforms in form of real exchange-rate appreciation and given the predominant role of exporters' interests in state-business relations, Colombian policymakers displayed their pragmatist inclinations by imposing temporary quantitative controls on capital inflows, the so-called *encaje* system or URR, in order to achieve exchange-rate stability and external competitiveness, thereby defying both the pure principles of neoclassical economics as well as the exhortations of the IMF.

An engrained sense of pragmatism has continued to shape economic policymaking in Colombia and thereby prevented the institutionalization of capital account openness as a long-term policy. In contrast to Peru, the freedom of international capital movements is not regarded as a symbolic, inalienable ingredient of the Colombian national economic identity. Instead, capital mobility is conditioned on its contribution to macroeconomic growth and stability. Once excessive capital inflows enter into tension or conflict with overall economic stability, Colombian policymakers do not hesitate to restrict them.

1.5 The Methodology of the Book

1.5.1 Achievements and limitations of large-N quantitative studies

The literature on the political economy of capital account policy is dominated by large-N quantitative studies based on global or regional samples of countries. As a result, the frequently used path for aspiring researchers is to assemble a database of quantitative indicators for their preferred explanatory factor(s) and a host of control variables and test them against a numerical measure of capital account openness. The usual end result of this exercise is that one causal factor somehow 'wins' over its competitors by way of a more significant statistical correlation with the values of the dependent variable. In other words, causality is adjudicated through the statistical co-variation between the numerical values of indicators of competing independent variables and the numerical measure of capital account openness. This has been the standard methodological approach in the literature (as indicative examples from different analytical traditions, see Haggard and Maxfield 1996, Brooks 2004, and Chwieroth 2007; Eichengreen 2001 provides a useful overview of the literature up to the late 1990s).

9 Pragmatism constitutes a "shared mental model" of the Colombian policymaking and business community. It provides "a framework that allows members of a group to make sense of social, political, and economic conditions" (Abdelal et al. 2006: 699) and to make decisions in accordance with their cognitive priors (Hall 1993; Denzau and North 2000). As a result, shared mental or cognitive models are an essential component of collective identities.

However, empirical results based on this approach have been ambiguous. On the one hand, they allow for the simultaneous consideration of a wide range of possible causal factors based on a relatively large sample of countries. Quantitatively-oriented researchers have made substantial progress in the construction of numerical indicators for independent variables thought to influence capital account policy. They have become increasingly sophisticated in tackling methodological problems associated with the operationalization of key theoretical concepts and have devised innovative ways to identify and analyze interaction effects between distinct causal factors on different levels of analysis.[10] In addition, they use increasingly fine-grained measures of capital account openness as their dependent variable.

On the other hand, methodological sophistication in quantitative analyses has not done away with the plethora of causal factors, all of which have received some form of empirical confirmation in large-N studies. The – still rather limited – integration of separate levels of analysis is restricted to only one ontological perspective, the "open-economy politics" framework that links interest- and (formal) institutions-based explanations of economic policies.

Quantitative studies of capital account policy have overwhelmingly focused on developed countries and are based on a rationalist-materialist epistemology. As a result, they have failed to consider social drivers of economic policies, most importantly cognitive and normative factors on the international and domestic level, mainly due to the difficulty to integrate them in a quantitative research design. In fact, some explanatory variables based on ideational and institutional accounts might not be susceptible to numerical measurement at all. As Eichengreen observed, "as is the case all too often in empirical economics, there may have been a tendency to focus on factors that are readily measured and quantified to the neglect of those that are more difficult to capture" (Eichengreen 2001: 351). Quantitatively-oriented scholars should also be aware that despite their best attempts to operationalize explanatory variables in order to enable their comparative assessment within a positivist research methodology, the concomitant costs in terms of the external validity of the resulting indicators are often substantial.[11]

In sum, not all causal factors identified in the literature are susceptible to empirical testing in a large-N, quantitative methodology. To be more precise, only a qualitative methodology based on in-depth analysis of individual, strategically selected cases allows me to include "social facts" such as collective identities in my analytical framework. On the other hand, the costs of such an approach compared with statistical studies lie in the limited capacity to generalize the research findings beyond the analyzed cases. However, since I

10 See, for example, the study by Mukherjee and Singer 2010 that tests the interaction between international and domestic drivers of capital account liberalization and addresses the endogenous nature of country participation in IMF programs.

11 Examples for the questionable operationalization of key variables to explain capital account policy include (i) using the size of specific sectors in the national economy as a measure to determine the influence of interest groups over economic policy outcomes; (ii) determining the influence of international actors such as the IMF on domestic policy decisions to the size or frequency of lending programs without analyzing the causal mechanisms leading to the domestic demand for these programs; and (iii) determining the policy preferences of foreign-trained economists without considering the possibility that economic ideas acquired abroad are subsequently transformed by the specific local context.

am less interested in contributing to a general theory of capital account policy and more interested in explaining the national variation of capital account policy between countries, the focus on a few, illustrative cases is justified. In this sense, this book is more oriented towards the explanation of individual cases than proving that a specific casual variable is a necessary or sufficient condition for determining capital account policy at the general, theoretical level.

1.5.2 Process-tracing in a comparative case study design

The explanation of capital account policy can be approached from different analytical angles (see Chapter 2). Each of them is based on distinct ontological and/or epistemological perspectives and offers a distinct causal mechanism for the explanation of capital account policy. Each mechanism, in turn, is related to an underlying driver. These drivers can either be specific actors or structures at the domestic and international level.

In my analysis, I focus on specific domestic and international actors and their influence on national capital account policy against the systemic context of a movement towards increased capital mobility. Purely structural accounts of economic policy choices predict homogeneity given similar incentives and constraints at the global level. Only the consideration of the interaction between interests, ideas, and institutions helps to account for the persisting national variation of capital account policy.

In order to assess the explanatory power of different clusters within a unified methodological framework, I apply a comparative or paired case study design in conjunction with the method of process-tracing (Tarrow 2010). Process-tracing aims at uncovering the causal mechanism connecting the explanatory and the outcome variables (George and Bennett 2005: 205–232; Gerring 2007: 172–185; Bennett 2008; Caporaso 2009). It analyzes or traces the process by which certain outcomes are produced, specifying alternative theoretical accounts or causal mechanisms of the decision-making process upfront, which are then interrogated against the empirical data. Based on extensive field research, tracing the process of how decisions on economic policies are taken provides a longitudinal analysis of the unfolding of political outcomes.

The principal advantage of in-depth, *in situ* qualitative research over large-N, statistical analyses of the causes of capital account policy is its ability to directly analyze and reconstruct the process of decision-making. In contrast to "data-set observations" – the basis of quantitative or regression analysis – process-tracing directly engages the empirical material with the aim to unearth causal mechanisms at play, rather than numeric correlations between variables (Brady and Collier 2004). Process-tracing seeks a historical explanation of individual cases with the goal to document whether the sequence of events or processes within a particular case fits the predictions by alternative theories (Mahoney et al. 2009). Last but not least, instead of a 'gladiatorial battle' where one theory 'defeats' its competitors, process-tracing allows for the simultaneous operation, observation and evaluation of different causal mechanisms producing a specific outcome – an important step towards my goal of analytic eclecticism (Sil and Katzenstein 2010a).

Each explanatory cluster makes unique predictions on what or who determines capital account policy. As a result, one can derive specific expectations in terms of observable implications from each cluster. Using these different expectations as the baseline, I ask which of them is able – either alone or in conjunction with other causal factors – to account for the decision-making process on capital account policy in each of the selected cases. This approach allows to eliminate possible causal factors as irrelevant for the explanation of the process leading to political decisions on capital account policy, and to take the interaction or co-determination between different causal factors into account.

I focus on the following three agents as possible determinants of capital account policy:

1. The International Monetary Fund;
2. Domestic economic interest groups;
3. The domestic community of (neoliberal) economists.

Each of them reflects a specific mechanism or process linking cause and effect in capital account policy. First, capital account policy is a function of the influence of international actors, in particular the IMF, over domestic policymaking, using both 'hard' (coercion) and 'soft' (persuasion) means of power. Second, cleavages and power struggles between domestic economic interest groups define capital account management as a salient policy issue. The 'winning' coalition of private economic interests is somehow able to 'capture' government decisions on capital account policy. And third, capital account policy is the result of a specific ideas-driven community of domestic-level economists that have gained access to high-ranking government positions. I consider the explanatory power of each causal mechanism, represented by a specific actor or group of actors, in my case studies on Peru and Colombia.

The empirical evidence or data used to assess the power of alternative explanations of capital account policy are based on more than fifty semi-structured, open-ended interviews with domestic and international policymakers and outside observers (see Appendix 2), the analysis of primary and secondary documents, press articles, surveys of economists in policy-relevant positions in order to probe their views on capital account management (see Appendix 3), and archival research. In each of the analyzed cases it is asked whether a specific causal mechanism, represented by a specific agent, is able to explain the decision-making process leading to a specific outcome in capital account policy. Table 1.1 below summarizes the alternative causal mechanisms, the expectations regarding observable implications, and data sources used in order to evaluate their explanatory power.

Yet as Marx's famous adage has it, individuals do not make their own history under self-selected circumstances, but under circumstances already existing, given and transmitted from the past. Agents are situated in an institutional context, both internationally and domestically. As a result, purely agency-based or voluntaristic accounts are insufficient explanations for capital account policy. Agent behavior has to be contextualized with the help of (formal and informal) institutions. The mutual interaction between institutions and agents, not their separate, independent effects, determines the process leading to specific outcomes in capital account policy.

Table 1.1 Alternative causal mechanisms

Causal mechanism/Driver	Observable implications	Data sources
Domestic interest groups	Policy outcomes reflect the material self-interest or the distributive preferences of specific economic groups	Interviews
IMF	Policy outcomes reflect IMF preferences or demands	Press coverage; interviews with policymakers; IMF Archives
Community of (neoliberal) economists	Policy outcomes reflect the position of a specific (neoliberal) epistemic community	Press coverage; surveys; interviews

The literature has made substantial progress in order to account for the impact of formal political and economic institutions on capital account policy. Existing analyses highlight the close connection between specific formal institutional arrangements, e. g., political partisanship and legislative fragmentation, and capital account policy. The relatively easy identification and quantitative measurement of formal institutions have facilitated large-N studies of their direct or indirect effects on economic policies. Yet, formal political and economic institutions might themselves be the result of underlying social institutions. In other words, they do not come into existence without specific social conditions. Hence, formal institutions act as *intervening variables* for economic policy outcomes. It is my explicit goal to delve into the domestic social foundations of capital account policy, above and beyond their visible representation in form of formal institutions.

However, how do we account for the existence of collective identities shaping capital account policy? Whereas formal institutions and their effects can be observed directly, no such straightforward identification and measurement is feasible for informal institutions. Or as Helmke and Levitsky (2004: 733) put it, "a country's constitution can tell us whether it has a presidential or parliamentary system of government, but it cannot tell us about the pervasiveness of clientelism or kinship network". Consequently, a case-oriented research design, employing methodological techniques ranging from extensive interviews with the actors who are affected by informal norms and rules to conducting large-N surveys, is best suited to establish the existence and content of shared identities, thus contributing to the analysis of the complex relationship between national economic identity and capital account policy.

1.5.3 Selection of case studies

Peru and Colombia are suitable cases for a paired comparison to show the explanatory power of alternative causal mechanisms for capital account policy. Both countries have historically taken different trajectories in capital account management, the outcome to be explained (see

Figure 1.7 below). Peru's capital account policy between 1970 and the early 1990s resembles a rollercoaster ride. Episodes of rapid liberalization were followed by equally drastic closednesss of the capital account, most notoriously during the second half of the 1980s with the full onslaught of the debt crisis and the application of heterodox economic policies during the (first) García administration. However, once the capital account was again liberalized in 1991 under the Fujimori government, apart from a brief interval of backlash in the mid-1990s, no major changes to the steady trend upwards occurred. Since 1997, Peru has consistently maintained the highest level of capital account openness among the bigger-sized countries in Latin America.

Figure 1.7 Capital account openness in Peru and Colombia, 1970–2007

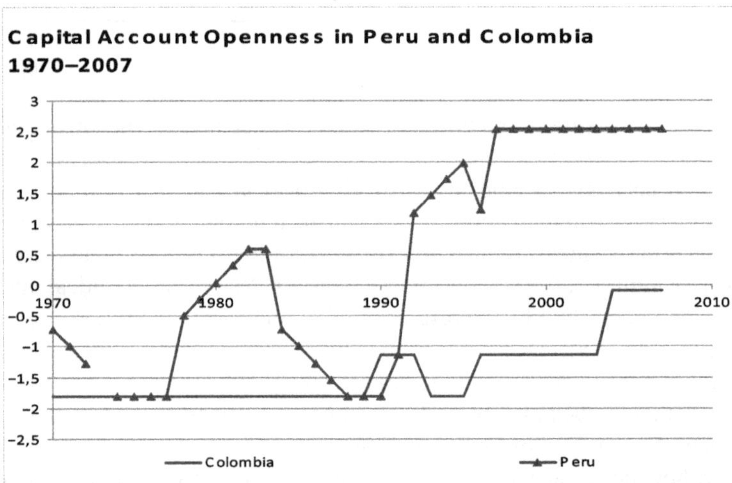

Source: Chinn and Ito 2008.

Now consider Colombia. Before 1990, Colombia was a stark contrast to Peru's erratic capital account policy. Long-term stability at a low level of capital account openness prevailed over frequent rollercoaster rides. In fact, the country's openness measure did not move at all for twenty years – an exceptional trend within Latin America. Both Peru and Colombia coincided in their initial opening process in 1991 and 1992. However, immediately afterwards the picture changes dramatically. While Peru continued with its rapid liberalization pace, Colombia first wavered and then slightly backtracked. To be sure, Colombia's overall trend was also upward, yet at a much slower speed than Peru and with frequent policy changes – something in common, albeit less dramatically, with Peru's trend before 1990.

The case studies address two questions in particular detail: (1) *why has Colombia historically lagged behind Peru in capital account openness, in particular after 1990;* and (2) *what explains the contrast between both countries after 1990 in terms of the sustainability of capital account liberalization?* Whereas Peru has sustained capital account openness until the present time, Colombia's initial opening of the capital account has been characterized by several reversals. Why is capital account liberalization sustained in Peru but not in Colombia?

Comparing economic policymaking in Colombia and Peru has a long academic tradition. Scholars were intrigued by the relative stability of economic policies in Colombia, compared with the frequent changes in economic paradigm and their resulting policies in Peru. Differences have been attributed to a variety of political-institutional factors related to the form and functioning of the political system, the organization of state-business relations, and the long-term influence of technocratic elites on economic policymaking (Thorp 1991; Thorp and Durand 1997; Dargent 2011). While useful to understand the different trajectories up until 1990, these studies are less helpful to answer the two questions posed above. Stability and continuity became an attribute of Peruvian, not Colombian, capital account policy in the recent past.[12]

A paired comparison requires the strategic selection of cases in order to reduce the high level of complexity surrounding social and political phenomena. Put simply, the selection of case studies cannot be done at will but must be justified in terms of methodological criteria. According to a *most-similar research design,* also called the method of difference after its initial proponent John Stuart Mill, cases with similar general characteristics and different values on the outcome variable are chosen (Van Evera 1997: 57–58; George and Bennett 2005: 153–160; Gerring 2007: 131–139; Gerring 2008: 668–671). The justification is to control for the effect of third variables that are not considered in the research design. Cases that are broadly similar in their political and historic characteristics but reflect different values or outcomes in terms of the phenomenon to be explained, facilitate the identification of the mechanism(s) connecting cause and effect. In other words, controlling for the possible effect of third variables in terms of the dependent variable is achieved through the selection of broadly similar cases.

Empirical analysis of capital account policy and its drivers is conducted within a paired comparison in order to trace the decision-making process on capital account management, thereby assessing the explanatory power of alternative causal mechanisms. Both Colombia and Peru are located in the same geographic region, which establishes an area of homogeneity with similar historical, political, social, economic, and cultural characteristics.[13] Given these overall commonalities, it will be easier to zero in on the remaining differences between the two countries – such as the depth and severity of the economic crisis affecting both countries in the late 1980s, state-business relations, and the form and long-term stability of formal and informal institutions – in order to assess their causal impact on capital account policy.

12 However, capital account policy might be the exception to the general rule that "public policies in Peru have been made arbitrarily, they have often been volatile, and they tend to be easily reversed" (Morón and Sanborn 2006: 22). Given this background, it is even more puzzling why capital account openness has been a stable, inflexible policy.

13 Weyland (2002a: 8) summarizes these similarities with the following list: "Iberian colonization, predominance of Catholicism, significant import-substitution industrialization, advanced 'social mobilization' [...], serious problems of debt and dependency, similar constitutional structures (for instance, presidential systems), and exposure to common ideational trends (for instance, the temporary attraction and later rejection of heterodox recipes)".

For the period under consideration (1990–2011), Colombia and Peru share a host of political and economic characteristics, which correspond to the first requirement of the method of difference:

- The status as medium-sized, middle-income countries;
- A high dependence on the export of primary commodities (oil in the case of Colombia, and copper and gold in the case of Peru);
- A fragmented political system with a high concentration of power in the executive and a weak legislature;
- The existence and historical strength of encompassing business associations;
- The personalist exercise of power by the president;
- Right-wing or center-right governments with a broadly defined (neo)liberal orientation in economic policy[14];
- Central Bank independent from executive interference;
- A floating exchange-rate regime combined with inflation-targeting[15].

The second requirement of the most-similar research design is variance of the dependent variable, allowing the remaining differences between the cases to demonstrate their causal impact. As discussed earlier, capital account policy in Colombia and Peru has reflected different trajectories, thereby assuming different values on the outcome variable. In particular, the macroeconomic situation of both countries during the initial adoption of capital account liberalization in the early 1990s was fundamentally different. Whereas Peru was treated as a pariah country in the aftermath of the heterodox economic policies applied by the García administration, Colombia emerged largely unscathed from the region-wide debt crisis of the 1980s. In other words, the context conditions at the beginning of the period under consideration were radically different. However, this fact alone cannot account for the divergent paths of capital account policy over time in both countries. Only the simultaneous consideration of other domestic-level factors as well as their interaction effects allows for the explanation of the *long-term* variation of capital account policy in Colombia and Peru.

Finally, some readers might wonder why a country such as Colombia traditionally plagued by specific political and economic characteristics such as an internal armed conflict and the importance of illicit economic activities related to drug trafficking can be compared to other countries in Latin America. In response, I posit first that Colombia's situation is

14 Starting in the late 1990s and early 2000s some left-wing governments in Latin America such as in Venezuela and Argentina have radically reversed course in capital account policy, re-introducing traditional administrative capital and exchange controls in order to defend a tenuous fixed exchange-rate regime. This policy reversal can clearly be attributed to their ideological, 'anti-neoliberal' stance. In other words, a fundamental political-ideological change of the national government leads to subsequent radical changes in capital account and other economic policies.

15 The Fujimori government in Peru adopted a (managed) floating exchange-rate regime as part of the initial economic stabilization plan in August 1990. Colombia changed the crawling peg exchange-rate regime in place since 1967 in favor of an exchange-rate band in 1991 before introducing a managed floating exchange-rate regime in 1999. Both countries adopted inflation-targeting in the early 2000s. While the Peruvian Central Bank thereafter shifted to "pure" floating, its Colombian counterpart continued to pursue managed floating aimed at maintaining real exchange-rate stability at a *competitive level* (Frenkel and Rapetti 2010).

not radically different from Peru's during the time period under consideration, which is why Colombia's inclusion in a most-similar research design is warranted. Peru also had a powerful military challenge from a left-wing guerilla group (the Shining Path) up until the early 1990s and its economy reflected a significant contribution from illegal, drug-related activities during the same period. Only the so-called balloon effect shifted the bulk of the illegal activities across the border to Colombia during the 1990s.[16]

Second, the illegal drug trade existed well before the 1990s and has been a constant within the Colombian economy until the present day. However, capital account policy has experienced some important changes during the same period. As a result, it is difficult to detect an independent effect of the illegal drug industry on economic policymaking in Colombia, for example by demanding capital account openness in order to facilitate the financial operations of the cocaine business. If the initial capital account liberalization in the early 1990s were a result of these demands, then the subsequent partial reversal of the opening policy cannot be explained with reference to illegal economic actors given that their interest in financial liberalization stayed the same and their economic strength all but increased during the 1990s.

1.6 Organization of the Book

The book is structured in five chapters that follow this introductory chapter. *Chapter 2* introduces a tridimensional matrix in order to review the state of the literature. Three distinct ontological frameworks – interests, institutions, and ideas – are linked to three distinct levels of analysis – individual, domestic, and international. Each possible combination between the two categories provides for a specific explanation of capital account policy. I briefly describe each possible explanation and assess its relative explanatory in terms of the sustainability of capital account liberalization. I especially focus on 'outside-in' explanations that analyze the impact of international forces on domestic capital account policy, highlighting two factors in particular: the role of the International Monetary Fund and neoliberal epistemic communities. I discuss their overall analytical purchase in light of theoretical and methodological considerations. I conclude that the literature has largely neglected the role of domestic informal institutions that refract the impact of international forces and thus lead to contingent outcomes in capital account policy despite uniform global and regional push and pull factors for capital account openness.

Chapter 3 introduces the concept of national economic identity as a variable in order to explain the variation of capital account policy in Latin America. The concept is based on a hitherto largely overlooked causal mechanism for the explanation of capital account liberalization – domestic informal institutions – as well as the analysis of state-business re-

16 The balloon effect is a direct result of the "war on drugs" in the Andean region declared by the United States government during the 1980s. Squeezing a balloon in one place makes it expand in another. Destroying drug crops in one country leads cultivation and the associated industry to move to another, spreading violence and corruption with it. Until the mid-1990s, Peru was the largest producer of coca in the world. The application of tougher eradication policies by the Fujimori administration let to a simultaneous rise of coca production in Colombia (The Economist, March 6, 2003).

lations. In other words, I combine the traditional focus on material factors with an analysis of social facts at the domestic level in order to understand capital account policy. On the one hand, shared understandings about legitimate economic policies constitute the essential social background for economic policies. If capital account openness is to be maintained over time, it needs domestic social legitimacy. The failure to receive social approval means that capital account liberalization will not be a durable feature of a country's macroeconomic landscape. On the other hand, state-business relations have to undergo a profound transformation towards favoring the material interests of pro-capital mobility actors within the domestic business community, who have come to dominate private sector interactions with the government.

Chapters 4 and *5* are dedicated to case studies on Peru and Colombia. Each chapter traces the evolution of capital account policy in the country over the last twenty years. In addition, each chapter assesses the explanatory power of 'outside-in' explanations. The analysis shows that both causal mechanisms found in 'outside-in' approaches – the role of the IMF and of the neoliberal epistemic community – fail to account for capital account policy in Peru and Colombia. I proceed to highlight the particular content and the impact of national economic identity on capital account policy in both countries. The Peruvian case study identifies a clear and decisive rupture with the previous national economic identity underlying capital account policy. A commitment to capital account openness was socially constructed as one of the critical lessons from the late 1980s economic crisis. Coupled with important changes in state-business relations providing privileged political access for economic actors with a preference for capital mobility over exchange-rate stability and external competitiveness, the sustainability of capital account openness in Peru was ensured. On the other hand, the survival of the pre-liberalization national economic identity during the economic liberalization process prevented that capital account openness became an enduring policy in Colombia. Specifically, the tradition of pragmatism and consensus-orientation among the political and economic elite of the country continued to inform decisions on capital account management, leading to policy instability with frequent changes between opening and closing.

Chapter 6 puts the two case studies in a comparative perspective, assessing the relative merit of alternative explanations of capital account policy. International forces highlighted in 'outside-in' explanations provide the structural context for changes towards the liberalization of capital account management in Latin America. However, international factors did not produce homogenous capital account policies. National and international agents pushing and pulling for capital account openness only find a fertile ground for their economic freedom campaign if the national economic identity changes in a way to include a new collective understanding and practice of economic policymaking where capital controls no longer have a home.

Chapter 2: Three Analytical Frameworks for the Explanation of Capital Account Policy: Interests, Institutions, and Ideas

The purpose of the present chapter is three-fold. First, I review the existing literature in political science regarding the explanation of national capital account policy with a view to (i) creating a typology based on broad analytical perspectives, and (ii) to signal an important lacuna with respect to domestic informal institutions that will be filled in the case studies on Peru and Colombia. Second, I provide a brief assessment of the major insights as well as the theoretical and/or empirical limitations of the existing explanatory approaches. Third, I show how different ontological foundations lead existing explanations to focus on different levels of analysis, key actors, or causal mechanisms driving capital account policy.

Given the dramatic upsurge in capital account liberalization since 1970, first in industrial countries and after 1990 also in developing countries, the literature has addressed this question with reference to three distinct ontological frameworks – interests, institutions, and ideas – operating at three distinct levels of analysis – individual, domestic, and systemic-international. This chapter introduces the different analytical categories and the main findings of the most relevant empirical studies in each cluster in terms of the determinants of capital account policy.[17] As a result of the review of the mostly quantitatively-oriented literature[18], nine possible explanatory clusters for what determines capital account policy are derived. The chapter concludes with a summary of the different causal mechanisms which can then be applied to the empirical material presented in the case studies.

Existing studies on the causes of capital account policy fall in one of three distinct analytical categories, each of them predicated upon specific ontological and corresponding epistemological premises.[19] Each of the three ontological positions can be linked to three broad levels of analysis, i. e., each can detect the main driver of capital account policy on the individual, the domestic, or the systemic-international stage. Both typologies are widely used in comparative politics and international relations theory (Waltz 1959; Blyth 2009), but are usually not combined in the same matrix. Interest-based explanations focus on rational choice assumptions about the determinants of economic policies. Institutionalist explanations emphasize the role of specific restrictions on autonomous agent behavior. Ideational explanations refer to the normative or sociological basis of economic policy decisions.

17 Note that I do not pretend to include all existing empirical studies on capital account policy into my analytical structure. What follows is a deliberately selective review of the literature in order to produce an indicative list highlighting the main drivers behind capital account policy.

18 My decision to focus on the findings of large-N, quantitative studies is owed to their explicit intention to generalize, which in turn makes it straightforward to subject them to a qualitative assessment.

19 In an overview article, Cohen (2002: 437–38) only uses the level-of-analysis distinction in order to identify different schools of thought in terms of the causes of financial liberalization. Conversely, Deeg and O'Sullivan (2009) only use the interests-institutions-ideas typology for a review of the recent literature on the causal forces shaping the political economy of global finance.

It should be said at the outset that the three analytical frameworks and levels of analysis are not mutually exclusive. Although they are based on different ontological and concomitant epistemological positions, more often than not their insights are complementary, not incompatible or contradictory. In other words, the shortcomings of one framework usually constitute the relative strength of another. I will come back to this important point in the conclusion of this chapter.

2.1 Interest-based Explanations

The first ontological framework refers to explanations of capital account policy based on interests. For many scholars, the interests of individuals and groups are the basic category for social science research. According to them, interests constitute the starting point for empirical analyses of political and social outcomes. Interests form the central element of the rational choice or expected utility framework. They enter the explanation of political phenomena as variables which determine the ranking of preferences over outcomes within strategic interactions. The actual formation of interests and preferences remains exogenous to the subsequent analysis. Their content is taken as given, in a somehow primordial fashion, and held constant during at least one round of interaction. Agents are usually attributed with so-called "thick rationality", i. e., assumptions about the specific content of their goals such as wealth-maximization or power-aggregation.[20]

Virtually all interest-based explanations of capital account policy follow the logic of "thick rationality". They ascribe materially-defined goals to social agents – individuals and groups – which, in turn, motivate their behavior. Put simply, individuals and the interest groups that represent them always prefer economic policies that raise their incomes to policies that reduce their incomes.

For the sake of parsimony – a criterion to which all rational choice theories aspire – interests are assumed to be objectively or exogenously given and relatively stable over time. In addition, actors encounter no substantive or procedural difficulties in knowing where their (materially-defined) interests lie and in drawing the 'right' conclusions for acting upon them in strategic interactions. The necessary abstraction from reality for the purpose of parsimonious theory-building is openly acknowledged: "This (the given-ness of preferences) is not meant as a description of reality but as an analytically useful bounding of the problem to be examined" (Frieden 1999: 44). In other words, the aspiration to "ruthlessly prune extraneous complexity" (Geddes 2003: 192) for the sake of "abstraction, simplification, analytical rigor, and an insistence on clean lines of analysis from basic axioms to analytical propositions to empirical implications" (Shepsle 2006: 32) is a characteristic trademark of interest-based explanations of economic policy.

20 Conversely, thin rationalists abstain from such judgments and take an agnostic point of view concerning the content of actor preferences. In their interpretation, agents are motivated by a variety of factors which can, at least theoretically, include altruistic goals such as justice or equality (Ferejohn 1991). What unites thin and thick rationalists, however, is the assumption that actors pursue their given goals in an instrumental, means-ends fashion with contextual factors influencing the costs and benefits associated with different behavioral options.

2.1.1 Interests at the individual level

Many empirical studies of capital account policy are based on ontological and epistemological premises predicated upon material self-interest. However, they differ in their chosen level of analysis, i. e., which are the main actors or processes determining capital account policy. Let me begin with the first category – the individual level. Here the focus is on domestic policymakers. Their principal interest is defined in terms of the desire to stay in power and/or to capture economic rents. In addition, governments are supposed to act in relative independence from special interest group pressure. In other words, capital account policy choices reflect the government's autonomy vis-à-vis the domestic and international society. The question then is why and under what conditions a government pursues an open or a closed capital account.

Early empirical studies focused on the causes for the governments' preference for financial repression or capital controls based on rent-seeking motivations. Alesina, Grilli and Milesi-Ferretti (1994) argue that governments impose capital controls in order to limit the ability of individuals to avoid the inflation tax and to facilitate the imposition of administrative measures designed to keep domestic interest rates artificially low. Government interest in seigniorage revenue from high inflation becomes the central motive behind the imposition of capital controls. Leblang (1997: 440) comes to a similar conclusion: "When governments repress the financial sector in an attempt to recycle debt, generate revenue, or distribute tax burdens, they are also likely to implement capital controls". In other words, capital controls provide a lifeline for economically struggling governments in order to stay afloat and an important source for patronage and state autonomy.

A more recent contribution that falls into the government-focused category is the "transitional cost" approach to capital account liberalization by Brooks (2004). She asks why developing countries have systematically stayed behind developed countries in opening up their capital accounts. Her answer points to greater transitional costs of international financial liberalization in those countries:

> leaders in developing nations under certain circumstances confront potentially greater short-term risks of economic disruption and systemic financial crisis: if they liberalize capital flows in the context of weak or repressed domestic financial sectors or if their governments possess inadequate resources with which to defend their currency, rescue banks, or alleviate the social costs of liberalization (Brooks 2004: 391).

In other words, governments everywhere weigh the macroeconomic costs of capital account liberalization against their benefits and subsequently choose the course of action that promises the country as a whole the highest return. A related expectation is that,

> political leaders (...) should advance capital account opening where macroeconomic fundamentals are positive rather than negative, in order to reduce the risk of economic calamity in the

> event of sudden reversals of capital flows, and thus to avoid as well the potential political backlash associated with such a crisis (Brooks and Kurtz 2007: 709).[21]

The principal problem with this sort of explanation is a striking empirical anomaly: countries that according to the transitional cost approach were best prepared to undertake financial liberalization moved rather cautiously in this direction, while countries that were institutionally and politically least prepared to shoulder the transitional costs, did move rapidly towards full capital account openness. The contrast between Argentina and Chile during the 1990s illustrates this point. Chile went through a dramatic liberalization period during the late 1970s and experienced the consequences of the rapid opening of the capital account without having the necessary institutional regulations of the domestic financial sector in place. Only after the establishment of these prudential regulations did Chile undertake capital account liberalization again after 1990. In contrast, Argentina's policymakers embarked on a full-scale liberalization program in 1990 without much regard for prudential requirements. In their hurry to leave high inflation and capital scarcity as a result of the 1980s debt crisis behind them, Argentine policymakers were hardly concerned with the "transitional costs" of capital account openness. In their mind, if such costs existed at all, they would be far inferior to the costs of not pursuing the radical opening of the capital account in times of economic dire straits. Brooks' approach presupposes a careful balancing of the benefits and costs of open capital accounts before governments take decisions regarding capital account liberalization. However, this is not a realistic assumption in most cases of capital account liberalization in Latin America during the 1990s. The rational calculation of the costs and benefits of capital account openness does not seem to be the only or perhaps not even the most important consideration for policymakers when contemplating fundamental policy changes.

2.1.2 *Interests at the domestic level*

According to interest-based explanations, policymakers have conflicting preferences vis-à-vis capital account policy. What has then turned the balance towards liberalization over the last thirty years, including in developing countries? Empirical studies addressing this question have turned to the wider domestic context. They posit that policymakers agree to capital account liberalization if they lack the capacity to resist societal pressure for financial opening. For example, Li and Smith argue that partisan governments lean towards financial liberalization if their core societal constituency increasingly supports it – skilled labor for left-wing governments, multinational corporations and commercial banks for right-wing governments. Skilled labor, multinational companies, and commercial banks may also influence capital account policy, regardless of whether 'its' political party is in power, if the group has broad national significance and captures government policymaking (Li and Smith 2002).

21 Mukherjee and Singer (2010) confirm Brooks' argument that capital account liberalization is conditional on the capacity of governments to off-set the negative distributional consequences of financial openness.

By far the most sophisticated interest-based framework operating primarily at the domestic level of analysis is the so-called "Open-Economy Politics" (OEP)[22] perspective. It subscribes to a pluralist or conflictive notion of the political process. Government policy is seen as the outcome of domestic power struggles and strategic interactions between state actors and societal groups. In other words, governments are merely the vicarious agent of societal interests and do not possess significant policy autonomy. As a result, agency is predominately ascribed to societal groups and the outcome of their battles to influence government decisions in their favor: "Politics, in this view, is primarily competition among various sectors of the economy" (Frieden 1991: 438). The crucial battle line runs between "integrationist" and "anti-integrationist" forces in the domestic political economy (Frieden 1991: 442).[23]

The chain of deductive reasoning used in OEP is captured in a three-stage process:

> OEP begins with firms, sectors, or factors of production as the units of analysis, derives their interests over economic policy from each unit's position within the international economy, conceives of institutions as mechanisms that aggregate interests (with more or less bias) and condition the bargaining of competing societal interests, and finally, introduces when necessary bargaining at the international level between states with different societally-produced interests (Lake 2004: 11–12).

As the first step, then, the political analyst identifies the relevant actors in the domestic economy according to sectoral cleavages, e.g., owners of capital, owners and workers in specific sectors, producers of traded and nontraded goods, as well as international investors, e.g., multinational corporations and foreign commercial banks. It is a central feature of all economic policies that some socio-economic groups will materially benefit while other groups will be negatively affected by them. Preferences over the outcomes of political processes can be assigned to actors and groups according to their position in the economy and how they are affected by the expected distributional consequences of policy measures. Their interests simply reflect the answer to the question of which policy decision would enhance their utility, as measured in increases in wealth or income, based on their position in the domestic economy.

According to interest-based explanations, interest groups face no substantial cognitive problems perceiving the implications of specific policies and hence ascertaining their concomitant costs and benefits in terms of the group's material utility. As a result, the formation of group preferences vis-à-vis specific policies is a straightforward process of calculating the distributive consequences of specific economic policies. The subsequent behavior of interest groups promoting or rejecting these policies is simply the reflection of their material position in the market. No other elements are needed in order to derive, i.e., to *assume* their policy preferences, and to predict their behavior. Cognitive uncertainty or confusion about one's interests and policy preferences are not foreseen in this elegant framework built

22 The term was coined by Bates (1997).

23 See Schamis (1999) and Treisman (2004) for applications of this approach in order to explain economic reform policies in Latin America during the 1990s.

on parsimonious, yet mostly untested 'as if' assumptions about actor interests (Blyth 1997, 2003).

Based on the differentiation of socio-economic interest groups in society, linkages are established between changes in the international economic arena, e.g., the rise in international capital mobility, and changes in domestic politics leading to a greater exposure of the national economy to global goods and capital markets (Frieden and Rogowski 1996). The operating logic follows the analytic tradition of the 'second image reversed' (Gourevitch 1978), i.e., events on the level of the international system have repercussions for the content and conduct of national policies. Greater capital mobility in the international financial system favors domestic economic groups with specific characteristics or assets (Frieden 1991).

As the last step, interest groups must be able to form powerful coalitions in order to overcome entrenched institutional arrangements favoring status quo politics. Whether they succeed in influencing the policymaking process is measured by the extent to which policy outcomes reflect their deductively derived, i.e., independent of observable behavior, interests. Following this logic, economic policy reforms are the result of a coalition-building process among self-interested participants. The successful initiation and stability of economic reforms depend on the degree to which the policy receives political support from key economic groups.

According to the OEP framework, financial internationalization has pronounced distributional consequences and is thus politically salient (Frieden 1991). On the one hand, groups that will be negatively affected by capital account liberalization include low-skilled, lower-income workers since they are less able to take advantage of expanded investment options to hedge against new risks attendant on financial openness. In addition, capital outflows in response to economic shocks can put wages at risk (Rodrik 1997). On the other hand, capital owners will increase their gains if the government decides to lower formal restrictions on international capital flows for it provides them with more investment opportunities.

To empirically demonstrate the influence of specific interest groups over economic policies, particularly on a cross-national level, has been a perennial problem for interest-based approaches. The standard approach in large-N statistical analyses has been to use aggregate economic features such as sector size as part of GDP as a proxy for the political importance or influence of business groups. This is a highly problematic indicator and more often than not distorts the facts on the ground. For example, the financial service sector represented around 10% of Colombian GDP in 2007, roughly identical to the size of the agricultural sector (Cárdenas 2009: 36), the most important traditional export sector of the country. However, the latter has apparently been more successful in terms of influencing government decisions on capital account management. In other words, using sector size as an indicator leads to indeterminate, inaccurate, or even wrong conclusions in terms of the leverage of interest groups over economic policymaking.[24]

24 Another example is the power of the agricultural sector over policymaking in the European Union. Despite its small size and contribution to GDP, the agricultural sector exercises a disproportionally high leverage over policymaking in the EU.

2.1.3 Interests at the systemic-international level

The final level of analysis on the horizontal axis focuses on systemic factors. According to this perspective, the causes of capital account policy lie outside specific countries. Either actors at the international level determine domestic policy, or systemic dynamics propel domestic actors pursuing their material self-interest to adopt and sustain specific economic policies.

In contrast to individual and domestic explanations of capital account policy, systemic approaches tend to be more sensitive to the specific situation of developing countries which traditionally have been exposed to asymmetric interactions with international public and private agents. They highlight the role of globally active economic actors such as large financial intermediaries or institutional investors, foreign governments, and international financial institutions.

The literature on the global diffusion of political and economic liberalism distinguishes between several causal mechanisms, each based on a common epistemological – rational choice – position and located on the same – international – level of analysis: coercion, competition, and learning. The effect of each mechanism leads to largely identical economic policies on a global scale (Simmons et al. 2008).

Coercion

The first mechanism refers to coercive power or the forceful external imposition of policies exploiting power asymmetries between actors. In other words, national policies and institutions are imposed by international agents through threat or use of physical force. As a result, national policymakers respond to material pressure from the outside in their specific policy decisions. In the case of international financial liberalization, especially in developing countries, the main actors in this regard are the International Monetary Fund and powerful states in the international economic system, in particular the United States. They have applied forceful measures in order to pressure national policymakers into liberalizing the capital account, mostly against the will of the latter. The aggressive push for financial opening in developing countries pursued by the US government and the IMF follows the logic of a like-minded vicarious agent for the specific interests of economic groups in industrial countries, in the particular the internationally-oriented financial sector (Bhagwati 1998; Wade 2001a; Stiglitz 2002, 2004).

The central instrument of coercive pressure is conditionality, i. e., reform conditions included as an integral part of IMF lending agreements with national governments. Economic conditionality gained prominence as part of the rapidly increasing number of structural adjustment programs during the Latin American debt crisis in the 1980s (Stallings 1992).[25] Proponents of the coercion mechanism emphasize how developed countries and the international financial institutions under their control have compelled developing countries to pursue liberal policies in trade and finance.

25 For earlier, descriptive studies on the relationship between the international financial institutions and Latin American countries, see Payer (1969) and Kofas (2002).

However, there are several analytical and methodological problems with the operationalization and efficacy of coercive power as seen through the eyes of IMF conditionality vis-à-vis developing countries. First, a country's decision to participate in an IMF program is based on 'nonrandom selection', i. e., the circumstances of countries that participate in IMF programs differ systematically from the circumstances of countries that do not. As a result, the challenge in ascertaining the influence of the IMF on a government's policy choices is that an IMF program itself may be epiphenomenal: that is, the factors that lead a country to select into an IMF program may also determine its subsequent policy behavior.

In fact, for a variety of political reasons countries may self-select themselves into IMF programs because they want conditions externally imposed on them, rather than the other way around (Vreeland 2003). For example, rather than being imposed as conditions by the IMF in loan negotiations, governments *voluntarily* commit themselves to economic reforms in the so-called 'Letters of Intent' (LOIs)[26] in order to use the political cover of the IMF to enact domestically unpopular reforms or to overcome internal divisions within the state apparatus (Remmer 1986; Woods 2005).

So it comes as no surprise that formal IMF conditionality – which is understood to mean prior actions, performance criteria, or structural benchmarks – rarely included capital account liberalization (Quinn and Toyoda 2008: 178). On the other hand, aspects of it were often included in the authorities' overall policy package presented to the IMF. A number of IMF-supported programs included references to aspects of capital account liberalization in the LOIs or accompanying policy memorandums (IEO 2005: 31). Put differently, capital account liberalization makes an appearance not as part of official IMF conditionality imposed on countries but as a voluntary commitment device sought by reform-oriented governments in order to overcome domestic resistance (Mukherjee and Singer 2010).[27]

In addition, the political and economic priorities of large IMF member countries shape the details, including the conditionalities, of IMF programs to a much larger degree than any objective criteria rooted in the economic situation of the country at hand (Stone 2002, 2008; Dreher et al. 2009; Pop-Eleches 2009; Copelovitch 2010). As a result, the traditional operationalization of IMF 'hard power' in quantitative studies in terms of the size and/or the frequency of disbursed loans has come under attack. The loans and their concomitant conditionalities are found to be in need of explanation before using them as an indicator for the Fund's power over developing countries.

Second, a number of empirical studies about loan conditionality have lent little support to the widespread assumption that coercive power enables international financial institutions (IFIs) to force their preferred economic policies down the throats of recalcitrant developing country governments. Regarding the adoption of policy reforms, these studies have consistently failed to establish a statistically significant association between the conditions set by the IMF for financial support and the economic policies of developing coun-

26 LOIs are statements of the national authorities' policy intention and do not constitute conditionality that links compliance with disbursements of funds.

27 However, see Wade (2001b) and Woods (2006: 125–128) for examples of the imposition of capital account liberalization by the IMF against the wishes of the national government.

tries (Remmer 1986; Killick 1995; Dollar and Svensson 2000; Bird 2003: 92–124; Vreeland 2006).

Thus, it is not surprising that large-N studies do not find any positive relationship between capital account openness in developing countries and 'hard' IFI influence as measured by the size of obligations owed to the IMF and the World Bank or the weight of IMF or World Bank loan flows as a share of country GDP (Brune and Guisinger 2003; Brooks and Kurtz 2007). As it turns out, the use of IMF credits is actually associated with restrictions rather than the liberalization of the capital account (Simmons and Elkins 2004: 186).[28] However, this finding most likely reflects the conditions that caused the country to seek IMF assistance in the first place rather than the influence of the IMF itself.

Yet it would be a premature assessment to conclude that

> it is difficult to sustain the argument that the waves of liberalization and restriction in these policy areas (capital account, current account, exchange rate regime) have been systematically influenced by direct or organizationally mediated hegemonic pressure (Simmons and Elkins 2004: 186).

For instance, the mere existence of an IMF financing arrangement with a specific developing country is positively related with the decision to open the capital account (Chwieroth 2005; Brune and Guisinger 2007; Chwieroth et al. 2009; Brooks and Kurtz 2012). This, in turn, indicates the importance of an institutionalized channel of communication and frequent interaction between national policymakers and representatives from the IMF as a condition for the adoption of externally desired policies (Broome 2010). I will return to this point when I discuss other, 'softer' ways of IMF influence on capital account policy.

Competition

The second diffusion mechanism refers to competitive pressure coming from the international level. National actors change policies and institutions due to economic peer pressure. In an effort not to lose out against key economic competitors and to preserve their countries as an attractive place for global investment, governments face strong incentives to choose 'market friendly' policies tailored to lure international investors (back). Once an economic competitor has adopted capital account liberalization, countries have strong incentives to respond in kind in order to prevent the diversion of capital flows to the competing nation.

Mosley (2003) argues that developing countries are particularly affected by this mechanism. Whereas developed countries are able to preserve significant wiggle room in terms of economic policies vis-à-vis capital market constraints, in developing countries the influence of financial markets on government policy autonomy is both strong and broad. The risk of default makes international market participants willing to consider a range of govern-

28 Rodrik explains why that might be the case: "external resources reduce the costs both of reform and of doing nothing – that is, avoiding reform. In addition, the *prospect* of aid can actually exacerbate the delay in stabilization, by inducing groups to postpone making sacrifices until aid actually materializes. The effect on reform is consequently ambiguous" (Rodrik 1996: 30).

ment policies in their investment decisions. As a result, in order to remain attractive as an international investment location, developing countries are forced to engage in 'competitive deregulation', including capital account liberalization. In turn, open capital accounts place substantial restrictions on the viability of heterodox economic policies or the ability to engage in expansionary fiscal policies.

In a large-N study, Simmons and Elkins (2004) find strong evidence that economic policies adopted by competitors for the same pool of global capital, in particular foreign direct investment, are quickly replicated by other countries with similar levels of education and infrastructure. However, using a different indicator for capital account openness, Brune and Guisinger (2007) find no support for the competition-for-capital hypothesis as the causal mechanism behind capital account opening. Similarly, Quinn and Toyoda (2008) find no evidence of competitive effects in their large-N, longitudinal study of international financial liberalization. Finally, Chwieroth et al. (2009), using competition in trade as the causal link, find no effect for capital account policy decisions in Latin America.

Yet the study periods, regional coverage and indicator of a country's competitors as well as the capital account openness measure of these three studies differ sharply from Simmons and Elkins (2004). The divergent findings regarding the 'competition effect' highlight the fact that different measures or specifications of the independent (competition) and dependent variable (capital account openness) employed in large-N studies can lead to dramatically different conclusions about the importance of specific causal mechanisms driving capital account policy.

Learning

The third mechanism emphasizes rational or Bayesian learning. National policymakers observe and interpret successful policy and institutional innovations in other countries and subsequently adopt these models in their own countries. As a result, they make optimal use of available information, update their prior knowledge and beliefs and revise their behavior accordingly. According to this perspective, capital account openness becomes a uniform policy choice across countries since it is increasingly perceived as a superior economic policy due to the salience of its apparent success. Thus, having learned the 'right' lessons from its own or other countries' experience with a specific policy, countries proceed to adopt and maintain it.

However, Meseguer (2009) finds that rational learning – about the global, regional and local consequences of capital account freedom in terms of economic growth – had little influence on the decision to adopt capital account liberalization.[29] As she put it,

> a high variability in observed performance under an open capital account was not a deterrent to adopting this policy. In fact, it is related to a greater likelihood of opening. [...] This behavior

29 However, rational learning seems to matter for sustaining an open capital account. Countries did pay heed to the experience of others in terms of the relative volatility of economic growth and especially regarding the impact of financial crises when contemplating the continuation of capital account openness (Meseguer 2009: 166).

> (...) hints at *nonrational behavior* related to unfounded expectations about performance under capital account openness (Meseguer 2009: 164–5; emphasis added).

Governments generally rushed to open the capital account without giving much thought to the previous experience of their own or other countries. To illustrate this point, consider the Latin American context during the late 1980s and early 1990s. The dramatic upsurge of capital account openness during that time could hardly be called a superior or consensual policy according to the academic literature at that time. Financial liberalization on a larger scale was tried before in some South American countries in the late 1970s – in Argentina, Chile, and Uruguay – with rather disastrous consequences (Díaz-Alejandro 1985). As a result, the high costs associated with capital account openness were well known in the region. Drawing the right lessons from this negative experience should have cautioned countries *against* the rapid adoption of capital account liberalization. With the possible exception of Chile, virtually no Latin American country in the early 1990s was prepared to assume the significant 'transitional costs' involved in opening the capital account (Brooks 2004). Yet many went ahead regardless – a conundrum for rational learning models (Meseguer 2009: 178).

An additional limitation of rational learning models is that rather than on a global basis, learning is more likely to occur among groups of peers who share information and whose experiences are more relevant to each other. As a result, similar policies are usually adopted in a regional context or between neighboring countries, with which close channels of information and communication exist (Quinn 2003; Brune and Guisinger 2007; Weyland 2007; Brooks and Kurtz 2012). Instead of rational learning based on fully available information about their costs and benefits, the spontaneous emulation of economic policies prevalent in a specific geographic region and based on incomplete information might be the driving force for diffusion. I will return to this analytically distinct causal mechanism when discussing the cognitive roots of capital account policy in the next section.

In sum, interest-based explanations of capital account policy operate at all three levels of analysis. Their common feature is that agent behavior is based on the *rational pursuit of material self-interest.* Within such a framework, each level of analysis emphasizes different drivers or causal mechanisms at work. The individual level focuses strictly on government actions; the domestic level broadens the horizon to include (coalitions of) economic interest groups and their influence over government policies. Finally, the systemic level introduces agents and dynamics outside the national context which drive national economic policies in a specific direction.

On the individual level, policymakers are the primary focus group. They make decisions on capital account policy based on their orientation toward national welfare, capturing economic rents, or political expediency. Yet policymakers do not make decisions based solely on their own volition. Instead, their decisions on economic policies generally, and capital account policy specifically, are shaped by other domestic and international actors. A domestic-level focus puts economic interest groups front and center in the analysis. Coalitions of domestic interest groups are expected to determine which capital account policy the government pursues. A focus on the systemic-international level locates the cause of domestic economic policy in forces or actors outside the country determining domestic policy choices. According to the three causal mechanisms – coercion, competition, and learning – the principal international actors are the IMF, economic competitor countries, or neighboring countries, respectively.

Table 2.1 Interest-based explanations of capital account policy

Individual	Domestic	Systemic-International
▪ Orientation of government (welfare vs. rent-seeking)	▪ Clashes between economic groups	▪ Coercion (though IMF) ▪ Economic competition ▪ Rational learning

2.2 Institutionalist Explanations

Institutions are commonly referred to as the humanly devised rules of the games that govern social interactions (North 1990: 3). They are more formally defined as

> a relatively enduring collection of rules and organized practices, embedded in structures of meaning and resources that are relatively invariant in the face of turnover of individuals and relatively resilient to the idiosyncratic preferences and expectations of individuals and changing external circumstances (March and Olsen 2006: 3).

Their function is to prescribe appropriate behavior for specific actors in specific situations based on the assumption that institutions create elements of order and predictability. As such they have a partly autonomous role from agency in political life.

Institutions come in different forms and sizes. They can range from bureaucracies and markets to kinship systems and religions. Besides formal institutions, informal systems of rules and procedures guide individual or group behavior and thereby shape social and political outcomes. However, what unites all forms of institutions is their capacity to fashion, enable, and constrain individual or group autonomous actions. In other words, they stand between human agency and social or political outcomes. As a result, institutions are rather static entities; they guarantee the stability and persistence of established patterns of interaction and impose a high, inertial cost for changing them.

At a general level, institutions are conceived of as multifaceted, exogenous and endogenous constraints on agents' range of autonomous actions. These barriers for individual or group actions can take several forms according to each level of analysis. On the individual level, cognitive constraints restrict the application of full rationality assumptions in terms of actor behavior. Cognitive filters channel the behavior of policymakers in directions which are not congruent with rational expectations. On the domestic level, institutions establish the formal rules governing the political process. These institutions constitute the filter between actors' interests and political outcomes. On the systemic level, institutions refer to structural constraints imposed by the specific position or integration of a country in the international economy.

2.2.1 *Institutions at the individual level*[30]

Individual actors face important cognitive barriers that constrain the application of perfect rationality assumptions to economic policymaking (Odell 2002; Walter 2005). Bounded rationality explanations of political decision-making inquire into the role of cognitive shortcuts and heuristics applied by individual decision-makers as well as the broader public. For them, the explanatory variable is the perception of risk by the chief government executive and public opinion. According to the most important insight of behavioral economics – prospect theory – actors faced with significant losses show a tendency for risk-taking, whereas they behave cautiously when faced with potential gains from their actions. In other words, long periods of economic deterioration shift people's propensity for assuming risk toward a demand for and acceptance of radical economic policies. Given a supply of such policy blueprints, rapid institutional change is expected (Weyland 2008).

Applying the insights of prospect theory, Weyland (2002a) relates the severity of the economic crisis in many Latin American countries in the 1990s together with the accession of new leaders to power to the adoption of drastic neoliberal reforms, including capital account liberalization. The crises put national leaders and the public at large in the domain of material losses and so exponentially increased their risk acceptance with regard to unorthodox policy measures. Hence, in this perspective economic reforms were not introduced due to rational cost-benefit calculations by governments or due to the pressure of economic interest groups but rather as a result of cognitive heuristics of policymakers. In other words, the adoption of neoliberal reforms was not the outcome of a thorough assessment of their fit with specific requirements and needs of a country but instead 'taken off the shelf' from prevailing policy prescriptions. Seen from this vantage point, prospect theory can provide a microfoundation for the interpretation of an economic crisis as a necessary variable for economic reforms through "people's situationally defined propensity toward risk" (Weyland 2002a: 45).

Prospect theory also sheds light on the sustainability of economic reforms. Market-based reforms are 'threatened by their own success'. While macroeconomic stabilization put state leaders in the domain of material gains, they became more cautious and risk-averse in its aftermath, "and therefore shied away from completing the program of drastic reforms recommended by their neoliberal advisers and the international financial institutions" (Weyland 2002a: 6). In other words, capital account opening gets stuck at a certain point when leaders and the broader public feel that they have left the domain of losses and are no longer willing to accept undue risks or the high costs associated with radical economic policies.

30 Labelling cognitive constraints on individual or group decision-making as institutions might be considered controversial. According to the conventional, Northian definition, institutions are consciously formed by human actors, i. e., they are a priori exogenous from individuals. On the other hand, cognitive constraints reside within individuals. I do recognize the deviation from the conventional notion of institutions in political science and economics when I apply the term to the individual level. However, I include a specific literature inspired by political psychology within an ontological framework with which it shares the emphasis on the constraining and enabling effects of institutions for political outcomes. To be sure, cognitive constraints are not the result of humanly devised rules but rather an endogenous factor affecting individual actors in pretty much the same way and thus according to predictable patterns for political decisions.

Cognitive-psychological explanations of economic policy choices have their inherent limitations, too. First, they encounter an empirical problem to account for cases where economic reforms took place without the prior occurrence of a profound economic crisis. Second, they have difficulties to explain where the cognitive shortcuts suggesting the details of a neoliberal reform package come from in the first place or who inserted these blueprints and how into the domestic political context. Weyland's sophisticated approach remains wedded to an individualistic-materialist account of political decision-making, emphasizing only cognitive constraints on policymakers. However, he fails to consider other types of institutional restrictions beyond the individual level for actor behavior.

2.2.2 Institutions at the domestic level

As mentioned before, there is a strong overlap between explanations which emphasize domestic interests and those which emphasize formal domestic institutions, at least in the "Open Economy Politics" framework. In essence, rational choice institutionalism is the extension of the interest-based approach. OEP maintains that political outcomes and processes cannot be explained solely on the basis of the actions of diverse, self-interested individuals and their influence on government decisions. Instead, institutional differences between countries and sectors determine distinctive patterns of economic policy, even when they are faced with similar challenges from international processes and domestic interest group pressure (Garrett and Lange 1996; Milner 2002 applies the OEP or "interests + institutions" framework to the explanation of national trade policy).

As a result, OEP interprets formal or what Shepsle calls "structured" institutions (Shepsle 2006) as the intermediary variable between the influence of interest-group coalitions and policy outcomes. Faced with societal pressure to implement specific economic policies, the outcome of the strategic interaction between governments and domestic interest groups is determined by certain executive characteristics such as political orientation (left-right) and the concomitant dependence on certain constituencies as well as specific features of the political system affecting the state's capacity to act autonomously vis-à-vis the domestic society (Katzenstein 1977). The crucial insight is that political outcomes can be varied by altering the procedures of interest aggregation through institutions. Policy choices are thus a function of pre-existing institutional arrangements.

OEP scholars have primarily focused on formal public or political institutions such as regime type, the constitutional powers of the president, electoral rules, as well as the composition, fractionalization and strength of the political party system (Haggard and Webb 1994; Haggard and Kaufman 1995; Haggard and McCubbins 2001). These institutions are "equilibrium ways of doing things" in the political game (Shepsle 2006: 26). They are supposed to filter or reconcile competing societal interests and transform them into collective choices.

Several quantitative studies have emphasized the role of domestic political and economic institutions as determinants of capital account policy, albeit many empirical findings have been derived from analyzing a subset of developed countries only. Five formal institutions are regarded as particularly relevant for changes towards liberalizing the capital account: (i) the fragmentation of the party system; (ii) central bank independence; (iii) a floating exchange-rate regime; (iv) right-wing governments in power; and (v) the absence of sophisticated inward-oriented development strategies.

An empirical study based on several OECD countries found that states with a higher number of veto-player parties in government enact fewer capital controls policy changes (Kastner and Rector 2003). Similarly, Brooks and Kurtz (2007) find that Latin American governments are most likely to pursue financial openness in countries where political authority in the legislature is fragmented. The reason is that ex post political responsibility for capital account reform enactment can be widely spread should an economic downturn emerge.

With the worldwide movement towards granting the central bank political autonomy from the executive, capital controls have been concomitantly reduced (Grilli and Milesi-Ferretti 1995; Quinn and Inclán 1997). The same trend occurred with the shift from fixed to (more) flexible exchange-rate regimes in Latin America (Frenkel and Rapetti 2010). According to the logic of the "Impossible Trinity"[31], governments in the developing world generally, and in Latin America specifically, increasingly preferred capital mobility and autonomous monetary policy over fixing their exchange rate as a nominal anchor (Eichengreen 2008: 178–183).

Quinn and Inclán (1997) show that societal demands, expressed through government partisanship, interact with resource endowments to shape capital account policy. Left-wing governments, representing labor, tended to maintain capital controls unless they were in countries with an advantage in skilled labor. Conversely, right-wing governments are more likely to enact capital account liberalization (Quinn and Inclán 1997; Leblang 1999; Li and Smith 2002; Brooks 2004; Kastner and Rector 2005) and, more importantly for my research question, function as the principal institutional guarantor for its sustainability (Brune and Guisinger 2007).

Finally, the legacies of post-World War II inward-oriented development strategies such as import-substituting industrialization (ISI) among Latin American countries condition the adoption and sustainability of neoliberal economic policies. Countries such as Brazil or Chile that have pursued "advanced ISI" are less likely to institutionalize a fully open capital account. The structural legacies of earlier economic development strategies have a significant imprint on the economic policies adopted during the liberalization period. The industrial deepening associated with advanced ISI created interest groups in export-oriented manufacturing or non-traditional sectors that adopt a middle-ground position between full economic liberalization and financial autarky. As a result, Latin American countries that pursued advanced ISI policies up until the onset of the continental debt crisis in the early 1980s are characterized by a historical legacy in form of internationally-oriented industrialists (Brooks and Kurtz 2012).

31 The term "Impossible Trinity" refers to the policy implications of the Mundell-Fleming model of a small open economy (Cohen 1996). According to the model, governments can only simultaneously pursue two out of the following three macroeconomic policies: (i) a fixed exchange rate regime; (ii) an independent monetary policy; and (iii) free capital mobility.

The position of export-oriented firms on capital account openness is, however, ambiguous (Frieden 1991: 444–5). While financial openness may offer access to lower-cost finance, it brings the risk of currency appreciation and exchange rate volatility, which harm exports. Given those mixed preferences of a politically influential domestic interest group, some – usually bigger – Latin American countries have been recalcitrant to fully liberalize their capital account (Brooks and Kurtz 2012). Yet, as the case of Argentina during the 1990s demonstrates, having been an advanced-ISI country is by itself no guarantee that governments refrain from liberalizing the capital account to a significant amount. Or put somewhat more succinctly, for every advanced-ISI country that only partially liberalized its capital account, there is another that went all the way down on the financial liberalization score.

At any rate, the cases of Peru and Colombia show a somewhat different pattern from the expectations of the extant institutionalist literature on capital account policy. Both countries have had fragmented legislatures, right-wing governments and central bank independence after 1990, yet show important differences in their capital account policies. This policy contrast despite formal institutional similarity emphasizes the need to delve deeper into the domestic context of the countries, in particular regarding the importance of 'unstructured' or informal institutions for policy outcomes, which the OEP approach tends to ignore.

2.2.3 Institutions at the systemic-international level

Various institutional constraints are imposed from the systemic-international level for the policy autonomy of national actors. In what specific forms do systemic-international rules of the game shape capital account policy in developing countries? And how can structural-level explanations account for the variation of capital account policy? I describe two different answers to these questions, drawn from rational-choice and sociological institutionalism, respectively.

Material constraints for national policy

In the context of increasing economic globalization, rationalist scholars emphasize material constraints on governments such as advances in communications and information technologies, increasing economic interdependence, and the rise of international capital mobility. They interpret these structural changes during the late twentieth century as unmovable, exogenous factors on the systemic level that affect all national governments in broadly similar ways. They refer to the increased mobility of capital brought on by the deregulation of national financial markets in the wake of the collapse of the Bretton Woods agreement in the early 1970s. The ease with which capital can be moved across national borders, these scholars suggest, has made it more difficult for governments to maintain traditional economic policies and institutions (Strange 1996). As a result, governments are left with little room for maneuver but to embark on financial liberalization (Andrews 1994). In addition, systemic forces privilege the interests and actions of certain domestic actors (Goodman and Pauly 1993). Given structural pressures from the international level, changing course drastically and abolishing capital controls is portrayed as an inevitable policy choice for national governments.

In the case of Latin American countries, these external constraints are related to the traditional dependence on foreign capital, related to historically low national savings rates and heightened by the aftermath of the 1980s debt crisis and the resulting balance-of-payments problems in many countries. Mahon (1996) interprets recurrent capital outflows in Latin America in the context of foreign debt crises as the impersonal, structural force for ensuing neoliberal reforms, including capital account liberalization. The exposure and vulnerability to often rapid changes in world capital markets has substantially reduced the room for policy maneuver at the domestic level, transforming orthodox economic policies into the only game in town.

However, policy convergence is not a foregone conclusion, even in dire circumstances. In fact, national variation in capital account openness persists. Empirical studies based on rational-choice institutionalism refer to the specific position of a country in the international economic hierarchy in order to account for policy variance. Even though economic globalization generally, and global capital mobility specifically are usually associated with uniform constraints on national economic policy, some countries are ostensibly better equipped to resist international financial market pressures than others. Whereas the structural forces driving increased capital mobility travel the globe in uniform patterns, national responses vary according to the specific form and depth of integration of each country into the international economy. This, in turn, constitutes an institutional filter generating path-dependent trajectories of capital account policy.

Haggard and Maxfield (1996) explain the differences in capital account policy across developing countries with reference to the ease of their access to international credit and foreign exchange markets. Countries with competitive export sectors, particularly in a commodity price boom, can resist international market pressure. Those countries do not need to cater to the interests of foreign investors and financial firms and can therefore allow themselves the 'luxury' of maintaining (some) capital controls.

Similarly, Lukauskas and Minushkin (2000) explain the variation in capital account policy despite uniform structural forces with reference to national economic conditions and the need for external funds. Both factors determine a government's bargaining power vis-à-vis international actors and domestic interest groups. Governments with low bargaining position due to poor economic conditions and/or a high need for external funds are forced to open their financial markets completely in order to attract or retain capital. Conversely, governments with high bargaining power vis-à-vis these groups are able to retain some forms of capital controls without losing access to foreign capital.

In sum, rational-choice institutionalist accounts operating on the systemic-international level delineate the macroeconomic scope conditions for autonomous government behavior. Countries with certain economic conditions, e.g., a large domestic market or limited needs for external funds, are better equipped to withstand the siren song of international financial liberalization. While structural forces at the international level, such as increased global capital mobility, push all countries towards liberalization, their particular rate and form of integration in the international economy determines the degree to which they need to pay heed to systemic forces.

Social constraints for national policy

Due to the widespread neglect of informal rules and norms in rationalist and historical versions of institutionalism, the study of social institutions has become the domain of sociological institutionalism (DiMaggio and Powell 1983; March and Olsen 1989). Sociological institutionalism provides a different conception and interpretation of institutions. It applies the core insight of sociology – that individuals behave according to scripts that are tied to social roles – to explain economic behavior (Dobbin 2004; Granovetter 2005; Smelser and Swedberg 2005). International monetary relations are not only an arena for power, material self-interest, and formal institutions (Kirshner 2000). Social processes operate also in the context of monetary policy or what is traditionally considered to be a rational-materialist world. As a result, sociological institutionalism assigns a central role to factors such as beliefs, norms, values, and culture.

The so-called World Polity school[32] is the leading protagonist of sociological institutionalism. It starts from the observation that similar institutional and political arrangements exist across countries in various policy areas. It locates the root cause for these similarities in the states' inclusion into a single world system that creates strong incentives for the homogeneity of institutional forms and policies. Adopting the same institutional structures is interpreted as a (collectively) rational decision in order to secure the state's existence in a capitalist world system. As a result, nation-states are understood as "constructions of a common wider culture, rather than as self-directed actors responding rationally to internal and external contingencies" (Meyer et al. 1997: 152). Instead of being the reflection of (aggregated) individual utility calculations of states, institutional homogeneity is the result of a symbolic attempt to attain international legitimacy. Importing foreign institutions and policies into the domestic environment regardless of actual functional needs and requirements for these policies and institutions is meant to demonstrate efficiency and modernity to the world (Meyer and Rowan 1977; Finnemore 1993).[33]

In other words, according to the World Polity school, liberalizing the capital account is not the result of political agency, neither on the domestic nor the international level, but structurally driven by a universal normative pressure that no policymaker can escape. Along with other liberal political and economic reforms, capital account openness becomes a signifier of modernity and is meant to provide developing countries with the symbolic legitimacy to become part of the league of modern nations.

However, sociological institutionalism suffers from several problems. First, based on methodological collectivism, it presents an "oversocialized" view of society and politics, which lacks sufficient room for political agency (Finnemore 1996a: 343). As a result, sociological institutionalism usually underestimates the significance of the domestic realm as a key battleground for political and social change. Political agents are treated as 'institutional dummies' unable to escape the constraints of formal and informal rules in world society.

32 Also called world culture or world society theory.

33 In their overview of causal mechanisms for the diffusion of liberal economic policies operating at the international level, Simmons et al. (2008) calls this *social emulation* and relate it to constructivism. However, they mainly emphasize cognitive, not normative factors driving the global emulation of liberal policies and institutions.

The structural perspective of sociological institutionalists prevents them from exploring the independent role of individual and collective actors.

> Rapid global changes across dissimilar units suggest structure-level rather than agent-level causes. They do not, however, prove them. One also needs to specify the mechanism of change and show the common source of the new preference and behavior. (Finnemore 1996b: 22)

Second, the major methodological tool of sociological institutionalism has been macro-quantitative analyses which grossly simplify or misspecify the multiple micro-mechanisms of international socialization as well as their failure (Finnemore 1996a: 339–340; Schimmelfennig 2003: 410–411). The result of these shortcomings of sociological institutionalism is its inability to explain significant cross-country variations of policies and institutions.

In spite of its shortcomings, sociological institutionalism makes clear that policymakers and domestic societies do not function in isolation from the world around them. Institutional constraints exist not only on the individual-cognitive or domestic-formal but also on the international-normative stage. Domestic economic policies are also shaped by informal institutional processes on the systemic level. The challenge, however, is to empirically demonstrate how social, non-material forces such as norms and ideas get translated into domestic policies and institutions.

In sum, institutions function as constraints on autonomous actor behavior. At the individual level, cognitive restrictions filter the economic policy decisions of political leaders. They only undertake significant changes to existing capital account policy if they perceive to be in the domain of losses, which stimulates risk-taking behavior. Once this perception subsides, 'business as usual' takes over again and dramatic policy changes are abandoned. On the domestic level, institutional restrictions are imposed by formal political institutions that condition the political game and thus shape the content of economic policies. Partisan politics and the degree of fragmentation of legislatures exert an inertial effect on capital account policy. Finally, on the systemic-international level, institutional constraints come in two forms. First, a country's specific integration in the international economy defines the range of economic policy options available to governments. Second, national policymakers are influenced by non-material, social forces at the international level that provide them with templates or scripts for economic policies.

Table 2.2 Institutionalist explanations of capital account policy

Individual	Domestic	Systemic-International
▪ Gain-loss perception of political leaders	▪ Fragmentation of legislature (high-low) ▪ Partisanship (left-right) ▪ Structural legacies of earlier development strategies (ISI)	▪ Dependence on foreign capital (low-high) ▪ Emulation of templates

2.3 Ideational Explanations

Ideas-based explanations seek to demonstrate that policy and institutional change cannot be explained without explicit reference to some sort of change in the ideas undergirding existing policies and institutions. They take their cue from Keynes' famous statement in the conclusion of the *General Theory* that

> the ideas of economists and political philosophers, both when they are right and when they are wrong, are more powerful than is commonly understood. Indeed the world is ruled by little else. Practical men, who believe themselves to be quite exempt from any intellectual influences, are usually the slaves of some defunct economist. Madmen in authority, who hear voices in the air, are distilling their frenzy from some academic scribbler of a few years back. I am sure that the power of vested interests is vastly exaggerated compared with gradual encroachment of ideas (...) it is ideas, not vested interests, which are dangerous for good or evil (Keynes 1973: 383–4).

Goldstein and Keohane (1993) define ideas in increasing order of malleability or regarding their propensity to change in three distinct, yet interconnected, categories[34]:

1. *World views* include the major religions and political ideologies. In terms of economic policy, neoclassical economics or Marxism could be labeled a world view.
2. *Principled beliefs* are "normative ideas that specify criteria for distinguishing right from wrong and just from unjust" (Goldstein and Keohane 1993: 9). In terms of economic policy, the efficient distribution of resources in an unfettered market could be labeled a principled belief (within neoclassical economics).
3. *Causal beliefs* are "beliefs about cause-effect relationships which derive authority from the shared consensus of recognized elites" (Goldstein and Keohane 1993: 10). In terms of economic policy, the positive link between international capital mobility and economic growth could be labeled a causal belief (within neoclassical economics).

In contrast to interest-based and institutionalist accounts, relatively few ideational explanations of specific economic policies exist. Scholars have grappled with the perennial methodological problems for the operationalization of ideas in any sort of causal research design (Yee 1996; Hall 1997: 185). What is more, there is still a widespread disregard for ideas as significant explanatory factors in mainstream political analysis. At best they are regarded as epiphenomenal, residual or functional variables, relegated to the supporting cast rather than the main protagonists in most analyses of economic policy reforms.[35]

---

34 Schmidt (2008: 306) proposes a related, three-category typology of ideas. At the most specific level ideas are policies. Programs, paradigms or frames of reference that underpin policy ideas encompass the second, intermediate level. At the most general level ideas are philosophies that undergird policies and programs with organizing ideas, values, and principles of knowledge and society. All three categories of ideas can be further distinguished between cognitive ('what is and what to do') and normative ideas ('what one ought to do'). For the latter point, see also Rueschemeyer (2006).

35 If considered in rationalist empirical analyses at all, ideas are usually depicted as "the hooks on which politicians hang their objectives and by which they further their interests" (Shepsle, quoted in Schonhardt-

For the typology of ideas-based explanations of capital account policy, I limit my discussion to only two levels of analysis: individual and systemic-international. In the next chapter I offer a detailed discussion of collective ideas at the domestic level which I refer to as informal institutions.

Ideas exist in the minds of individuals but can only become politically relevant when adopted by a larger group of politically influential people at the same time. *Individual explanations* focus on how specific groups of people who share a particular economic idea, e. g., Keynesian or neoclassical economics, rise to the top of the political hierarchy and are thus able to determine economic policies according to their preferred ideology. In other words, the emphasis is on the fate of the individual carriers of ideas – not the ideas themselves. The more powerful the promoters of specific economic ideas become in the political hierarchy, the more likely it is that these ideas are enacted in international or domestic arenas (Sikkink 1991; Goldstein 1993; Berman 1998; McNamara 1998; Parsons 2003; Schonhardt-Bailey 2006; Darden 2009; Wedel 2009).

Ideational scholars critical of the purely individualistic, 'Weberian' perspective on ideas have demanded to take ideas, i. e., their actual content, seriously and not only consider their usefulness to connect diverse interest groups for the purpose of a common political goal. They argue for a truly independent category of analysis for ideas – fully transcending functionalism and methodological individualism – in the explanation of political, economic and institutional change (Blyth 2002; Campbell 2002; Hay 2006; Schmidt 2008, 2010; Béland and Cox 2010). As a consequence, *systemic-international explanations* start their analysis at the socially-defined structural level, emphasizing the constitutive role of norms in the international state system. They then seek to trace the impact of international norms on specific domestic policies. This perspective is usually associated with social constructivism in international relations theory (Wendt 1999). Constructivists argue that ideas or norms, not immutable 'material facts', determine actor behavior. Political and economic interests are not automatically given by 'objective' circumstances but rather the result of a process of social construction, where ideas play a crucial role.

The two forms of ideational explanation often overlap in empirical analysis. International norms and economic ideas enter the domestic realm through a variety of formal and informal channels. The main difference between the two perspectives is whether they focus on the "political power of economic ideas" (Hall 1989), or more precisely of their carriers, within the domestic context, or on the power of international norms to generate compliance on part of individual states. The first perspective is located within the disciplinary background of Comparative Politics or Comparative Political Economy, whereas the latter stems from International Relations.

Bailey 2006: 25). In other words, what matters is their strategic use to advance given material interests, not their independent or causal effects on actor behavior (Krasner 1993; Jacobsen 1995, 2003).

2.3.1 Ideas at the individual-domestic level: norm entrepreneurs and epistemic communities

Several studies of changes in economic policies have alluded to the crucial role of individual reformers with specific principled and causal beliefs about economic policy. The rise of foreign-trained economists ('technocrats') and economic teams, the so-called "technopols" (Domínguez 1997), to top-level positions within the state bureaucracy has been regarded as a necessary condition for the implementation of neoliberal economic reforms in many developing countries (Williamson and Haggard 1994: 594). It is through their activities that a common "cosmological heritage" based on a liberal international economic order can be established in the domestic context (Lal 2001: 241).[36] Individual economists who became convinced of the new, neoliberal creed have thus acted as "norm entrepreneurs" (Finnemore and Sikkink 1999) for the idea of economic liberalization.

The meteoric rise of a new generation of economists to powerful government positions has indeed been a common feature of many Latin American countries during the 1980s and 1990s (Markoff and Montecinos 1993; Montecinos 1997; Centeno and Silva 1998; Montecinos and Markoff 2010). Beginning in the late 1970s, 'técnicos' have increasingly replaced 'políticos' in important political positions for the management of economic affairs (Grindle 1977; Grindle and Thomas 1991). Mostly trained abroad at US graduate programs in economics, they have formed a closely-knit community with shared world views as well as principled and causal beliefs about 'good' or 'correct' economic policies which they implemented as soon as they reached politically influential positions in government. In other words, foreign-trained economists turned politicians became the central transmitters of the neoliberal economic doctrine for domestic policymaking (Drake 2005).

Going beyond the focus on norm entrepreneurs and their individual position in the state bureaucracy, the literature on epistemic communities emphasizes the collective identity of a coherent group of individuals pushing a specific agenda and striving for political influence. In other words, this literature illuminates the supply-side of the economic ideas-policies link. Epistemic communities are domestic and transnational networks of knowledge-based experts with a similar set of principled (normative) and causal beliefs and access to the political decision-making process (Haas 1992). They have also been called the "cognitive baggage handlers of constructivist analyses of politics and ideas" (Haas 2001: 11579). Peter Haas, the main protagonist of the concept in international relations theory, points out that epistemic communities can serve as better conduits for policymakers compared with traditional interest groups in politics since their knowledge is

> politically untainted, and thus more likely to 'work', in the political sense that it will be embraced and followed by political authorities concerned about the need for appearing impartial, and also technically (Haas 2001: 11580).

36 Thirty years ago, Evans coined the term "compradors" in order to describe the domestic allies of external actors, e.g., foreign banks, neoliberal US think-tanks, other states, or the international financial institutions (Evans 1979). During the debt crisis of the 1980s combined with a more prominent role of the international financial institutions in domestic affairs, their role became even more pronounced in Latin American politics (Haggard 1986).

A number of country and cross-country qualitative studies have tried to parse out the independent role of specific economic ideas, primarily neoclassical economics, for economic policy outcomes in Latin America by analyzing the fate of their representatives – professional economists – within the political machinery (Hira 1998; Babb 2001; Teichman 2001; Fourcade-Gourinchas and Babb 2002; Biglaiser 2002a).[37] Based on their shared beliefs about economic policies, these individuals initially form an epistemic community amongst themselves or what Hira calls "living social communities of like-minded professionals" (Hira 1998: 13). Upon being parachuted into the political establishment, they go on to build "international policy networks" with powerful, like-minded outsiders such as members of the national business community and international actors such as the IMF and the World Bank (Teichman 2001, 2004; Woods 2006: 65–69). Usually brought into the state bureaucracy by political leaders looking for 'fixers' in dire economic circumstances, neoliberal technocrats quickly become important mobilizers of policy reform, acting in relative political insulation from parliamentary or societal oversight or influence. In other words, economic policy reforms, including capital account liberalization, are the result of ideas-driven individuals who shape political outcomes according to their intrinsic beliefs, not as vicarious agents of powerful economic interests.

In addition, these studies emphasize the link between economic ideas, their inherent characteristics and their fit into the national or structural context. Put differently, the availability of a receptive institutional and intellectual environment in the target countries and the suitability of ideas for strategic use by domestic actors in their struggle for power and influence against opponents are seen as important conditions for their impact on domestic policy (Kingdon 1995; Hall 1989; Sikkink 1991; Dezalay and Garth 2002; Gourevitch 2005: 25–30).

Chwieroth (2007) uses a large-N, quantitative approach to analyze the influence of neoliberal economists turned technopols on capital account policy in emerging market countries. He posits that individual preferences in terms of economic policy are determined by professional training in graduate schools. In other words, the preference of future policymakers for an open capital account is established during their graduate studies at "neoliberal" US universities.[38] Upon re-insertion into the domestic context and forming a "coherent economic team of like-minded economists" able to shape government policy, this domestic-level community of neoliberal economists rapidly moved capital account policy towards openness.[39]

---

37 Chile, Argentina, and Mexico have received particular attention in this regard (Silva 1991, 2008; Valdés 1995; Silva 1998; Biglaiser 2002b; Dezalay and Garth 2002; Williams 2002; Estrada Álvarez 2005a).

38 The survey findings reported in Colander (2007) seem to corroborate the assumption that students in elite US graduate programs in economics become (a) politically more conservative, and (b) economically more inclined towards neoliberalism as a result of their training. However, Klein and Stern (2007) find that only a small percentage (8%) of members of the American Economic Association actually hold free-market policy views.

39 Kogut and Macpherson (2008) make a similar argument for the decision to privatize. They posit that the number of American-trained economists generally and University of Chicago-trained specifically among the overall population of national economists raises the likelihood that privatization is adopted in a specific country. However, their study suffers from serious methodological shortcomings. First, they only include members of the American Economic Association in their survey sample. Second, no measure of policy access for American-trained economists is provided in their analysis. Their sheer number is regarded as

In other words, not only the specific professional background of policymakers per se but also the place of their studies is assumed to make a difference for their behavior in economic policy. Imbued with the dominant paradigm of the location of their postgraduate training in economics, decision-makers will favor economic policies that correspond to the prescriptions internalized during their professional studies.[40] Biglaiser puts this relationship in more general terms,

> (T)o predict which policies economic policymakers favor, we need to evaluate the training of policymakers. If most economic policy makers earned degrees at virtually the same schools and share similar beliefs with regard to economic policy, we can establish a close connection between the ideas of policy makers and the policies they initiate (Biglaiser 2002a: 181–2).

However, the nascent quantitative literature on domestic-level neoliberal epistemic communities suffers from important analytical and methodological shortcomings:

- Neoliberalism is a broad church and often fails to capture important nuances of economic policies (Boas and Gans-Morse 2009). Policymakers do not have to subscribe to the entire array of neoliberal policy prescriptions despite having earned their postgraduate degrees at Chicago and other 'neoliberal' US universities. For instance, Chile's capital account policy during the 1980s and 1990s reflects a clear deviation from the teachings of the 'Chicago School' despite the fact that the country has otherwise been the poster-child of neoliberalism in Latin America mainly due to the influence of the 'Chicago boys' during the Pinochet regime (Valdés 1995). In addition, which economic doctrine prevails over others might depend on the specific institutional location within the state, rather than the professional training of the people in charge of the institution. In other words, neoliberal thinking has not necessarily penetrated all state institutions after 1990. In fact, neoliberalism might co-exist with heterodox thinking within different state institutions in the same country in Latin America (FitzGerald 2005). As a result, the notion of a uniform, tightly-knit neoliberal hegemony, e.g., in Marxist or neo-Gramscian analyses, is certainly overblown and too stark to capture the complex reality of policymaking in an era of economic globalization (Gill 1995; Estrada Álvarez 2005a).
- University graduates might adopt a specific economic world view well before or even after attending foreign universities. This is related to the problem of reverse causation or self-selection: "...although some adjusting to the school view does occur in graduate school, unless the changes occur in the first year, the predominant factor in determining the beliefs of a graduate school student is self-selection. Graduate schools modify those beliefs somewhat, but often reinforce previously existing views" (Klamer and

proxy for political influence and considered sufficient to determine economic policy decisions at the national level.

40 MacKenzie et al. (2007) analyze the "performativity of economics", i.e., how the discipline of economics actually produces the phenomena it seeks to analyze. It does so by presenting a stylized view of the economy generally, and financial markets specifically that, once internalized by students of economics or market participants, become self-fulfilling.

Colander 1990: 25).[41] The available quantitative studies ignore the possibility of self-selection into graduate programs at specific schools and might therefore exaggerate the educational socialization mechanism or 'Chicago effect'.[42]

- More often than not there is a substantial time lag between the professional education and the accession to the higher levels of the domestic political bureaucracy. As a result, foreign-trained economists might adopt a more 'politicized' view on the content and execution of economic policy, which does not necessarily reflect the orthodox perspective that they developed during their professional training. In other words, "an international consensus may prevail on 'best practice' but local political realities may mean that this consensus cannot take root in policy development (...) In short, there may be transfer of policy knowledge but not a transfer of policy practice" (Stone 2004: 549).

In sum, explanations of capital account policy located at the individual level emphasize the carriers of specific economic ideas in the domestic context. They detect the origins of economic ideas in the professional training received abroad and trace their subsequent ascent toward the upper echelons of the national political bureaucracy. In such a perspective, a coherent team of neoliberal economists given sufficient access to and autonomy in political decision-making is behind the recent move towards capital account liberalization in developing countries. However, the epistemic community theory overstates the causal effect of foreign training on economic policy decisions. It only considers changes in government personnel and from that deduces the likelihood of capital account liberalization. Epistemic communities-based arguments neglect the wider domestic context – both in social and material terms –, in particular the social beliefs and practices governing economic policymaking and the specific set of state-business relations, in which decisions on capital account policy are situated.

The epistemic community theory is able to shine some new light on the overall trend towards capital account liberalization in developing countries, but fails to account for the variation of capital account policy. Whether capital account openness is a durable domestic policy goes beyond differences in the educational profile of policymakers or the direct political influence of foreign-trained neoliberal economists.

---

41 In a re-run of the 1985 survey among economics PhD students at elite US universities, Colander (again) found that the large majority of students (78 %) did not change their political views in graduate school. However, in terms of economic perspectives, more students (+7 % overall) found themselves believing that neoclassical economics had become more relevant compared with their view before entering graduate school (Colander 2007: 32).

42 See, for example, Biglaiser's bold assertion that: "(h)aving spent 2 years in courses that stressed the benefits of free market economics, and having had many occasions to interact with professors in formal and informal settings on the importance of free trade policies and private ownership, most of these [Chilean] students became devout monetarists" (Biglaiser 2002b: 275). That implies that students' attitudes before their professional training are unimportant or easily malleable.

2.3.2 Ideas at the systemic-international level: the power of international norms

The literature about the effect of international norms on domestic policies is vast. Rather than studying the power of ideas as encapsulated in individuals on the domestic level, social constructivism in international relations theory represents a structural perspective similar to the 'world polity school' within sociological institutionalism. Ideas must become codified at the international level, serving as cognitive filters through which actors or states come to interpret their environment and derive standards of appropriate behavior. In other words, ideas must harden into norms on the systemic level in order to affect a wide range of states and their policies (Finnemore and Sikkink 1999).

Norms shape the range of possible, appropriate, acceptable, or legitimate actions, thus 'constituting' them in the first place. They provide the yardstick to which actors refer to when trying to legitimize or justify their behavior. For example, the legitimacy and usefulness of controls on international capital movements receive a different treatment within the framework of neoclassical economic theory as opposed to the concept of "embedded liberalism" rooted in Keynesian economics (Ruggie 1983). As more and more policymakers in industrial countries adopted the former framework as a reference point for national economic policy, their views on the legitimacy and usefulness of capital controls changed accordingly (Best 2004; Widmaier 2004; Abdelal 2007).

The main vehicles for the emergence, worldwide diffusion and subsequent institutionalization of norms about financial liberalization are international organizations. Individual norm entrepreneurs inside and outside international organizations (IOs) are crucial for the adoption of specific ideas as norms within IOs (Park and Vetterlein 2010). Once the organization as such subscribes to the idea and transforms it into an emergent norm circumscribing 'appropriate' state behavior, the diffusion process follows suit.

The capital mobility norm cascade started in Western Europe and the OECD (Helleiner 1994). Those organizations are tasked to monitor the compliance of members with the new norm, thereby helping to regulate and constrain their behavior. In the context of the IMF, while capital account openness was never codified as a norm, the organization nonetheless influenced the social context of the international financial system by fixing the meanings of 'appropriate' capital account policy, thus defining for its members the range of legitimate policies at specific points in time, globally disseminating the reigning financial orthodoxy with a view to institutionalizing it in member-states.

Constructivist scholars substantially diverge from the ontological conception of IOs in interest-based approaches. IOs exert power not only or primarily through coercive means but also through their normative authority vis-à-vis national governments (Barnett and Finnemore 2004). States emerge as eager followers of international trends that are actively promoted by IOs without these ideas necessarily being forced upon them. As a result, the mechanism of *persuasion* better captures compliance with international norms rather than overt coercion. The IMF exercises this kind of 'soft', 'discursive', or 'normative' power through regular policy consultations with and the technical training of national economic elites. 'Soft power'[43] can supplement or even supplant the coercive instruments in the hands of the IMF (James 1995: 775–6; Killick 1996: 226).

The so-called policy dialogue with state authorities is regarded as the most important instrument of World Bank and IMF soft power vis-à-vis developing countries (Nelson 1996: 1553–1558; Killick 1998: 180–181).[44] Policy dialogue or advice usually takes place in the context of IMF surveillance or so-called Article IV missions to member countries, normally on an annual basis. Unfortunately, there has been no systematic attempt to study the conditions under which the 'soft power' of the IMF can bring about policy change. While various scholars stress the importance of the IMF's policy influence for the start of economic reforms in developing countries (Ikenberry 1990: 103; Nelson 1990: 27; Kahler 1992: 123), they concede that this concept is slippery and hard to measure with the positivist methodological toolkit.[45] As a result, it is usually excluded from consideration by empirical studies of IMF influence over domestic policy decisions. The only exception is Chwieroth (2006). However, his quantitative analysis of IMF 'soft power' using various channels of direct ("teaching") and indirect influence ("cheerleading") shows only limited evidence for the organization's influence on capital account policy in developing countries.[46]

In sum, ideational systemic-domestic explanations see international norms as the drivers of capital account policy. Norms first emerge within international organizations and are then diffused to its member states using 'soft' or discursive channels of influence. The principal agent is the IMF, yet with a radically different conception of its power vis-à-vis national policymakers. Rather than coercing states into compliance, the IMF engages in a discursive process aimed at persuading national policymakers to adopt globally legitimate or 'appropriate' standards for capital account management.

Table 2.3 Ideational explanations of capital account policy

Individual-Domestic	Systemic-International
▪ Norm entrepreneurs forming a coherent epistemic community of economists with access to political power	▪ Existence of international norms ▪ IMF 'soft power' and its domestic institutional scope conditions

43 The term 'soft power' was popularized by Nye. He succinctly defines it as the ability to "getting others to want the outcomes that you want, co-opting people rather than coercing them" (Nye 2004: 5).

44 Other instruments may include stints of future national policymakers within the organization and the technical training of staff from finance ministries and central banks at the IMF training institute (Killick 1998: 184).

45 For example, in a quantitative study on the causes of pension privatization, Madrid (2005) uses the number of World Bank missions a country has received in order to measure the ideational or discursive influence of the Bank on local pension policy (which turns out to be statistically significant) – a questionable approach since more 'talking' does not necessarily amount to increased influence over the counterpart.

46 He does, however, find that the IMF's indirect influence ("cheerleading") as a channel of information and technical support for reform-oriented domestic policymakers has been a significant factor for capital account liberalization in Latin America. Similarly, in a case study on Mexico, Woods (2005) argues that the influence of the IMF and the World Bank is related to an ideational contest expressed in domestic bureaucratic battles. International organizations can empower certain bureaucratic groups, aligned with their own economic ideas, using 'soft' power instruments. Cheerleading is probably the apt term to describe this role.

2.4 Conclusion

Table 2.4 below provides a summary of the causal mechanisms according to each ontological framework and level of analysis. While they focus on different dynamics as drivers of capital account policy, there is some overlap in terms of the specific actors under consideration.

The literature on the drivers of capital account policy presents a highly heterogeneous picture. Interest-based and institutionalist approaches largely dominate the explanatory scene. However, almost all the potential causal factors discussed earlier have received some empirical confirmation in the existing literature. No single explanation has been completely rejected. As a result, we are confronted with the apparent over-determination of the dependent variable. In addition, almost all factors point in the same direction towards capital account liberalization.

Table 2.4 Summary of analytical categories to explain capital account policy

Level of Analysis/ Ontological Framework	**Interests**	**Institutions**	**Ideas**
Individual	▪ Orientation of government (welfare vs. rent-seeking)	▪ Gain-loss perception of political leaders	▪ Norm entrepreneurs forming a coherent epistemic community of economists with access to political power
Domestic	▪ Clashes between economic groups	▪ Fragmentation of legislature (high-low) ▪ Partisanship (left-right) ▪ Structural legacies of earlier development strategies (ISI)	
Systemic-International	▪ Coercion (through IMF) ▪ Economic competition ▪ Rational learning	▪ Dependence on foreign capital (low-high) ▪ Emulation of templates	▪ Existence of international norms ▪ IMF 'soft power' and its domestic institutional scope conditions

However, the significant national variation in capital account policy – both between developed and developing countries and within the developing world – has been insufficiently addressed in the literature. Systemic-international explanations only consider structural forces pushing and pulling countries in the same policy direction. They are certainly important but insufficient accounts of domestic-level policy outcomes.

In the context of the global financial crisis of 2008–9, a behaviorally informed Keynesianism – or what Cassidy calls "reality-based economics" as opposed to "utopian economics" (Cassidy 2009) – has made a strong comeback. Instead of rational, self-interested, utility-maximizing actors, powerful social-psychological forces, including social identities and norms, drive the economy as a whole and financial markets in particular (Akerlof and

Shiller 2009; Akerlof and Kranton 2010). As a result, scholars increasingly doubt the ontological and epistemological foundations of traditional interest-based explanations – the 'Holy Trinity' of rationalism, materialism, and perfect information.

The dominating epistemological – positivism – and methodological approaches – large-N, quantitative studies – to explain capital account policy have intrinsic problems to operationalize analytical concepts derived from non-rationalist approaches. As a result, there is a dearth of empirical studies based on cognitive and normative factors to explain capital account policy, though often plagued by their own methodological problems. The well-known trade-off between theoretical parsimony and analytical rigor on the one hand, and understanding the actions of 'real people' imbued with both material *and* social motifs on the other, rears its head in this regard.

A glaring lacuna in the existing literature concerns informal institutions at the domestic level – the shaded area in Table 2.4. In contrast to formal institutions as well as global norms and ideas, the role of domestically shared rules and understandings has largely been neglected. Yet as I aim to show, intersubjective beliefs and rules about 'appropriate' economic policies and policy instruments are a crucial factor to explain the sustainability or fragility of capital account openness.

While blending analytical approaches is certainly a desirable path in order to grasp the reality of economic policymaking, the challenge has been defined as showing the relative weight of different causal forces in influencing actor behavior (Deeg and O'Sullivan 2009). Unfortunately, the available methodological approaches and instruments to separate causal forces in terms of their impact on capital account policy are underdeveloped at best and unviable at worst. It is the interaction or complementarity between causal mechanisms embedded in contending research traditions, not their artificial separation by assigning indicators of relative weight that fundamentally drives capital account policy. As a result, analytic eclecticism is a more promising approach instead of theoretical or paradigmatic purity, even if it comes at the cost of losing some rigor and parsimony (Sil and Katzenstein 2010a).

I aim to show that domestic-level causal mechanisms based on interests, institutions, and ideas *together* provide a better, i. e., more complete, understanding of the variation of capital account policy than any of them on their own. More precisely, the change of national economic identity consisting of (i) informal institutions defining the boundaries of legitimate economic policies and (ii) a specific set of state-business relations is a prerequisite for durable capital account openness in Latin America during the last two decades.

Chapter 3: National Economic Identity and Capital Account Policy

> Rather than a dialogue of the deaf in which each side tries to marginalize or subsume the other in the name of methodological fundamentalism, the challenge now should be to combine insights, cross boundaries, and, if possible, synthesize specific arguments in hope of gaining more compelling answers and a better picture of reality (Fearon and Wendt 2002: 68).

I am cognizant of the fact that the explanation of capital account policy is characterized by extensive endogeneity and the ubiquity of complex interaction effects. As a result, instead of privileging one particular theoretical approach outlined in the previous chapter to account for the cross-country variation of capital account policy, I make use of "analytic eclecticism" (Sil and Katzenstein 2010a, 2010b). This research strategy "invites us to figure out how different types of mechanisms normally explored in isolation from one another might interact as part of more complex configurations in a given context" (Sil and Katzenstein 2010c: 23). My aim in this chapter is to provide an analytically richer and at the same time more realistic account of the drivers of capital account policy in Latin America. As a result, my approach does not follow any of the neat theoretical categories outlined in the previous chapter. Instead I pretend to fuse causal mechanisms found in nominally competing research traditions such as rationalism (or interest-based approaches) and constructivism (or ideational approaches) with a view to arrive at a better picture of reality, as the quotation at the beginning of this chapter asks for. Hence, my simultaneous usage of rationalist and constructivist terminology such as material interests and national identity does not wish to signal a theoretical potpourri but rather a deliberate attempt at analytical bridge-building for a better understanding of a complex reality. By doing so, I deliberately eschew an epistemological discussion as to whether rationalism and constructivism are compatible in the first place.

In order to engage in this effort, I focus on causal mechanisms found at the domestic level. International factors are undoubtedly important to explain the general trend towards greater capital account openness in the world in general, and in Latin America in particular during the last two decades. However, they are insufficient to understand why countries have either maintained, or at least partially retracted from capital mobility after the initial opening in the early 1990s. In a similar vein, while the international political and academic discourse in the aftermath of the contemporary global financial crisis turned critical of capital mobility, its effect on national capital account policies is neither direct nor immediate. In fact, I submit that domestic-level factors play a much larger role than international ones for specific outcomes in capital account management. In the two case studies on Peru and Colombia I demonstrate the limited explanatory power of causal mechanisms located at the international level to explain capital account policy in Latin America.

International norms and ideas propagated by international organizations such as capital account liberalization need a specific social *and* material context in order to shape domestic economic policies over the medium and long run. On the one hand, I draw on constructivist scholarship in international relations and comparative politics to argue that so-called norm entrepreneurs for the cause of capital freedom need domestic social legitimacy. In other words, a societal majority has to accept the unfettered flow of international capital as a legitimate part of the country's macroeconomic policies. Social legitimacy for international capital mobility at the domestic level is, in turn, embedded in informal institutions governing economic policymaking (Seabrooke 2006). In other words, a societal consensus – articulated in shared understandings about legitimate economic policies and instruments – exists that capital account openness is part and parcel of the national economic identity. Given the failure to reach this consensus, capital account liberalization might still be initiated in a country, but is unlikely to be sustained over time.

On the other hand, the explanation of the emergence, maintenance, and change of domestically shared understandings about legitimate economic policies requires an interest-based complement. How did a specific interpretation of the national economic identity become dominant and what are the pillars of its stability? Put differently, an analytical focus on informal institutions needs to be supplemented by an actor-based account. Domestic structures do not come into existence or are maintained on their own – they need agents with (i) specific interests vis-à-vis capital account policy and (ii) privileged access to the arenas for economic policymaking. Taken together, shared expectations about legitimate capital account policy are inextricably linked to specific state-business relations.

The mutual constitution of social (shared expectations) and material institutions (state-business relations) requires a reconsideration of traditional accounts of causality (Wendt 1998). According to structuration theory, the attribution of cause-effect relations becomes virtually impossible. The only viable, although deficient, way in order to empirically ascertain how economic agents and domestic informal institutions interact is through careful process-tracing.

3.1 What is National Economic Identity?

The concept of collective or social identity has a long pedigree in the social sciences. Theoretical and empirical analyses about the role of national identities are particularly ubiquitous. Scholars have tried to explain their emergence, change, and specific effects for individual and group behavior. There is little doubt that collective identities are important *social facts* of the world in which we live. They enable actors to literally see and interpret the world in a specific way, thus guiding their decision-making process.

Constructivist scholarship has tried to apply the concept of collective identity as a causal factor in international relations (Katzenstein 1996; Wendt 1994, 1999). In this interpretation, states are seen as equipped with social motifs based on specific identities that shape their material and instrumental interests, and subsequently their actions in international politics. While most constructivist scholars have limited themselves to analyze the effect of systemic norms on state identity and subsequent behavior (outside-in explanations),

I focus on the domestic foundations of national economic identity and its effects on foreign economic policy, or more precisely capital account policy - in other words, an inside-out explanation of state behavior in international economic relations.

I do not wish to engage in an elaborate exegesis of the identity scholarship at this point. Rather I take the pragmatic position that collective identities have both ideational *and* material foundations. In other words, actors influenced by collective identities are driven by both normative and instrumental concerns. The important point here is to recognize that (i) collective identity has non-trivial effects on actor behavior, and (ii) material interests contribute to the formation, stability, and change of social identities.

I stress that one important element of the content of collective identity is what Abdelal et al. call *social purpose*, i. e., "the goals that are shared by members of a group" (Abdelal et al. 2006: 696). Social purposes are particularly relevant in the context of foreign economic policymaking where governments face a host of complex decisions whose outcomes are uncertain and for which unambiguous guidelines or instructions are therefore mostly missing (Blyth 2003). Given the absence of clearly predictable outcomes of foreign economic policy choices, the social purpose element of national economic identity helps governments to make and socially justify specific policy decisions (Abdelal 2001). Capital account policy is a case in point.

Defenders of capital account liberalization, based on neoclassical economic theory, have argued that it allows for an efficient allocation of capital and the diversification of risk boosting investment and economic growth (Obstfeld 1998, 2009; Mishkin 2009). Conversely, Neo-Keynesian scholars have argued that capital flows are inherently volatile and that opening the capital account may thus lead to instability and does not promote economic growth (Stiglitz 2000).

National economic identity informs whether states privilege the free flow of international capital as a source of domestic wealth creation, or instead give priority to overall macroeconomic stability and external competitiveness. In other words, the specific content of national economic identity helps governments to resolve the dilemma between opening the capital account on a sustained level for the sake of attracting foreign capital flows, or regulating capital flows in order to maintain macroeconomic and exchange-rate stability. Given the largely unclear relationship between capital account liberalization and economic growth in developing countries (Rodrik 1998; Prasad et al. 2003, 2007; Kose et al. 2006, 2009), governments cannot base their decision regarding this dilemma on an existing consensus in the academic literature, similar to the one that exists on the general benefits of free trade.

Faced with external norm advocacy to liberalize the capital account, especially from the IMF during the early 1990s, national economic identity constitutes a crucial *social* filter in order to determine whether capital account openness will be a durable feature of a country's political economy. The social purpose element of national economic identity, in turn, defines whether the goal of economic policymaking is to prioritize the free flow of foreign capital at all costs, or rather to defend overall macroeconomic stability, especially of the exchange rate. Depending on the specific social purpose engrained in their national economic identity, governments interpret their macroeconomic situation through particular lenses, making them more or less inclined to keep the capital account open over time.

3.2 What are Domestic Informal Institutions?

The rational-choice perspective on institutions only focuses on formal rules that shape actor behavior (Weyland 2002b). However, in order to fully comprehend the actions of political and economic actors, scholars need to take the existence and evolution of unwritten, collective understandings, assumptions, rules, and norms within the domestic context into account. The analysis of informal institutions such as clientelism, corruption and neopatrimonialism has a long pedigree in comparative politics generally, and in the Latin American context in particular, usually emphasizing their negative or distortionary effects for the democratic political process. However, specific informal institutions can have positive, stabilizing consequences for the domestic economy, thereby increasing the margins of maneuver for policymakers (Helmke and Levitsky 2006a).

Unfortunately, the existing literature on capital account policy pays only scarce attention to domestically shared beliefs and expectations about legitimate economic policies. Yet social facts not only exist at the global level where ideas, beliefs, and norms shape actors' interests and behavior but at the domestic level, too. Like globally operating norms and ideas, intersubjective beliefs and rules among the national policymaking and business elite exist alongside and independent of individual beliefs and have the potential to influence the subsequent behavior of an individual or a group through "a power of coercion, by reason of which they control [sic] him" (Durkheim, quoted in Chwieroth and Sinclair 2008: 10). I argue that domestic informal institutions are a crucial factor behind the stability or instability of capital account openness over time.

I define informal institutions as *socially shared rules and understandings underpinning and legitimizing economic policies.* An institution is "a relatively stable collection of practices and rules defining appropriate behavior for specific groups of actors in specific situations" (March and Olsen 1999: 308). In my usage of the term, informal institutions are essentially equivalent to what social constructivists call "intersubjective beliefs" (Searle 1995). While most scholars working in comparative politics focus their attention on specific practices associated with informal institutions such as clientelism or graft, I posit - in line with sociological institutionalism - that the term institution signals a link between collective beliefs and subsequent actor behavior. In other words, if capital controls enjoy social legitimacy among the political and economic elite of a country, the government will be hard-pressed to defend capital account openness on a long-term basis if it threatens the social purpose embedded in the national economic identity. If the defense of national economic autonomy in general, and exchange-rate stability in particular constitute important elements of the national economic identity, the concomitant informal institutions ensure that policymakers contemplate and utilize an important instrument in order to defend national economic autonomy: capital controls.

It is important to emphasize the distinction between informal institutions or intersubjective beliefs on the one hand, and norms on the other. The two concepts are closely related but their difference is linked to aggregation:

> the norm definition isolates single standards of behavior, whereas institutions emphasize the way in which behavioral rules are structured together and interrelate (Finnemore and Sikkink 1999: 251).

Put differently, informal institutions are a collection of practices and rules and not just a specific norm that governs actor behavior vis-à-vis a specific policy issue, such as human rights or environmental standards. As a result, the term 'informal institution' in form of collectively held beliefs and understandings is meant to inform the behavior of a wide range of actors in terms of broad policy areas. In other words, national economic identity is associated with a number of informal institutions, all of which with the aim to fulfill the social purpose of the identity.

Similarly, the emphasis on domestic informal institutions is distinct from arguments about transnationally operating epistemic communities based on collectively shared ideas and the influence of these groups over policy outcomes (Haas 1992). Some scholars have emphasized the crucial role played by politically influential economists trained abroad in "neoliberal economics programs" for the shift towards capital account liberalization in developing countries generally, and Latin America specifically (Biglaiser 2002b; Chwieroth 2007). In contrast, I argue that the shared ideas of the neoliberal epistemic community must be socially embedded within the domestic context, i.e., above and beyond the nominal representation of members of this group in high-ranking government positions, in order to shape capital account policy over the medium and long run. Put differently, I aim to demonstrate in the following case studies that the mere presence of foreign-trained neoliberal economists in influential government positions is not a sufficient condition for the durability of capital account openness but requires the embeddedness of their ideas in socially shared rules and understandings (Granovetter 1985). Specific economic ideas acquired during professional training abroad must thus be subjected to the test of *domestic social resonance* (Cortell and Davis 1996, 2000). Depending on the particular social context, neoliberal ideas about capital account management encounter either a receptive or a recalcitrant terrain.

The longevity of capital account openness is based on an informal agreement among the country's political and economic elite that restricting international capital movements is an idea whose time has gone. The durability of capital mobility is predicated upon the collectively shared belief that capital controls have lost not only their overall effectiveness but more importantly their legitimacy as instruments of macroeconomic policymaking. The extent to which this conviction has become entrenched within a country's discourse and practice explains the sustainability of capital account openness over time. The institutional foundation for the sustainability of capital account openness only exists if the prevailing economic discourse and its concomitant social rules, understandings, and practices reflect the illegitimacy of capital controls. In other words, the embeddedness of the principled belief in capital account openness constitutes an indispensable *social* condition for maintaining an open capital account.

In contrast, if the informal institutions underwriting pre-liberalization capital account policy survive the initial adoption of capital account liberalization, it is unlikely that capital account openness will last over time. Informal institutions dating back to the reign of the import-substituting industrialization model stand in the way of making open capital accounts a general and permanent feature of the Latin American political economy.

Informal institutions do not change on their own volition. Gretchen Helmke and Steven Levitsky point to two sources of informal institutional change which are particularly relevant for the discussion of capital account policy. First, "(i)f actors' shared expectations about the costs and benefits of an informal rule should change (...), then informal institutions – even long-established ones – may change quickly" (Helmke and Levitsky 2006b: 24–25). Here I come back to the received wisdom that an economic crisis facilitates market-oriented reforms (Williamson and Haggard 1994: 564). I build on this argument by positing that an economic crisis has the potential to undermine the domestic informal institution legitimizing capital controls. Whereas previously restrictions on international capital movements constituted a socially accepted instrument of macroeconomic management, an economic crisis whose origin or aggravation can discursively be associated with the existence of capital controls provides a congenial context for the successful legitimization of capital account openness. As I show in the case study on Peru, the profound economic crisis that afflicted the country at the end of the 1980s became associated with the existence of capital controls which, in turn, undermined their social legitimacy on a long-term basis.

Second, "(d)evelopments in the external environment may change the distribution of power and resources among actors, weakening those who benefit from a particular informal institution and strengthening those who seek to change it" (Helmke and Levitsky 2006b: 24). As I argue in the next section of this chapter, state-business relations underwrite capital account policy. Specific economic interest groups provide the informal institutions legitimizing or delegitimizing capital controls with private sector support. Sustainable capital account openness is thus predicated upon a change in state-business relations towards establishing a dominant position for those private sector actors materially benefitting from the free flow of international capital.

3.3 The Role of Actor Interests and State-Business Relations

For informal institutions to persist over time, scholars need to identify those actors or groups who underwrite their existence. Put differently, if capital account openness is to survive within the national political economy, specific actors must ensure that its social legitimacy remains unchallenged. These actors come from various backgrounds, be them members of the domestic neoliberal epistemic community or representatives of international financial institutions. In line with interest-based accounts at the domestic level, I argue that a crucial actor, or rather a coalition of actors, for the durability of capital account openness is located within the private sector. As long as this pro-capital mobility group is able to dominate state-business relations, private sector demand for capital account openness, and against defending national economic autonomy, will be forthcoming.

As is the case for many economic policy choices, domestic interest groups exhibit different preferences when it comes to capital account liberalization. Some groups have an unequivocal preference for capital freedom, while others oppose it vehemently. However, given the opaque technical nature of capital account policy and substantial collective actions problems, it is unlikely that broad, class-based coalitions form and clash over this issue.[47] A cleavage between holders of specific assets in the economy whose income is directly and visibly affected by international capital flows is more likely (Frieden 1991; Haggard and Maxfield 1996).[48] Owners of fixed assets generally, and competitive export sectors specifically, initially stand to benefit from increased capital mobility for it provides access to new, cheaper sources of credit from abroad to fund their economic activities. However, since capital account and trade liberalization usually occur in conjunction in developing countries, the exchange rate experiences a dramatic nominal appreciation induced by the rise of imports and foreign capital flows into the country. As a result, over the medium and long term, the export-oriented sector is negatively affected by increased capital mobility.

On the other hand, large financial intermediaries such as banks (both inside and outside the country), owners of mobile assets, institutional investors, and domestically-oriented corporate borrowers stand to benefit from capital account liberalization for it provides them with access to cheap(er) foreign capital without having to worry about the exchange-rate implications to a significant extent.[49] Hence, the central cleavage in terms of capital account liberalization as portrayed in the extant interest-based literature runs between two economic interest groups: *the export-oriented sector versus the financial industry.* According to this perspective, the balance of power between these two competing sectors determines capital account policy. In this interpretation, capital account policy is a direct function of the influence of each interest group coalition over government decision-making.[50]

However, in the context of market-oriented reforms in Latin America during the last thirty years, the traditional cleavage within the business community between the financial sector embracing capital account openness on the one hand, and recalcitrant exporters on the other has become blurred. The organizational structure of the corporate sector in many Latin American countries has experienced a profound transformation towards economic concentration, thereby leading to the dominant position of a few very large private companies, so-called conglomerates or economic groups (Fernández and Hogenboom 2007a). These new actors are defined "as an assembly of companies that function largely independently yet operate under some form of centralized control" (Fernández and Hogenboom 2007b: 5). Conglomerates are usually made up of entities that operate in different sectors of the economy, usually including the financial sector and sometimes also including the mass media. As a result, the two allegedly competing sectors in terms of financial liberalization – export-oriented vs. financial sector – have largely become united under the single roof of

47 Political mobilization is unlikely to form around capital account policy since the costs of capital account liberalization for the mass public – in contrast to other, redistributive policy areas – are widely distributed, uncertain, and (when they appear) often very delayed.

48 Empirical studies in other economic policy areas, especially in foreign trade, have shown that asset specificity has a significantly greater political salience than class cleavages notwithstanding the fact that winners and losers in terms of class structures are more pronounced in those areas (Hiscox 2001).

49 However, while domestic financial intermediaries support capital account openness for its reduced cost of capital, at the same time they oppose the entry of foreign competitors into the domestic financial market. In other words, domestic banks want the access to foreign capital but without the entry of foreign competitors (Pepinsky 2009).

50 As it is common in the OEP framework, the government is regarded as a mere vicarious agent for the specific interests of powerful corporate groups.

a conglomerate. Thus, ascertaining the specific preferences of a conglomerate or economic group transcends the traditional cleavage among domestic interest groups in terms of capital account policy.

In a similar vein, I eschew the notion that there is a unified "neoliberal community" within a country's private sector that has somehow "captured the state", implying that this community exercises full control over all types of economic policy decisions (Durand 2010). For example, authors such as Jairo Estrada (2005a) suggest that both domestic business actors *and* multinational corporations form part of this community, unified by common material interests and beliefs in the superiority of market-based or neoliberal reforms. In other words, both groups within the export-oriented sector of the economy are supposed to share the same interests and preferences when it comes to macroeconomic policies – a necessary condition, one would think, in order to capture the state. I submit, however, that important differences of interests and preferences vis-à-vis specific macroeconomic policies persist among the members of a generally market-friendly community such as the export-oriented sector of the economy.

As a result, rather than following the conventional logic of putting the export-oriented sector *as a whole* in a specific category in terms of its preferences vis-à-vis capital account policy, I consider the interests of distinct groups within this sector. In fact, in contrast to accounts portraying the private export sector as "(t)he single most powerful source of domestic support for market-oriented reforms" (Remmer 1998: 11), its preferences vis-à-vis capital account openness are far from unambiguous.

Countries face a policy dilemma after the initial liberalization of the capital account. Confronted with real exchange-rate appreciation, they can either decide to privilege the continued inflow of foreign capital based on a restrictive monetary policy, e. g., with a view to achieving low inflation and remaining attractive for foreign investors, or focus on macroeconomic stability, policy autonomy, and external competitiveness by – at least temporarily – restricting the inflow of foreign capital. Exporters face a similar dilemma: while capital account liberalization may provide them with access to cheap(er) financial resources abroad, they are negatively affected by exchange-rate appreciation in the aftermath of capital account opening. Put differently, an initial enthusiasm for capital freedom over time gives way to a more cautious view, demanding government restrictions on capital inflows in order to bring exchange-rate appreciation under control.

Thus, capital account policy – while certainly not possessing the same degree of political salience as, for example, trade policy – puts economic interest groups at loggerheads. It then depends on the specific nature of state-business relations which interest group – and its concomitant preferences vis-à-vis capital account policy – is able to influence government decision-making. For capital account openness to be sustainable over time, the interests of economic groups worried about the appreciation of the nominal exchange rate induced by trade liberalization and increasing capital inflows must be marginalized in favor of other groups for which the stability and, above all, competitiveness of the exchange rate are not primordial concerns. This group of actors forms the backbone of support for durable capital account openness within the domestic business community.

In contrast to accounts that treat the export-oriented sector as a homogenous group for which policy preferences and straightforward predictions on political behavior can be deduced, I separate the sector in two groups according to *corporate size*. Size, I submit, is the critical factor when it comes to export-sector preferences in terms of capital account policy. On the one hand, big, economically diversified actors such as multinational corporations (MNCs) and domestic conglomerates – together commonly known as 'big business' – prefer full and sustained capital account openness given their multisectoral business activities. Their preferences vis-à-vis capital account policy are shaped by both a primordial interest in international capital mobility and a relatively low sensitivity to exchange-rate volatility. On the other hand, small and medium-sized business actors, usually concentrating their export activities on one specific product or industry, prefer partial and temporary capital account openness, or more precisely demand controls on capital inflows in order to secure a stable exchange rate for their external competitiveness.

Taken together, for the government to establish full and sustained capital account openness, MNCs and large domestic economic groups (DEGs) must become its principal interlocutor and ally within the private sector. These economic actors must dominate formal and informal state-business relations, thus excluding other business actors from meaningful or significant political access.

Durable capital account openness is predicated upon a profound transformation of state-business relations that undermines the collective representation of the private sector in general, and of the export-oriented sector in particular. Whereas formal interactions dominated state-business relations during the import-substituting industrialization period, the rise of 'big business' in the aftermath of the wave of privatizations in Latin America during the early 1990s has undermined collective action within the domestic business communities (Schneider 2010). In turn, MNCs and DEGs benefitted from the diversification of interests within the private sector and have been able to either dominate the agenda of economy-wide and sectoral associations, or by privileging informal or individual interactions with the government contributed to their declining relevance for state-business relations.[51] In other words, the more 'big business' is able to exercise control over crucial entities for the collective representation of private sector interests, the more a concern for exchange-rate stability and external competitiveness gives way to a preference for capital mobility within these entities.

Conversely, if small and medium-sized actors within the export-oriented sector of the economy are able to maintain close access to the economic policymaking process, durable capital account openness is at risk. In other words, in countries where state-business relations are conducted by institutionalized, iterated interactions between the private sector – usually represented by encompassing business associations (Silva and Durand 1998) – and the government, capital account openness is unlikely to persist over time. Crucially, economy-wide, umbrella organizations that aggregate sector-specific associations must give pride of place to the interests and preferences of smaller-scale economic actors, especially from the export-oriented sector. Put differently, the more business associations resemble repre-

51 It is important to note, however, that state-business relations cover both formal and informal channels of interaction between the political and the private sector (Offe and Wiesenthal 1980). The latter category is associated with private sector activities such as legislative lobbying, campaign contributions, networks, going all the way to corruption (Schneider 2010).

sentative entities of *all* private sector actors and are not co-opted or marginalized by MNCs and DEGs in their interactions with the government, the more likely it is that the concern for exchange-rate stability and external competitiveness takes precedence over the interest in capital mobility within the business community.

3.4 Conclusion: The Domestic Foundations of Capital Account Openness

My aim in this chapter has been to construct an analytically eclectic argument that combines specific causal arguments from competing theoretical approaches in order to explain the cross-country variation of capital account policy. I have suggested that national economic identity plays a crucial role for the durability or fragility of capital account openness over time. Domestically shared understandings provide a crucial institutional fundament for the social legitimacy of economic policies in general, and capital account policy in particular. Domestic societies are based on informal institutions that structure the "rules of the game", i. e., the range of legitimate actions and instruments in terms of economic policies. In other words, a consensus among the political and economic elites of the country determines whether capital account openness forms part of the social purpose of the national economic identity, or alternatively whether it plays second fiddle compared to other policy goals such as national economic autonomy or exchange-rate stability. The social purpose of national economic identity defines macroeconomic priorities for a country which, in turn, lead to the durability of capital mobility, or to its fragility.

National economic identity, in turn, is closely related to a specific set of state-business relations. State-business relations provide socially shared ideas and expectations about legitimate economic policies with a material foundation. Put differently, specific material interests within the business community underwrite a social consensus on the legitimacy of capital mobility or capital controls, respectively. For capital mobility to last in the domestic political economy, private sector actors equipped with a specific interest in the openness of the capital account must gain the upper hand in state-business relations, thus relegating the interests of actors in favor of exchange-rate stability and external competitiveness to the background. Given their seize and diversified activities, multinational corporations and domestic conglomerates have a clear preference for capital mobility over exchange-rate concerns within the export-oriented sector of the economy. If those actors manage to dominate state-business relations, thereby undermining the collective representation of the domestic business community irrespective of firm size, the social legitimacy of capital account openness is based on powerful private sector support.

In addition, the campaign for durable capital account openness is reinforced by the occurrence of an economic crisis leading not only to the onslaught of market-oriented reforms but more importantly to the thorough delegitimization of government restrictions on international capital movements. In other words, economic crises whose causes or consequences can be associated with the existence of capital controls provide argumentative support for outlawing such restrictions once and for all. As a result, the discursive association between capital controls and economic crisis in the collective memory of a society helps to embed capital mobility within the national economic identity.

Conversely, while the absence of an economic crisis will not necessarily prevent capital account liberalization from occurring in the first place, it will nonetheless act as a social obstacle for the institutionalization of capital mobility within a country's political economy. In turn, capital controls remain socially legitimate instruments of economic policymaking based on the shared understanding that macroeconomic stability in general, and exchange-rate stability and external competitiveness in particular must receive priority over guaranteeing the free flow of international capital in and/or out of the country. In countries without a social consensus on the priority of capital mobility over other macroeconomic goals, state-business relations are dominated by encompassing and sectoral business associations which primarily reflect the interests of private sector actors for whom capital account openness is not a primordial material concern over the medium and long run.

Taken together, the absence of an economic crisis in the run-up to market-oriented reforms and state-business relations characterized by powerful business associations representing all sizes of corporate actors constitute the material background for the lack of a socially shared understanding that views capital mobility as an inalienable element of the national economic identity. As a result, at least temporary restrictions on international capital movements remain legitimate instruments to be used by policymakers in order to ensure macroeconomic stability and autonomy.

Chapter 4: Capital Account Policy in Peru. The Institutional Legacies of the Economic Crisis

In line with several other countries in Latin America, the traditional pattern of economic policymaking in Peru has been a stop-go cycle with abrupt oscillations between market-oriented reforms and the subsequent return to protectionist policies. For Latin American standards, Peru had a relatively open economy until the late 1960s when the leftist military dictatorship under General Juan Velasco Alvarado assumed power. The military government attempted to reduce dependence on foreign capital, eliminate oligarchic power and accelerate industrial development. To accomplish these goals, it empowered the state and introduced protectionist and nationalist economic policies, following the then dominant Import-Substitution Industrialization model. The economy was successively restructured along protectionist lines and international economic transactions, including capital movements, heavily regulated. The end of the dictatorship and the return to democracy in 1980 brought a political and economic opening of the country. President Fernando Belaúnde launched a pre-'Washington Consensus' package of economic policies, including the liberalization of capital movements. However, his presidency ended in economic turmoil due to the accelerating debt crisis affecting the entire region. The result was a backlash against liberal economic policies with the election of President Alan García in 1985. He promised and delivered a strict nationalist course whose most visible demonstration was a partial debt moratorium and strict controls and regulations in many part of the economy, including capital account transactions. Yet the application of the so-called heterodox model ended in even bigger economic failure.

With the election of President Alberto Fujimori in 1990 began yet another cycle back to the market. Since then, however, liberal economic policies, including capital account liberalization, have had a much longer life span. The radical liberalization of the capital account introduced in 1991 has proved to be a durable policy despite several changes in government, including left-leaning presidents such as Ollanta Humala (since 2011), and external economic conditions. In this chapter, I argue that two long-term consequences of the economic crisis preceding the initial liberalization phase help to explain this surprising outcome: (i) the restructuring of state-business relations providing the financial and mining sectors with a veto-player position for economic policymaking in Peru; and (ii) the social construction and successful societal embedding of an economic discourse delegitimizing capital controls, denouncing them as an alleged slippery slope toward economic chaos and mismanagement. In other words, I argue that the explanation for the longevity of capital account openness in Peru can be found in specific institutional changes accompanying the initial opening of the economy. The legacy of the profound economic crisis during the late 1980s gave rise to a new socially shared understanding about the illegitimacy of capital controls in the contemporary political economy of Peru.

This chapter is organized as follows. Section one describes the context and the content of the initial adoption of capital account liberalization in the early 1990s. It emphasizes the social construction of capital account freedom as a crucial lesson from the economic crisis of the late 1980s. Section two discusses competing explanations for the sustainability of capital account liberalization in Peru: on the one hand, the influence of the International Monetary Fund, and the political strength of the neoliberal epistemic community on the other. I show the limited influence of the IMF over capital account policy decisions and the entrenched discursive, though not necessarily political power of the neoliberal epistemic community. Based on survey data, I document the strong commitment of the foreign-trained community of elite economists to the principle of capital mobility. Section three analyzes the institutional foundations for the durability of capital account openness over time: (i) changes in state-business relations favoring the interests of the financial and mining sectors over those of the industrial or non-mining export sector; and (ii) the social embeddedness of capital account freedom in contemporary Peru. Section four concludes.

4.1 The Rise of Capital Account Openness from the Ashes of Economic Chaos

4.1.1 The national trauma

There can be little doubt that Peru lived through a dramatic economic crisis at the end of the 1980s (Crabtree 1992). President García's heterodox economic policies resulted in a desperate economic and social situation.[52] In his inaugural speech in July 1985, García promised a 'home-grown solution' to the inflation problem as opposed to IMF orthodoxy. The central element of the ensuing heterodox program was a partial moratorium limiting service payments on Peru's medium- and long-term public debt to no more than 10 % of annual export earnings. In addition, the program contained the direct administration of prices and wages as well as the strict regulation of imports and foreign exchange. As a result, debt service-payments decreased substantially and several economic and social indicators showed some improvement between 1985 and 1987. At the same time, however, loan disbursements from international financial institutions became negative and the default on service payments for public and private debt turned Peru into a pariah of the international financial community.

Beginning in late 1987 public finances collapsed within the context of an increasingly desperate foreign-exchange situation and García's erratic policy decisions. In July 1987, the president announced his intention – against the background of high levels of capital flight – to nationalize all commercial banks as well as all finance and insurance companies. At the

52 However, not all problems facing the country should be blamed on García's policy mistakes. As Carol Wise (2003: 176) points out, three structural problems have beset the Peruvian economy since the late 1960s: (i) a strong dependence on external financing, especially foreign direct investment, to support government programs; (ii) a high amount of savings in foreign currency leading to informal dollarization of the economy; and (iii) a conflictual relationship between the state and domestic entrepreneurs, resulting in a low domestic investment rate. Add to that the periodic pendulum swings between orthodox adjustment and heterodoxy that had a profoundly negative effect on economic growth (Ortiz de Zevallos 1989; Gonzales de Olarte and Samamé 1991; Pastor and Wise 1992).

same time, borrowing abroad by private banks was substantially limited and the cash deposit requirement was reimposed. The decision to nationalize the banks resulted in García losing the support of virtually all of his political allies and marked the beginning of an 'antipopulist backlash' and the rise of a conservative opposition movement (FREDEMO) led by novelist Mario Vargas Llosa.

Between 1988 and 1990, per capita GDP in real terms fell by 25%, all the way back to the level of the early 1960s. Real GDP in 1990 was similar to the one in 1978. Between 1988 and 1990, Peru's industrial production contracted by 30% and exports per capita were lower overall than they had been in the 1950s (Rossini and Paredes 1991: 285). Tax receipts amounted to only 3% of GDP by the end of García's term (Klarén 2000: 407). There was a substantial drop in public investment, especially in public health and education. The public-sector deficit reached 11% of GDP by 1988 due mainly to the rapidly shrinking tax base. Annual inflation approached 2,000% by late 1988, more than 3,000% in 1989 and peaked at approximately 7,500% in 1990. The stock of net international reserves at the end of July 1990 had a negative balance of US$ 163 million (Ledesma 2001: 9).

The social costs of the economic tail-spin were enormous: real income dropped 22% between 1987 and 1989, falling to the 1960s levels. Wages of public employees fell by 60% between 1985 and 1990. By 1990, a full 70% of the workforce was either unemployed or underemployed (Klarén 2000: 395).

Table 4.1 Macroeconomic indicators for Peru, 1985–1990

Year	Growth of real GDP (constant 2000) in annual % change	Inflation, Consumer price index (in %)	Trade balance (millions of US$)	Debt service of % of exports of goods, services and income (in %)	Investment as % of GDP	Fiscal deficit as % of GDP	International Reserves (annual % change)
1985	2.8	163.40	980	27.69	19.28	−3.47	−35.84
1986	10	77.92	−404.83	21.07	20.65	−5.82	−95.50
1987	8	85.82	−871.03	13.27	20.68	−8.83	−917.02
1988	−8.70	667.02	−466.46	9.44	22.33	−5.49	−201.42
1989	−11.70	3398.68	938.95	8.92	18.58	−9.49	48.65
1990	−5.14	7481.66	33	10.81	16.47	−7.95	145.50

Sources: World Development Indicators, International Financial Statistics, Banco Central de la Reserva del Perú.

Not being able to freely exchange their local currency for US dollars not only enraged the external sector but also the population at large. One characteristic element of García's heterodox program was increasingly tougher restrictions on international capital transactions. Driven by the attempt to stem rising levels of capital flight, the administration introduced a variety of capital and exchange controls. For example, immediately after taking office, the government froze all dollar accounts forcing them to be turned into local currency only at the new, devalued exchange rate plus a 3 % premium.

A direct, if unintended consequence of the capital and exchange controls was a sharp rise of the informal or *de facto* dollarization of the Peruvian economy at the end of García's presidency. People increasingly lost faith in the stability and value of their domestic currency and started a 'flight to quality' by substituting their local currency for US dollars, not only to preserve the value of their assets but also as a medium of exchange and as a unit of account. Similar to countries such as Bolivia or Argentina during the same period, dollarization in Peru emerged as a response to macroeconomic instability, particularly high levels of inflation and a rapidly depreciating exchange rate, first during the late 1970s and in a rather dramatic fashion during the hyperinflation period at the end of the 1980s.[53]

Within a relatively short period of time, the dollarization ratio of the Peruvian economy increased dramatically: after the end of the military regime in 1980, the dollarization ratio steadily rose during the second presidency of Belaúnde (1980–1985) to about 60 % in 1985. The ratio fell to less than 10 % between 1985 and 1988 as the result of the forcible conversion of foreign currency banks deposits into domestic currency, accompanied by a range of foreign exchange and capital controls that limited the issuance of new foreign currency deposits. People who could not transfer their foreign currency abroad in order to avoid the confiscation of their deposits preferred to keep their dollars outside of the financial system. As a result, the controls regime failed in its attempt to de-dollarize the economy and the government eventually re-allowed foreign currency deposits in September 1988. The consequence was that dollarization rapidly increased between 1988 and 1990 reaching its old level of 60 % in 1991 and has since remained between 65 % and 75 % (Quispe 2000), though recently falling to levels around 50 % (IMF 2010: 34–56).[54] Against the background of the substantial dollarization of the Peruvian economy – an institutional legacy of the 1980s crisis – the effectiveness of controls on international capital movements in and out of the country invariably suffers given people's choice to move portfolio from foreign to national deposits and vice versa within the domestic financial system.

4.1.2 The initial liberalization of the capital account

García's successor as president, Alberto Fujimori, was left with little room to maneuver in terms of economic policies. The country was considered a pariah by the international financial community. Since García had inaugurated the debt moratorium, the country run

53 Dollarization follows a well-defined pattern: first agents replace domestic currency as reserve of value, holding usually dollars outside the financial system ("under the mattress"). Then, the dollar is used in some transactions, typically involving real estate and durable goods, and eventually some prices are set in dollars. Most governments later on allow banks to issue deposits in foreign currency to avoid financial disintermediation (Savastano 1996).

54 For comparison, due to legislation prohibiting foreign currency loans, except for on-lending, and a ban on foreign currency deposits, financial dollarization in Colombia is virtually non-existent. In 2004, just 2 % of all deposits were in foreign currency and 6 % of all loans were denominated in foreign currency. The same numbers for Peru were 64 % and 74 %, respectively (Rennhack and Nozaki 2006: 15).

up arrears with the IMF and was declared ineligible to borrow funds in 1986. After having won the presidential election on a gradualist reform platform, Fujimori quickly changed course once being sworn into office and ominously shortly after a trip as president-elect to New York in June 1990 where he met the leaders of the IMF, the World Bank, and the Inter-American Development Bank. There he was told that "if the new president tried to avoid an immediate, painful adjustment, his administration would run the course of Alan García's. If he did not adjust, he ought not to turn to the international financial institutions for help (...) In other words, if the government did nothing, it would face continued isolation; if it did everything the international financial institutions wanted, it could count on them for full support" (Stokes 1997: 217; Abusada 2000: 130). The subsequent switch from a gradualist stabilization program to a neoliberal 'shock therapy' is widely considered the direct consequence of this trip.[55]

The international financial institutions clearly demarcated the terms of financial rapprochement along the lines of the 'Washington Consensus'. As Wise puts it, "once he (Fujimori) was elected it took just ten days for the newly inaugurated administration to realize that hyperinflation had rendered gradualism a foreclosed option. The complete collapse of state finances, combined with the halt of capital flows to Peru, meant there was *zero financial room to maneuver*" (Wise 2003: 204; emphasis added). Binding structural constraints and the policy limits set by the international financial institutions were a major impetus behind the wave of neoliberal economic reforms in Peru during the early 1990s.

The majority of the Peruvian population was willing to go along and accepted a high political and economic risk in order to get out of the dire straits (Weyland 2002a: 116–118). Rising like a phoenix from the ashes of economic chaos, Fujimori seemed destined to bring about this radical turnaround.[56] Immediately upon taking office in August 1990, he launched an all-out reform program – the so-called *Fujishock* – intended to stabilize the run-away economy. The explicit purpose of the draconian adjustment program was a quick fix for hyperinflation.[57]

Capital account liberalization was not part of the initial stabilization plan. Even though hyperinflation was reduced in the aftermath of the adjustment program, inflation levels remained rather high – 24% per month in early 1991 – and came down only slowly. As a result, when the initial 'shock treatment' "proved insufficient for curing inflation, Fujimori intensified the dosage" (Weyland 2002a: 117). He fired Juan Carlos Hurtado Miller as Minister of Economy and Finance in February 1991 and appointed the outspoken free-market

55 Interview with Felipe Ortiz de Zevallo, June 8, 2005.

56 Note, however, that Fujimori's 1990 election campaign was based on gradual economic reforms. In fact, his contender during the elections, Vargas Llosa, promised much more radical reforms to stabilize the economy. Hence, one should be careful to associate the domain of losses with a higher risk-seeking attitude of the population (Weyland 2002a). In fact, during the presidential elections the majority of the population voted for the candidate that apparently constituted a lower risk in terms of the painfulness of the economic adjustment.

57 Unlike other successful macroeconomic stabilizations in Latin America at the same time, the Peruvian program did not fix the exchange rate but controlled the money supply via a restrictive monetary policy. Subsequently, the Central Bank only intervened by attempting to depreciate the currency to a degree that was consistent with the objective of reducing inflation.

enthusiast Carlos Boloña as his replacement. Boloña describes his approach to financial sector management in the following way:

> The objective of the money market reform is to obtain a financial system that is efficient, profitable, competitive, open to foreign markets, and characterized by solvency and prudence. These reforms aim to eliminate financial repression and create a new system that covers financial needs in the short and long runs. We also seek to develop a capital market that can play a significant role in the financing of businesses. The financial sector must be an efficient private savings intermediary so that both private and public savings finance the different economic sectors (...) To achieve these objectives, it is necessary to liberalize interest rates, eliminate quantitative and qualitative controls, and reduce the required reserve ratio to normal levels (Boloña 1996: 201).

Boloña wasted no time to implement his liberalization strategy. One month after his nomination, he introduced a string of structural reforms in various sectors of the economy, including the full liberalization of the capital account (Morris 2000: 315). Under the Foreign Investment Promotion Act of 1991, foreigners were allowed to invest in almost all economic sectors and repatriate all profits and capital equipment as they saw fit. Additional legislation was passed that protected all investors, domestic and foreign, from sudden changes in existing laws and established procedures for the resolution of investment disputes (Manzetti 1999: 251).

Boloña's main intention was to reassure the international financial community and to regain its trust in the country, especially in the context of ongoing negotiations over debt rescheduling. With the surge of structural economic reforms, Boloña wanted to signal to investors that Peru had made an irreversible choice for a free-market economy and he hoped to attract new capital inflows in order to reignite economic growth (Boloña 1996).

The effect of the reforms in terms of monetary policy was characterized by a fundamental conflict between the economic objectives of low inflation, on the one hand, and a competitive exchange rate on the other (Hnyilicza 2001). Having introduced a restrictive monetary policy and abandoned interest-rate ceilings during the first wave of reforms, real domestic interest rates went up rapidly. That certainly helped to bring down inflation and stimulated capital inflows, yet at the same time contributed to a real appreciation of the exchange rate, thereby hurting the country's external competitiveness (Sheahan 2006). The declared strategy of the government and the Central Bank to reconcile both economic objectives was to bring inflation down slowly in order to prevent a strong currency appreciation. Yet when push came to shove in macroeconomic decision-making, the clear preference of the government and within the Board of the Central Bank was to reduce inflation at all costs, assigning a secondary role to exchange-rate stability (Sheahan 1994; Gonzales de Olarte 1998: 73; Rodríguez et al. 2000: 109).

The restrictive monetary policy led to massive capital inflows: 1,226 million US dollars in 1993, 3,838 million in 1994 (2,241 million alone from privatizations), 2,551 million in 1995, 4,080 million in 1996 and 2,736 million in 1997 (Rodríguez et al. 2000: 106). In contrast, exports increased by only 17 % in 1994 and 7 % in 1995, resulting in a substantial current-account deficit, 5.6 % of GDP in 1993 and 7.3 % in 1995. Only the burst of privatization-related foreign direct investment helped to finance this deficit.

Table 4.2 Macroeconomic indicators for Peru, 1991–2007

Year	Growth of real GDP (constant 2000) in annual % change	Inflation, Consumer price index (in %)	Trade balance (millions of US$)	Debt service of % of exports of goods, services and income (in %)	Investment as % of GDP	Fiscal deficit as % of GDP	International Reserves (annual % change)
1991	2.17	409.53	−601	25.05	17.29	−2.56	53.47
1992	−0.43	73.53	−914	20.28	17.31	−3.89	37.04
1993	4.76	48.58	−1325.68	58.53	19.31	−3.65	108.55
1994	12.82	23.74	−1545.35	18.17	22.25	−3.17	16.15
1995	8.61	11.13	−2974.72	15.93	24.82	−3.39	28.61
1996	2.52	11.54	−2657.42	34.54	22.82	−1.44	19.07
1997	6.86	8.56	−2497.35	35.59	24.09	−0.80	−9.69
1998	−0.66	7.25	−3119.05	24.25	23.61	−1.13	−8.49
1999	0.91	3.47	−1210.62	28.15	21.09	−3.14	−2.66
2000	2.95	3.76	−1137.51	25.80	20.16	−2.79	5.30
2001	0.21	1.98	−1141.49	22.21	18.77	−2.80	11.43
2002	5.02	0.19	−672.68	33.54	18.40	−2.14	6.21
2003	4.03	2.26	−14.06	21.60	18.43	−1.74	23.90
2004	4.98	3.66	2272.56	17.13	17.95	−1.25	11.61
2005	6.83	1.62	4451.81	26.54	17.89	−0.70	22.54
2006	7.74	2.00	8152.60	12.83	20.04	1.46	60.28
2007	8.86	1.78	7428.65	25.02	22.92	1.84	12.67

Sources: World Development Indicators, International Financial Statistics, Banco Central de la Reserva de Peru.

The architects of the economic reform program defend the simultaneous launch of the entire range of structural reforms, including capital account liberalization, emphasizing political expediency and the need to mend relations with the external creditors as quickly as possible by signaling a credible commitment to comply with their demands, and, in fact, to go well beyond them.[58] As Boloña explains:

58 Interview with Roberto Abusada, former adviser to the Minister of Economy and Finance, June 7, 2005.

> I was convinced not only that the reforms had to parallel the stabilization process but also that they had to be completed in as short a time as possible (…). Reforms not made in the first difficult moments of the stabilization process are never made (Boloña 1996: 185).

4.2 Competing Explanations for the Sustainability of Capital Account Openness

There is a relatively good understanding of what drove the initial opening of the capital account in Peru, but much less knowledge about the reasons for its persistence given changing political and economic circumstances. In this section, I consider two 'outside-in' explanations that emphasize the role of causal mechanisms located at the international level – the influence of the IMF and of the foreign-trained epistemic community of economists – before turning to the role of domestic institutional factors.

4.2.1 Relations with the IMF: liberalization from the outside?

Peru had very close interactions with the Fund during the early 1990s. Between 1990 and 1993 it was heavily engaged in negotiations with the IMF about the restructuring of the external debt burden that the García administration had piled up (Abusada 2000). In the context of these close interactions, did the IMF, either through 'hard', i.e., loan conditionalities, or 'soft' power, i.e., persuasion and policy dialogue, force or convince the Peruvian government to adopt and maintain an open capital account?

External constraints on the country were clear and present when Fujimori took office in August 1990. Essentially, Peru was in a bind: due to Garcia's antagonistic, confrontational stance it had lost all credibility with the international financial community. Given the chaotic situation, the new government urgently needed to restore trust and regain confidence on the international stage. As a result, the main objective on the international economic front during the first years of the Fujimori administration was to again become eligible for IMF loans after negotiating the rescheduling of the existing arrears. These negotiations were the cornerstone of the relations between Peru and the IMF from 1990 to 1993.

However, the conventional image of a weak country, trapped in economic chaos, whose economic policies are subsequently dictated by powerful international financial institutions needs modification. As mentioned earlier, clear signals from the World Bank and the IMF were an important element behind the abandonment of the 'no shock' campaign promise by Fujimori. In addition, the initial adjustment program in 1990 was developed in close collaboration with IMF and World Bank advisers (Abusada 2000: 130).

Peru resumed payments to the multilateral financial institutions as early as September 1990. The first tangible result of the negotiations with the Fund came in September 1991 when the IMF's Board of Directors approved the so-called Rights Accumulation Program (RAP) for the period between October 1991 and December 1992. Under such a 'shadow program' the country committed itself to specific targets in monetary and fiscal policy whose compliance does not result in disbursements but instead in the accumulation of borrowing rights. Once the process had been successfully completed, the country was able to access

Fund resources. Having successfully completed the goals set out in the RAP at the end of 1992, the IMF approved the first loan to Peru after 1985 for US$ 1,395 million for the period between March 1993 and March 1996 under an Extended Facility Program (Abusada 2000).

However, capital account liberalization was not and legally could not be on the list of reforms that the Fund required Peru to implement in order to restart relations with the country. In fact, Boloña's 1991 economic reform package went well beyond what was asked of the Peruvian government by the IMF at the time (Weyland 2002a: 105–6).[59] Instead, it was a home-grown initiative by the Fujimori government intended to woo foreign investors back with a credible commitment to liberalized markets (Bartolini and Drazen 1997). While certainly not speaking out against capital account liberalization, the IMF had little direct influence or control over its content, let alone its rapid implementation schedule. To put it bluntly, Peru 'jumped the gun' by unilaterally going all the way down on the international financial liberalization front without explicit pressure or even implicit nudging from the IMF.[60] When the Rights Accumulation Program with its attendant conditionalities was approved in September 1991, the capital account was already liberalized for half a year. Neither coercive nor discursive power from the IMF was required for the liberal policy change to take place.[61] Trapped in a desperate economic situation, the Fujimori administration had liberalized virtually all accounts of the balance of payments at once.

Generally speaking, during the past twenty years the IMF followed a *hands-off approach* to capital account management in Peru, after having seen its liberalization agenda exemplary implemented by the local authorities. According to the IMF staff reports, the topic was barely raised during the annual Article IV consultations with the Peruvian government. However, while not arguing against capital account liberalization on principle, in its policy consultations the IMF did highlight the attendant risks of an open capital account by, for example, urging the authorities to "move rapidly in implementing plans to strengthen financial supervision and prudential control" (IMF 1993: 15). Yet both sides – the Peruvian government and the IMF country team – agreed that removing restrictions on international capital movements as fast and comprehensibly as possible was a desirable policy for the country. While not being the causal force behind this policy change, no objection, let alone protest, was ever registered from the IMF.[62]

An interesting modification to the Fund's passive stance occurred in early 1998, i.e., in the midst of the Asian financial crisis. The IMF staff team recommended the imposition of capital controls in order to deal with speculative capital inflows – a somewhat surprising move given the organizational climate advocating unrestricted capital flows at the time. In its Article IV report for 1998, the IMF team suggested – copying a measure already in place

59 Interview with Roberto Abusada, June 8, 2005, and written communication from Luis Durand-Downing, IMF Mission Chief for Peru 1991–1996, August 3, 2007.

60 Scholars defending the external imposition argument might argue that the Peruvian government merely applied some sort of anticipatory obedience vis-à-vis the IMF when introducing capital account liberalization in 1991. However, in my interviews or written communications with former IMF as well as Peruvian government officials I could not find any evidence that the preference for capital account openness was informally communicated by the IMF before the Peruvian government adopted capital account liberalization.

61 Written communication from Luis Durand-Downing, August 3, 2007.

62 Interview with Roberto Abusada and based on a review of all IMF Article IV consultations staff reports from 1990 onwards.

in Argentina – to extend the coverage of the marginal reserve requirements on foreign currency deposits to foreign borrowing, while at the same time lowering the percentage rate charged in order to deal with rapid credit expansion (IMF 1998: 15). The staff argued that such a measure should be considered a prudential regulation instead of a conventional control on capital movements.[63]

However, the IMF's call for caution fell on deaf ears. The staff report notes that "the (Peruvian) authorities viewed the increase in bank borrowing abroad as part of the process of internationalization of the banking system and they did not favor extending the coverage of the reserve requirement, on the grounds that it might be construed as a step toward capital controls, which they wanted to avoid" (IMF 1998: 15). According to a member of the Fund's team at the time, the Peruvian government did not want to restrict international capital mobility as a matter of principle, even if such restrictions were couched in the language of prudential regulation. Their fundamental resistance to such measures seemed to have deep-seated ideological reasons.[64]

In sum, the adoption and maintenance of capital account liberalization in Peru was not directly imposed or indirectly insinuated by the IMF. Instead, the process followed a domestic-level logic. In their quest to lure foreign investors back to their country at virtually any cost, Peru's policymakers went far beyond the call of duty demanded by the IMF for restoring relations and assuring financial support for the economic reforms (Weyland 2002a: 19–22). The direct influence of the IMF on the initial adjustment program in 1990 rapidly waned and increasingly domestic free-market enthusiasts such as Finance and Economy Minister Boloña dominated the reform agenda. Their ideological convictions combined with the perceived need to re-attract foreign investors account for the adoption of capital account liberalization during the early 1990s. The hands-off stance adopted by the IMF in terms of capital account management also minimizes its role for the maintenance of capital account freedom. As a result, the drivers behind the sustainability of capital account openness in Peru must be found elsewhere.

4.2.2 Foreign-trained economists' views on capital account policy

Is capital account policy in Peru determined by neoliberal economists trained at foreign universities and occupying influential positions within the state bureaucracy? In other words, are neoliberal ideas imported from abroad and represented by high-level members of the government the drivers of capital account policy in Peru?

In order to assess the 'orthodox temperature' in terms of capital account management among foreign-trained economists in Peru, I applied an online survey among the recipients of the Central Bank scholarship for graduate studies abroad in September 2005 (see Appendix 3). The Human Resources Department of the Peruvian Central Bank provided me with a list of 46 names and email addresses of people who previously worked at the Central

63 Interview with Gilbert Terrier, Member of the IMF Peru mission during the 1990s, July 5, 2007.
64 Interview with Gilbert Terrier, July 5, 2007.

Bank and studied abroad with its financial sponsorship.[65] From this list, 18 people (39 %) completed the survey. 67 % of the respondents indicated that they were able to shape capital account policy in Peru from positions in the political bureaucracy, i. e., within the government or the Central Bank.

The survey participants were asked whether they agreed or disagreed with a number of propositions regarding capital account management. Asked about their current view on capital account policy, 72 % of the respondents either strongly or mostly agreed with the efficient market hypothesis compared with only 59 % immediately after their graduation. A whopping 94 % strongly or mostly agreed that government restrictions of international capital movements should be abolished; 76.5 % believed this after graduating. An overwhelming majority, both presently and after graduation, considered capital controls as ineffective and unnecessary for the preservation of national autonomy. Almost 90 % believed that market mechanisms, not government intervention, should determine capital flows, and that restrictions on long-term capital flows are not essential to foster domestic welfare. None of the respondents thought that quantitative limits, e. g., caps on foreign investment, are essential for the stabilization of the domestic economy.

This strong neoliberal sentiment becomes a bit more nuanced in terms of short-term capital flows. Concerning the question whether restrictions on short-term portfolio capital flows are necessary to address international capital market volatility, the responses indicated only a slight majority rejecting the proposition, both presently and immediately after graduation. However, a clear majority (83 %) of the respondents spoke out against price-based restrictions, e. g., taxes on capital inflows, with a somewhat smaller majority (65 %) immediately after graduation. Almost 90 % of the respondents acknowledged the need for prudential regulations in the domestic financial market, while 40 % recognized that capital controls can easily be disguised as prudential regulations.

72 % of the respondents attributed their views on capital account policy to their studies abroad. Yet 50 % believed that it only had a moderate influence. On the other hand, 87.5 % indicated that the domestic economic context strongly influences their views. 61 % said that the experiences of other countries did so.

33 % of the respondents attended courses on capital account management at the IMF. Yet 55 % saw little or no influence of the IMF on their views on capital account policy. A similar result was obtained regarding the influence of domestic business groups.

Taken together, the results of the survey demonstrate an overwhelming rejection of almost all types of both traditional and new, i. e., price-based capital controls among foreign-trained Peruvian economists. An unambiguous preference for orthodox capital account management comes out in their responses. In accordance with the expectations of sociological or constructivist approaches, the negative view on capital controls perpetuates after receiving professional training abroad. Can we then safely conclude that the persistence of capital account openness in Peru has its origin in the foreign training of elite economists

65 Unfortunately, the list did not contain the names of current employees of the Central Bank nor did it indicate the institutional affiliation of the 46 people. However, judged by the email addresses, most people were located in the Peruvian economy and finance ministry as well as other government agencies, private commercial banks, consulting agencies, and academia.

– steeped in the neoclassical orthodoxy – who have occupied important positions within the political machinery?

4.2.3 The neoliberal epistemic community: social rather than political power

Postgraduate professional training and mutual identification as economists are rather recent phenomena in Peru. Professional economists with master's or doctoral degrees only appeared during the 1970s. By that time, the disciplinary discourse was still dominated by the theoretical backbone of the Import-Substitution Industrialization (ISI) model, i. e., CEPAL structuralism as well as Keynesianism and a significant dose of orthodox Marxism. Only the decay of the military government and the beginning of Peru's prolonged economic crisis in the mid-1970s slowly shifted the discourse to include neoclassical or orthodox economic theory. However, "the political tenor of the 1970s and 1980s in Peru was not especially propitious for the development of any particular widely-shared consensus on economic policy either inside or outside the academy, and especially not one in the neoliberal direction" (Conaghan 1998: 148). While people began to question the statist and populist economic policies of the military regime after 1976, these policies were not completely discredited within elite circles or in the broader public opinion as demonstrated by their resurrection during the first García administration in the late 1980s (Webb 1994: 372–373).

One important factor behind both the increased professionalization of the discipline as well as its turn towards neoliberalism among the elite segment of the profession was postgraduate education abroad. However, in comparison with Chile and the external formation of a closely knit 'monetarist or Chicago-style school' at the Catholic University in Santiago de Chile, Peruvian economists were trained at a diverse set of institutions in the United States – ranging from Boston University, Iowa State, Rochester, Pittsburgh, Wisconsin, and Brown to the New School for Social Research – and only occasionally as economists in the first place (Conaghan 1998: 147; Cortázar 2006). Given this heterogeneous composition of the elite segment of the economics profession, "there was no single shared language or binding set of basic assumptions that located professionals on a common ground in the 1980s" (Conaghan 1998: 148). Cacophony rather than the uniformity of views on economic policy characterized the intellectual landscape of Peruvian economists at the end of the 1980s.

Yet only a few years later, such a uniform, neoliberal view emerged and quickly came to dominate the academic and political discourse on economic policies. As Conaghan aptly put it, orthodox economists were the "stars of the crisis" (Conaghan 1998). The 1980s economic crisis energized and radicalized the free-market discourse of a new breed of economists and simultaneously provided them with public credibility and political support to carry out their preferred reforms. The first phase of Fujimori's term in office between 1990 and 1993 is generally seen as the heyday of orthodox technocracy's influence on government economic policies (Mauceri 1997). From its 'home base' in the Ministry of the Economy and Finance, a relatively small group around Minister Boloña provided the ideological basis for the first wave of economic reforms.[66]

However, due to the institutional and disciplinary variety of the professional training of elite economists, it is rather unlikely that the neoliberal view on capital account policy is the direct result of their foreign education. Only a small fraction of the economic team during the Fujimori administration obtained professional degrees from foreign universities. In addition, the composition of the team reflected a high degree of disciplinary heterogeneity. Several members were not even trained in economics or only at the undergraduate level.[67] A professionally coherent neoliberal team as a causal factor behind capital account liberalization certainly looks different (Chwieroth 2007).

In addition, the rise of neoliberal technocrats to public stardom and direct policy control was rather short-lived. Changes in the political calculation of President Fujimori at the beginning of 1993 ended Boloña's brief career in politics as swiftly as he rose to the forefront in the first place.[68] Boloña's meteoritic rise and fall in politics seems to confirm the widespread association between the fate of specific economic ideas, the people associated with them, and their usefulness for the political calculations of executive leaders (Bates 1993).

However, despite firing Boloña, Fujimori left capital account policy unchanged. In other words, the survival of capital account openness was not tied to the political fate of ideas-driven individuals. Instead, the view that capital freedom is and must remain an essential characteristic of economic policymaking became a generalized phenomenon in the Peruvian economics profession during the 1990s.

Despite losing its prominent place in government, the neoliberal epistemic community was able to lay the intellectual foundation for a largely consensual interpretation of specific economic policies. The public voice and political influence of the so-called 'liberal camp' has dominated the public and intellectual discourse on economic policymaking beyond the end of Fujimori's presidency.[69] In fact, the difference between the diversity and rivalry of the economic discourse during the 1980s and today's intellectual monoculture and interpretive predominance of the 'liberal camp' is striking.[70] Even the corruption charges and nu-

66 In fact, closely knit elite cliques have remained a characteristic of the Peruvian economic policymaking process until the present time. As a result, open discussions, flexibility and pragmatic decisions beyond a narrow range of ideologically acceptable policy options are the exception, not the rule (Morón and Sanborn 2006; Wise 2003: 224).

67 See the biographies of the authors in the volume by Abusada et al. (2000).

68 There is some uncertainty as to why Fujimori decided to fire Boloña in January 1993 given his successful track record as minister. Some observers indicate that Boloña simply became too orthodox for the taste of the president and the business sector as the economy stabilized and executive priorities began to change (Arce 2003: 341), while others believe that Boloña developed too much of a political profile or personal ego for Fujimori to stomach (Conaghan 1998: 160). Somewhat ironically, after winning his third presidential term in a rigged election in April 2000 Fujimori brought Boloña back from political retirement to serve in his old job in July 2000. However, only a few months later in November 2000 Fujimori resigned in the midst of political turmoil caused by a bribery scandal. Boloña then ran as a presidential candidate for the elections in April 2001 (obtaining 1.7% of the vote) and was later charged with corruption as well as plotting a coup against Fujimori.

69 Interview with David Rivera, editor-in-chief of the economic journal PODER 360°, October 16, 2009.

70 The incarnation of change *par excellence* is Alan García himself. He has publicly recanted his heterodox policy views of the 1980s and irrespective of his 2006 campaign promise to introduce a "social change" to

merous convictions of former members of Fujimori's cabinet, including *all* ministers of the economy and finance, have not fundamentally undermined the social legitimacy of capital freedom in Peru.[71]

Today both the orthodox (neoclassical) and the non-orthodox (structuralist or Neo-Keynesian) camps in the economists' community agree on certain macroeconomic fundamentals.[72] Especially prominent among them is the preservation of capital freedom. Even when so-called non-orthodox economists held politically influential positions in the Central Bank and in the Ministry of the Economy and Finance during the administration of Alejandro Toledo (2001–2006)[73] and in the current administration of Ollanta Humala, their policy decisions did not reflect any intention to fundamentally change this principle of economic policymaking.

In fact, it is quite striking how the Humala administration that came into office in August 2011 on a left-leaning, nationalistic electoral platform has largely continued the macroeconomic course of its predecessor governments since Fujimori. The personnel in charge of economic policy largely hails from the previous García administration, including the economy and finance minister and the head of the Central Bank. Humala does not enact a profound transformation of the pre-existing economic model in Peru with its significant dependence on mineral exports and capital inflows. Rather he takes the existing model as given and implements incremental changes for redistributive purposes such as higher taxes for multinational corporations in the mining sector. Towards the end of 2011, less than half a year in office, Humala looks to have abandoned his left-wing intentions for good and largely purged his government of its heterodox members to replace them with "solidly centrist technocrats" (The Economist, December 17, 2011). Put differently, another sign that the existing economic order, including the freedom of international capital movements, is safe in Peru – notwithstanding the initial fears about Humala's campaign announcement to engender a "great transformation".

---

the existing development model, including modifying the restrictive economic provisions of the 1993 Constitution, has continued the orthodox macroeconomic policies introduced during the Fujimori era.

71 Conaghan exaggerates the impact of the corruption charges as 'the end of neoliberalism in Peru' (Conaghan 2005; 2006). Despite public indignation about the "immoral economy" that reigned under Fujimori, his neoliberal economic policies have proved rather resilient. In contrast to countries such as Argentina, the neoliberal discourse has not lost its social legitimacy in Peru. There is no strong, sustained groundswell within the population against neoliberal economic policies. Despite the fact that Peru's population is the second most dissatisfied in Latin America with the economic situation generally and the political response to the current economic crisis specifically, a – slightly declining – majority continues to support market-based over state-based economic policies (Latinobarómetro 2009).

72 The consensus between the two camps has its limits, though. Policies to de-dollarize the economy and higher taxes for the financial and extractive industries constitute a red flag for the liberal camp.

73 The most important examples were Oscar Dancourt, first as member and then as president in charge of the Board of Directors of the Central Bank, and Kurt Burneo as Vice-Minister of the Economy and Finance.

4.3 Institutional Changes as Determinants of Sustainable Capital Account Openness

4.3.1 Changes in state-business relations: the weakening of collective entrepreneurial representation

The nature of state-business relations is an essential element for the persistence of economic policies. Specific economic interests play an important role when it comes to the sustainability of neoliberal economic reforms (Arce 2003). The move from crisis-induced reforms to their consolidation is affected by shifting governing coalitions and changes in the interactions between state and business. For example, Moisés Arce has shown how the dominance of different societal groups across different phases of the economic restructuring process helps to account for the mixed record of market reforms in Peru (Arce 2005).

Here I consider this relationship and the origins of business sector support for capital account openness. After a period of distrust, uncertainty, and conflict between business elites and the government before 1990, the Fujimori administration reached out to the business community as a key political ally for its economic reform program. As a result, organized business played an active role in backing policy shifts during the 1990s. Yet the business community is notoriously divided over many issues, including capital account liberalization and its consequences for specific economic sectors. The durability of capital account liberalization requires the support of the dominating alliance of economic sectors within the domestic business community. Capital account liberalization acquires a material fundament in society only if interest groups supportive of capital controls lose their influence over government policy to economic sectors that are unambiguously in favor of capital freedom. Peru after 1990 provides a showcase example for the reconfiguration of state-business relations as a domestic institutional condition for consolidating capital account openness.

As a result of Boloña's departure as minister of the economy and finance and his subsequent replacement by a former business sector executive (Jorge Camet), the influence of orthodox technocrats within the Fujimori government declined and somewhat more heterogeneous business interests came to dominate the state bureaucracy and economic policies (Arce 2005). However, capital account openness never came under threat. How can we account for this outcome?

Starting in 1991 and especially after his 'self-coup' in April 1992 Fujimori actively courted the business community in order to broaden the base of political support for his semi-authoritarian regime. The Confederation of Private Entrepreneurial Institutions (*Confederación Nacional de Instituciones Empresariales Privadas;* CONFIEP), the business sector umbrella association created in 1984, became the primary interlocutor for extensive government-business cooperation. At its peak, CONFIEP represented twenty-two business associations *(gremios)* and was widely recognized as the unified voice of the private sector.

However, behind the public image of a unified business community, CONFIEP has been characterized by internal tensions between rival economic interest groups. During the second part of the 1990s, *gremios* that represented more mobile factors of the economy, e. g., the financial sector or producers of commodities such as large-scale mining companies, started to dominate the organization, imposing their preferences over economic policies on the rest of the *gremios* assembled in CONFIEP, including several founding members of the organization (Cotler 1998a, 1998b, Gonzales de Olarte 1998).[74]

This institutional development occurred against the background of a relative de-industrialization and the return to the dominance of traditional exports in the Peruvian economy since the early 1990s (Abugattás 1999). Nontraditional exports occupy a distant second place compared to traditional ones, primarily mineral commodities which account for 60% of all export gains. In fact, Peru is now known as a "mining country", highly penetrated by multinational companies and domestic conglomerates. It is therefore no surprise that the interests of these players have prevailed over others in shaping government policy.

Owners of mobile factors of production and producers of nontradable goods directly profited from the first generation of neoliberal reforms, including capital account liberalization. In particular, the large-scale privatization program starting in 1991 and extending until 1997 led to a large inflow of foreign capital, especially in the mining and banking sectors. Multinational companies that came to dominate these sectors have been direct beneficiaries of capital account openness. Their primary concern has been with the free inflow and outflow of capital rather than a focus on the negative effects of capital account liberalization for the stability and competitiveness of the exchange rate. Their economic rationale is tied to the preservation of a stable investment climate with as little state intervention as possible. In addition, the highly dollarized cost structure of the mining sector makes it less sensitive to exchange rate fluctuations. As a result, important members of the Peruvian business community such as large, foreign-owned mining companies do not seek or support government actions to stabilize or devalue the nominal exchange rate (Pascó-Font and Ghezzi 2001: 259). While the real exchange rate in Peru certainly maintained stability during the last twenty years, it did so at a *non-competitive level*, i.e., in the context of a significant nominal appreciation of the exchange rate (see Figure 4.1 below).

On the other hand, producers of tradable goods, e.g., labor-intensive exporters of nontraditional goods, suffered from lower tariffs and the elimination of tax rebate subsidies for nontraditional exports. As a result, their business associations such as the National Society of Industries (SNI, composed of industrialists) and the Association of Exporters (ADEX, composed of nontraditional exporters) have demanded promotional policies for their more sophisticated, value-added products. These industries have been negatively affected by the restrictive monetary policy pursued by the Central Bank – justified in terms of inflation control – and the resulting appreciation of the exchange rate.

74 Most importantly, the business associations of the mining, oil, and fishing industries as well as the banking and insurance association. In addition, newly established *gremios* such as the Chamber of Foreign Trade (COMEX) and the Association of Private Pensions Funds (AAFP) who joined CONFIEP during the early 1990s fall into this category.

Figure 4.1 Peru bilateral real exchange rate with the US, 1980–2008, deflated by CPI indexes (Index 1 = average 1980–2008)

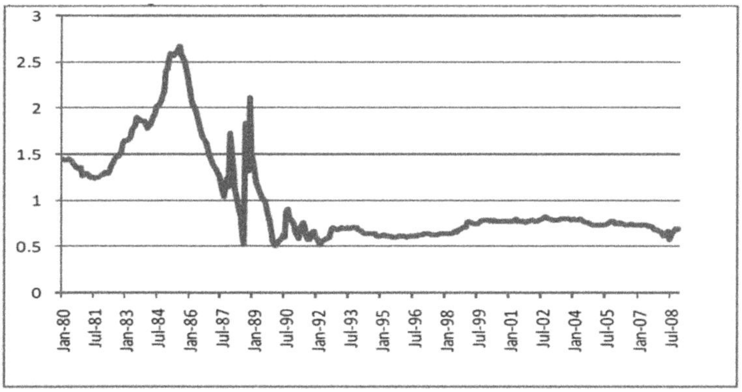

Source: Frenkel and Rapetti 2010.

Despite representing a much larger share of the economy compared to the first group of industries, SNI and ADEX have been systematically marginalized within CONFIEP (Arce 2003: 343–344; Durand 2002, 2010: 173–5). Their interests and concerns related to the volatility of the exchange rate were simply not included in the policy consultations between CONFIEP and the government.[75] As a result, potential measures to address exchange-rate volatility, including capital controls, were never tabled by CONFIEP in its interactions with the government. Given this structural divergence within the organization and the inability to get a fair hearing for their policy proposals vis-à-vis the government, ADEX, SNI and the Chamber of Commerce of Lima (CCL) decided to leave CONFIEP in 2000 – amidst political discussions within CONFIEP about whether or not to support the Fujimori administration in its final crisis – hoping that bilateral interactions with the government would yield an improved pay-off. This split significantly weakened the representative power of CONFIEP which from then on could no longer claim to be the unified, encompassing private sector entity in state-business relations. In what remained of CONFIEP, the interests of large companies the mining and finance sector took precedence over those of small and medium-sized firms, primarily located in the industrial and nontraditional export sector.[76]

In addition, the decay of CONFIEP as the collective voice of the Peruvian private sector was hastened by the preference of the Fujimori government and its successors for direct and permanent dialogue and discussion–at the highest level–with business associations representing the "finance-exporters' bloc" (Durand 2010: 174), dominated by multinational companies, such as the American Chamber of Commerce (AMCHAM), the Chamber of Spanish

75 Interview with Carlos González, Chief Economist of ADEX, October 15, 2009.

76 Interview with César A. Ferrari, former Member and General Manager of the Board of Directors of the Peruvian Central Bank, April 19, 2007.

Companies (COECE), the North American-Peruvian Business Council (NAPBC), and most importantly the National Society of Mining, Oil and Energy (SNMP). Even though ADEX decided to re-join CONFIEP in 2003, it simultaneously formed a policy coalition – the so-called Entrepreneurial Alliance for Development – together with SNI and CCL. Yet even this parallel lobbying strategy has not substantially changed the political powerlessness of the industrial and nontraditional sectors vis-à-vis the traditional export sector, allied or in fact fused with the financial industry.

Given the asymmetric power structure within CONFIEP, a specific coalition of industries profiting from the free flow of international capital and largely unaffected by exchange-rate fluctuations has been able to usurp the voice of the domestic business community, granting them privileged access to economic policymakers. As a result, the appreciation of the exchange rate in the aftermath of financial and trade liberalization was not regarded as a business community-wide concern, but instead as an unfortunate but somewhat inevitable consequence of the economic liberalization process. The business groups suffering from its consequences over the medium and long run and hence the ones with an interest in modifying the unbridled flow of international capital have been politically sidelined (Durand 2004, 2010).[77]

4.3.2 The long-term effects of the 1980s crisis: the social embeddedness of capital freedom

In virtually every interview I conducted with current or former economic policymakers as well as outside observers, the 'national trauma' of the late 1980s invariably appeared as a critical juncture to understand the trajectory of capital account policy during the last two decades. The economic chaos left behind by the García administration and its concomitant economic policies have served as the political-intellectual legitimization for an orthodox capital account management. The specter of the late 1980s continues to shape what Peruvian policymakers and the population at large consider to be socially acceptable economic policies today. Every policy instrument that is remotely reminiscent of this 'dark period' is automatically considered illegitimate and hence excluded on principle from the macroeconomic policy toolkit in contemporary Peru. No substantial discussion about the potential usefulness of capital controls is allowed to take place in economic and political circles due to the construed fear that economic chaos will be the inevitable result. In short, a national taboo surrounds specific aspects of macroeconomic management that are discursively linked with the economic disaster of the late 1980s.

There can be little doubt that much of the economy's tail-spin in the late 1980s was the result of President García's so-called heterodox experiment, which imploded with a bang. The most visible sign of the economic crisis that afflicted the country was hyperinflation.

77 A related problem concerns the pride that the main institutions in charge of macroeconomic policy – the Ministry of Economy and Finance and the Central Bank – take in their allegedly unbiased, technical analysis of specific proposals made by some business associations in order to address exchange rate volatility. Exporters' associations such as ADEX thus prefer to try their luck in interactions with line ministries such as Foreign Trade or Production (Interview with Carlos González, October 15, 2009).

The memory of this dramatic experience is etched into the collective consciousness of the Peruvian society. In their desperate situation the majority of the population was willing to support radical measures with the prospect of a quick recovery from the crisis. After his 'neoliberal turn', President Fujimori could build his personal popularity as well as the legitimacy of his radical economic policies on the widespread feeling of despair. However, conventional wisdom suggests that such feelings do not last forever and dissipate as soon as the first signs of economic recovery appear. As a result, the sustainability of neoliberal reforms is threatened by a change in public sentiment and the resulting turn toward risk-avoidance and truncated economic reforms on part of the political leadership (Weyland 2002a). Yet why have some neoliberal reforms escaped this logic and instead become embedded in the domestic political economy? The persistence of capital account openness highlights how the association of specific economic policies with 'national disasters' permanently removes them from the public discourse. Consequently, capital controls are not considered legitimate instruments for macroeconomic management well beyond the immediate aftermath of the economic crisis.

Until the present time policymakers and observers alike refer with disdain to the 'dark period' of economic management during the first García administration. They invariably associate the resulting economic and social chaos with the underlying heterodox policies, including substantial restrictions on international capital movements. The disastrous consequences of García's economic management are extended to all forms of non-orthodox economic policy instruments such as providing subsidies, introducing price controls or fixing the exchange rate.[78]

The remaining non-orthodox economists are seen as tainted by their direct or indirect association with the heterodox policies of the 1980s. As a result, their rather modest policy suggestions, e. g., temporarily putting a brake on international capital flows for the purpose of stabilizing the exchange rate, are an easy target for the representatives of the reigning orthodoxy. Their standard response to capital account policy suggestions that do not 100% conform to the pure gospel of neoclassical economics is to dismiss them out of hand with the argument that 'heterodox policies' have been discredited once and for all during the first García administration. Since the current economic development model crucially depends on foreign capital investment, any policy measure that ostensibly threatens to 'scare investors off' must be rejected *on principal grounds,* i. e., without any need to engage in a detailed discussion about them.

The widespread opposition to the capital and exchange control system in place during the late 1980s has been strategically used by the neoliberal epistemic community to associate any criticism of its orthodox capital account policy with the failed economic model of yesteryear, leading to "economic holocaust" in the parlance of one of its members.[79] Linking the existence of capital controls to economic chaos has become a staple in the dominant crisis narrative. In fact, Fujimori "was able to use a radical version of market reforms as jus-

78 Interview with Javier Abugattás, former Vice-Minister of the Economy and Finance during the first García administration, October 12, 2009. For example, the National Accord on State Policies, signed in 2001 by government officials, leading opposition parties, business, labor and other civil society representatives, explicitly commits the state to maintain a flexible exchange rate (Policy No. 22).

79 Interview with Roberto Abusada, October 16, 2009.

tification for the liquidation of social, political, and institutional norms associated with what he considered the country's 'disastrous populist past'" (Tanaka 2003: 221–222). Against the background of a plethora of government interventions in day-to-day financial transactions, capital account liberalization was introduced and defended as a clear sign of economic freedom for the business community and the "common man and woman". Taking away this "freedom" is thus officially portrayed as an attack on a fundamental economic liberty for the population at large.

The discursive outlawing of capital controls also reached the formal institutional level. The charter of the Peruvian Central Bank *(Ley Orgánica)* commits it to a strict anti-inflation objective, which in turn has translated in the application of a restrictive monetary policy and the 'benign neglect' of the exchange rate. The inflow of foreign capital has been unambiguously regarded as a sign of the renewed confidence of the international financial community in the country. In addition, the Central Bank has considered the appreciation effect on the exchange rate as moderate and acceptable for the maintenance of macroeconomic stability and growth.[80]

Last but not least, the Constitution approved in 1993 includes several articles that restrict the discretionary power of the state in terms of macroeconomic management. The inclusion of these provisions was the intellectual brainchild of the team surrounding Minister Boloña, just before he was fired by President Fujimori. Article 64 guarantees Peruvian individuals and corporate bodies "the free availability, use and disposal of foreign currency as well as the guarantee of free convertibility of foreign currency at a single exchange rate". The immediate purpose of these constitutional regulations was to facilitate the repatriation of capital that left Peru during the 1980s and to stimulate financial intermediation.[81] On the other hand, they constitute a substantial limitation for the executive authority to use the full range of instruments for macroeconomic management. Capital freedom became a constitutionally guaranteed right in Peru, thereby perpetuating its removal from economic scrutiny and political debate.

4.4 Conclusion

Hyperinflation in the late 1980s induced large numbers of Peruvians to swallow the painful economic medicine prescribed by President Fujimori. However, what explains the longevity of neoliberal reforms in Peru after their initial adoption in dire circumstances? I have argued that neither the influence of the International Monetary Fund nor the occupation of high-ranking government positions by members of the neoliberal epistemic community provide satisfactory answers to this question.

The adoption of capital account openness in the early 1990s and its maintenance until the present day have been "driven by the country authorities' own economic and political agendas" (IEO 2005: 4). The IMF pursued a largely passive, hands-off approach given that

80 Interviews with Adrian Armas, Chief Economist, Peruvian Central Bank, June 8, 2005, and Hugo Santa María, Chief Economist, APOYO Consultoria, October 13, 2009.

81 Interview with Hugo Perea, Chief Economist, BBVA Banco Continental, October 14, 2009.

the ideas and policies it promoted were already entrenched in and practiced by the Peruvian authorities after 1990. While foreign-trained economists exhibit clear preferences for neoliberal capital account management, their direct political influence was rather short-lived. Instead, I posit that two domestic institutional factors help to account for the stability of capital account openness in Peru.

First, state-business relations were restructured in the context of the economic liberalization process during the Fujimori era. The traditional business alliance composed of industrialists and exporters of non-traditional goods demanding government interventions in order to stabilize and devalue the exchange rate lost its politically influential position and was replaced by 'big business' actors with a different set of distributive preferences, favoring the free flow of international capital over the stability and competitiveness of the exchange rate. In the context of the general opening of the economy and large-scale privatizations programs in the early 1990s, the financial and mining sectors came largely under foreign ownership. Given the increasing dependence of the Peruvian economy on foreign capital investments, these economic actors occupy a veto-player position in terms of capital account policy. This skewed balance of power in the Peruvian business community affecting state-business relations has prevailed until the present day.

Second, I have argued that the socially shared association between capital controls and economic disaster has provided the informal institutional foundation for economic policymaking in Peru during the last twenty years. Stephan Haggard and Steven Webb put it succinctly:

> [Y]ears after any traces of a direct effect on the economy have faded, economic successes or failures of the past continue to mold politicians' views on policy reform. Economic experiences – whether "golden ages" or "nightmares" – provide elites with lessons and analogies that shape their current decisionmaking, however different the conditions (Haggard and Webb 1993: 154).

As Kathleen McNamara has shown for the case of Germany's rigorous low inflation stance in the run-up to the European Monetary Union, the political, social, and economic trauma associated with hyperinflation leaves a visible mark on the national consciousness and casts a long shadow over economic policymaking (McNamara 1998). Similarly, Peruvian policymakers and citizens alike are prone to remember the 1980s García presidency through the lens of hyperinflation and economic chaos that ought to never befall the country again.[82] Put differently, the social construction of collective memory shapes how policymakers and the public at large approach economic policymaking in the present time. The discursive association between capital controls and economic chaos has led policymakers to exclude otherwise viable policy options from the available menu on principal grounds. As a domestic social convention, capital controls are not only considered ineffective but more importantly *illegitimate* instruments for macroeconomic policymaking. In other words, Peru's status as

82 The head of the consulting branch of the influential APOYO Group has a collection of bills from the García era displayed in his office. With both irony and contempt, he reminds visitors of the galloping inflation rate during that time. Interview with Gianfranco Castagnola, June 8, 2005.

a capital mobility enthusiast is inextricably linked to the social power of the 'capital controls = economic chaos' association.[83]

83 In contrast to both Chile and Singapore, Peruvian policymakers did apparently not protest against the ban on capital controls that the US government has mandated in its trade and investment treaties with developing countries since 2003 (Kevin P. Gallagher, Control That Capital, http://www.foreignpolicy.com/articles/2010/03/29/control_that_capital, accessed March 30, 2010). Apparently, the Peruvian government saw no problem whatsoever in tying its hands on macroeconomic policy as a result of the 2008 free trade agreement with the United States.

Chapter 5: Capital Account Policy in Colombia. The Institutional Legacies of the Pre-Liberalization Period

Colombia's political and economic history in the 20th century has long been considered an outlier among Latin American countries (Palacios 2006). The oldest democracy in the region, virtually free of military dictatorships, coups d'etat, and populist governments, with a stable two-party political system but also with the longest armed conflict in the region, a country that managed to avoid profound economic crises for most of the second half of the 20th century. It was the only major country in Latin America that emerged relatively unscathed from the 1980s debt crisis, preserving positive real GDP growth rates during that traumatic period for the region. A country with a long history of financial agreements with the International Monetary Fund during the late 1940s and 1950s that nonetheless broke off relations with the Fund in the mid-1960s and pursued an autonomous form of macroeconomic policymaking until the 1990s, which, as one observer described it, was "based on selective but firm government intervention, that neither fully choked the private sector with over-regulation, nor allowed it to flourish" (Edwards 2001: 28).

In this chapter I briefly review the history of capital account policy in Colombia before and after 1990. In line with virtually all countries in Latin America, Colombia started to radically open its economy in the early 1990s. Many restrictions on international capital movements that characterized the previous economic model based on ISI were abolished. The opening process – called *La Apertura* – also extended to the political realm trying to rebuild the political system with new, more participatory elements.

However, capital account openness has not been a sustained feature of the Colombian political economy after its initial adoption in 1991. Against the background of large private capital inflows and the resulting appreciation of the real exchange rate, the government decided to impose restrictions on capital inflows in order to maintain external competitiveness. Effectively, Colombia copied the Chilean model of an implicit tax, the so-called unremunerated reserve requirement (URR) or *encaje.* The URR has not been a constant feature of Colombian capital account policy, though. Depending on changing circumstances, it was either operative with varying degrees of force or lay dormant. However, the *encaje* system has formed part of the macroeconomic policy toolkit in Colombia since its introduction in 1993.

In order to account for Colombia's role as a capital mobility laggard, I first consider explanations located at the international level. I analyze the influence of the International Monetary Fund on the one hand, and the role of the foreign-trained neoliberal epistemic community on the other. I find little support for a decisive role of the IMF in Colombian capital account policy. The results of a survey among foreign-trained Colombian economists show a moderately negative perspective on capital controls. However, the traditionally prominent representation of foreign-trained economists in the state bureaucracy and in high-ranking government positions did not ensure that the free flow of international capital became an enduring attribute of the Colombian political economy.

As an alternative explanation, I stress the critical role of an informal institution – *pragmatism* – as a crucial mechanism for embedding (emerging) international norms and ideas into the domestic polity. Pragmatism as a "shared mental model" (Denzau and North 2000) has long characterized the policymaking and business elites in the country. It was initially based on a consensual arrangement between the two main political parties after the end of a bloody civil war during the 1950s. In addition, state-business relations have been relatively free of structural conflicts guaranteeing not only the access of the business community to the political elite but also a largely consensual view on the main content and instruments of macroeconomic policy. Most importantly, the tradition of pragmatism has survived the opening process of the economy in the early 1990s and continues to shape economic policymaking until the present time, including capital account management.

This chapter is organized as follows. Section one discusses the puzzle of initiating market reforms without a prior economic crisis and provides a short overview of the pre-liberalization system of capital account management. Section two describes capital account policy during the liberalization era, emphasizing the content and frequent use of the *encaje* system. Section three analyzes the role of the IMF for capital account policy in Colombia. Section four reports the results of a survey among foreign-trained Colombian economists regarding their views on capital account management. Section five describes the domestic culture of pragmatism and consensus-orientation that characterizes economic policymaking and state-business relations, laying the informal institutional foundation for capital account policy in Colombia. Section six concludes.

5.1 The Colombian Puzzle: Market Reforms without Economic Crisis

Remarkable consistency and relative stability have traditionally characterized economic policymaking in Colombia (Stallings 1990; Thorp 1991; Urrutia 1991). As a result, the radical economic liberalization process that started in 1990 constitutes an intriguing, though largely understudied puzzle for most political economy approaches. The frequent argument that a severe economic crisis is a necessary condition for the start of structural reforms is contradicted by the Colombian case.[84] In contrast to virtually all other Latin American

84 The crisis analogy is appropriate for the Colombian context, though, in terms of the political situation during the late 1980s. The illegal drug trade, most visibly the power of the Medellín cartel led by Pablo Escobar, besieged the country and led to rapidly increasing levels of political violence. Several presidential candidates were assassinated between 1987 and 1990, among them the front-runner in the polls for the elections in 1990, Luis Carlos Galán. Given the widespread violence and the threat of the collapse of the existing institutional order, many people shared the impression that the country was indeed at the edge of chaos. However, justifying the economic opening of the country with reference to the existence of a *political* crisis seems rather far-fetched (Edwards 2001: 33–4). To use a historical analogy, the political crisis after the assassination of presidential candidate Jorge Eliécer Gaitán in 1948 that led to a period of widespread political and criminal violence in the country prompted several institutional innovations, most importantly the creation of the *Frente Nacional* (National Front) of the Liberal and Conservative parties, but no corresponding changes in the *economic* model.

countries, Colombia was not significantly affected by the debt crisis of the 1980s (see Table 5.1 below). It was the only country in Latin America with no declining GDP during that period. Average GDP growth stood at 3.4% between 1980 and 1989. In addition, a relatively moderate level of inflation – 21% on average during the 1980s – was ensured through a variety of formal and informal price indexation mechanisms.

As a result, the pressure on the government to implement drastic economic reforms in light of an unbearable debt and/or inflation burden and in the context of US-led debt restructuring initiatives (Baker and Brady Plans) did not apply to Colombia. Individual-level explanations based on cognitive psychology are also built on the assumption that policymakers undertake drastic economic reforms only when faced with a dramatically negative state of the economy (Weyland 2002a). However, Colombian policymakers and the public at large during the late 1980s were not focused on the urgency to reduce run-away inflation as in other Latin American countries. In addition, according to the traditional political economy perspective, the electoral system prohibiting the reelection of presidents should provide little incentives for incoming administrations to implement radical reforms.[85]

However, notwithstanding conventional wisdom, Colombia enthusiastically embraced the teachings of the 'Washington Consensus' during the administration of President César Gaviria (1990–1994). Economic liberalization was situated in the context of a wider modernization project for the country, including the state and its institutions (Juárez 1993; Urrutia 1994). The "full insertion of Colombia into the world" became the dominating mantra of the Gaviria government right from its start. Free-market reforms went hand in hand with structural reforms of the state, its roles and functions as well as its institutional apparatus. These political, economic and social changes were enshrined in the new Constitution of 1991. Structural reforms were declared unavoidable in order to achieve the status of a 'modern country' on par with its neighbors in the region, let alone the developed countries, after the end of the Cold War (Cohen and Gunter 1992).

Unable to justify the need for structural reforms with the actual state of the economy, reforms were portrayed as indispensable in order to increase economic growth in the medium and long run and to maintain macroeconomic stability in the short run. The slogan of the time was: "La economía va bien, pero el país va mal" ("the economy is doing well, but the country is doing badly"). Colombia was said not to be able to afford a closed economy any longer given that the world was changing rapidly toward democracy and economic freedom. Nothing less than a revolution, albeit a peaceful one, was considered necessary to make the leap forward into modernity (Gaviria 1990).

85 The 1991 Constitution prohibits the reelection of the Colombian president. However, a constitutional change allowing the reelection of President Álvaro Uribe for one term was approved in 2004. Uribe was subsequently reelected for a second term in May 2006. The attempt to yet again change the Constitution in order to allow Uribe to run for a third term in office was rejected by the Constitutional Court in February 2010.

Table 5.1 Macroeconomic indicators for Colombia, 1985–2007

Year	Growth of real GDP (constant 2000) in annual % change	Inflation, Consumer price index (in %)	Trade balance (millions of US$)	Debt service of % of exports of goods, services and income (in %)	Fiscal deficit as % of GDP	International Reserves (annual % change)
1985	3.09	24.05	−595	41.76	−2.00	24.43
1986	5.84	18.87	1346	32.13	−1.18	58.99
1987	5.37	23.30	1325	36.82	−0.36	3.14
1988	4.06	28.11	565	44.23	−1.08	11.75
1989	3.42	25.87	1200	48.40	−1.24	−1.55
1990	6.04	29.15	1821	40.88	−0.68	23.31
1991	2.28	30.37	2740	36.26	−0.20	39.64
1992	5.03	27.02	1188.70	38.82	−1.47	22.03
1993	2.37	22.44	−1458	33.81	−0.65	0.84
1994	5.84	22.85	−3277.47	45.29	0.63	0.11
1995	5.20	20.89	−3718.52	31.53	−1.93	3.15
1996	2.06	20.80	−3284.69	36.94	−2.48	18.87
1997	3.43	18.47	−4138.08	28.38	−2.75	−0.88
1998	0.57	18.68	−3911.32	29.84	−4.39	−10.51
1999	−4.20	10.87	571.58	40.77	−4.62	−7.98
2000	2.92	9.22	1411.24	27.70	−4.89	18.07
2001	2.18	7.97	−812.16	35.07	−5.14	6.92
2002	2.46	6.35	−1128.44	39.31	−4.78	9.01
2003	4.61	7.13	−883.46	44.70	−4.20	1.48
2004	4.66	5.90	−333.52	32.97	−3.88	22.24
2005	5.72	5.05	−506.94	35.58	−4.07	7.30
2006	6.94	4.30	−1796.65	30.74	−3.04	11.56
2007	7.55	5.54	−3203.42	21.98	−1.15	29.92

Sources: World Development Indicators; Banco de la República de Colombia.

It thus comes at little surprise that rationalist-material explanations of economic policy reforms have problems with the Colombian case (Williamson and Haggard 1994: 563). Sociological explanations that link reforms to the desire of domestic elites for the social recognition as a modern country by the international community seem more adequate (Meyer and Rowan 1977; Meyer et al. 1997). In order to achieve the sought-after recognition and to overcome the widespread image of a 'narco-state', the Gaviria administration emulated the policies and institutions befitting a 'modern country' according to the list of the recently approved 'Washington Consensus', but without a genuine domestic need for them. Unlike Peru, the adoption of capital account liberalization in Colombia was not related to pressing economic circumstances or powerful business interests. Instead, the economic liberalization process had complex sociological, not narrow rationalist-materialist foundations. It was the symbolic rather than the utilitarian value of capital account liberalization that motivated its initial adoption.

5.2 The Fall of the pre-1990 Capital and Exchange Control Regime

Given the 'revolutionary' mood during the early 1990s, several traditional institutions for economic policymaking in Colombia were quickly brushed aside. Perhaps the most notorious and best-known example of the previous economic model was the management of international capital flows. In March 1967, in the midst of a severe balance-of-payments crisis with negative foreign exchange reserves and after failed negotiations with the IMF who pressed for the introduction of a floating exchange rate regime, the government of President Carlos Lleras Restrepo broke ranks with conventional wisdom and introduced the so-called crawling peg exchange rate regime based on frequent, pre-announced mini-devaluations of the currency (Nelson et al. 1971: 215–261; Currie 1981: 96–99; Thorp 1991: 145–158). In order to sustain the fixed exchange rate regime while simultaneously preserving the autonomy of monetary policy, capital mobility had to be limited. The result was the 'Decree-Law 444' – the *Estatuto Cambiario* – that governed every aspect of Colombia's foreign exchange and trade transactions and was the center of the country's external sector policy for more than thirty years.

The *Estatuto Cambiario* had four major components (Montenegro 1990: 357–358):

1. Control of all foreign exchange operations through the Central Bank. It was illegal for private citizens to hold and trade foreign exchange domestically or abroad. All exporters had to declare their foreign exchange earnings in advance and remit them to the Central Bank in exchange for pesos or so-called "Certificates of Exchange";
2. Strict quantitative restrictions on imports through government provision of import licenses;
3. Monopoly of the Central Bank over all international capital movements and strict limits on private indebtedness;
4. Strict regulation of foreign direct investments. All investments of more than US$ 100,000 required the prior approval of the National Planning Department according to pre-established criteria.

The principal goal of these measures was to avoid real exchange rate overvaluation as the result of the crawling peg exchange rate regime. The results of the *Estatuto* were rather impressive: the system was credited – both by Colombian and foreign observers – with allowing the country to maintain a stable real exchange rate and avoiding recurrent balance-of-payments crises as well as the accumulation of large quantities of international reserves (resulting from export booms) without negative effects for the inflation rate. In addition, the system was flexible enough to successfully steer the domestic economy both through good and bad times in the international economy and helped to keep external indebtedness under control. The upshot was a stable, coherent macroeconomic policy and the absence of economic populism that beleaguered Colombia's neighbors in Latin America.

However, the widely shared perception that the capital and exchange control regime was an important fundament for the country's economic success story changed dramatically and rapidly at the end of the 1980s. As late as 1987, the head of the Central Bank, Francisco Ortega, emphatically declared on the occasion of a conference celebrating the twentieth anniversary of the introduction of the *Estatuto Cambiario:*

> The positive results of its application are well known, given that it allowed the country to avoid new exchange rate crises. Phenomena such as external debt have been regulated, most importantly in the critical aspect of private debt (…) I dare to anticipate that the [criticisms and suggestions coming out of the conference] have more to do with the actual operation of the various instruments contained in the *Estatuto* than with its conception and philosophy (Ortega 1987: 20; my translation).

In fact, while some analysts proposed modifications of the *Estatuto,* nobody seemed to question the overall legitimacy of the existing regime. As Rudolf Hommes, the finance minister in the Gaviria administration put it, the *Estatuto Cambiario* constituted a "social totem, practically untouchable" among the economic profession and business community of the country (Hommes 2002: 286; my translation).

Yet several economists who only a few years earlier defended the regime on the basis of its positive track record in preventing balance-of-payments crises suddenly changed course and spoke of a "structural stagnation of the Colombian economy". Specifically, they considered the capital and exchange control regime an anachronism: "the majority of Colombians violated it almost daily and it stopped being a useful instrument to deal with the economic problems of the 1980s and 1990s. It became more an instrument of sectoral rather than macroeconomic intervention, and with time, a mere formality, with little or no compliance on part of the population" (Hommes 2002: 286; my translation).

In addition to being rendered ineffective, it was argued that exchange and capital controls provoke the misallocation of resources. Armando Montenegro, the head of the National Planning Department in the Gaviria administration highlighted the paradox that Colombian policymakers were facing in 1990 when proposing to scrap the *Estatuto:*

> In a few years the consensus that existed in public opinion, among businesspeople and economists about the virtues [of the *Estatuto*] changed substantially. One moved from the assertion that the Decree-Law 444 of 1967 has been fundamental for overcoming the exchange rate crisis

> of the 1960s and useful for the management of the economy for twenty years to the recognition that it has developed into a straightjacket for Colombia during the 1990s (Montenegro 1990: 352; my translation).

Just like in Peru at the same time, justifying the abolition of the *Estatuto* was couched in the language of economic freedom for the business community and the population at large (Restrepo 1991). If people were allowed to travel abroad, why were they not allowed to freely acquiring the needed financial resources? Given the existing legal restrictions in the country, most people simply turned to the parallel ('black') market for their foreign financial transactions (Grosse 1992). Most well-to-do citizens had illegal bank accounts outside the country. The *Estatuto* was allegedly made redundant by the technological advances of globalization and the relatively easy access of private citizens and businesses to foreign sources of finance.[86] In addition, the decline in the investment rate at the end of the 1980s served as a pretext for allowing domestic agents to look for funds abroad. Given the lack of competition in the domestic banking sector – where foreign banks could not establish subsidiaries – and heavy state intervention through directed credit schemes, neoliberal reformers aimed at breaking the monopoly of public banks through the liberalization of foreign direct investment in the banking sector, providing domestic agents with cheaper credit through the direct access to foreign banks.[87]

The fate of the capital and exchange control regime was sealed since no distinguishable economic interest group directly profited from it. In addition, President Gaviria lured the external sector with the promise of increased access to external finance to support the abolition of the regime.[88] Given this constellation, once Gaviria publicly stated his intention to abolish the *Estatuto*[89], no political or economic veto-player stepped forward and defended the regime. As Sebastian Edwards put it,

> (f)rom a political economy perspective, the importance of the reform of the Exchange Rate Statute was not related to what happened after it was enacted, but what *did not* happen. There was no generalized outcry, nor accusations that a major institution had been abandoned, nor charges of excessive neoliberalism. Almost nothing happened (Edwards 2001: 71; emphasis in original).

It seemed as if the Gaviria administration merely formalized what was already a widespread informal practice. In addition, apart from a few economists linked to the introduction of the

86 Interview with Roberto Junguito, former Minister of Finance (1984–1986 and 2002–2003), October 1, 2004.

87 Interview with María Mercedes Cuéllar, former minister of Foreign Trade, member of the Board of the Colombian Central Bank (1991–1996) and currently head of the private financial sector association (Asobancaria), March 13, 2007.

88 Interview with Guillermo Perry, former Minister of Finance (1996–1998), September 21, 2004.

89 In his inauguration speech as president in August 1990, Gaviria used the phrase "reforming the *Estatuto Cambiario*" instead of abolishing it. He said: "We will reform the *Estatuto Cambiario* which has provided the country with a framework that significantly contributed to the development of foreign trade and to the stability of the exchange rate. With this change we will abandon the pretension to control everything, which today is a bit utopian, beyond the reality of an economy that is now bigger, more diversified and more solid compared with the one when the *Estatuto* was in place. This reform is required for the sake of developing our foreign trade and the financial markets for goods and services" (Gaviria 1990; my translation).

Estatuto in the 1960s and the leadership of the Central Bank, in particular President Ortega who criticized the reform, nobody else seemed to even take notice at the time.[90]

5.3 Capital Account Policy in the post-1990 Era: the Encaje System

During the late 1980s and early 1990s Colombia experienced a profound transformation from a coffee-based to a petroleum-based economy. The discovery and subsequent exploitation of large oil fields in the south of the country quickly replaced coffee as the major export product. Starting in the 1930s and up until the mid-1980s, coffee constituted more than 50 % of Colombian exports (Arango 2005). As a result, macroeconomic management was built around coffee: when the international price was high, the country accumulated reserves, increased taxes, and tried to prevent the currency from appreciating in order to safeguard its non-traditional exports. Conversely, when coffee prices were low, the government pursued deficit spending, borrowed, and tried to prevent exchange rate depreciation (Nelson et al. 1971; Palacios 1980; Thorp 1991).

The descent of this long-standing arrangement was inextricably linked with the rise of oil as the major export product and the volatile, decreasing international coffee price in the aftermath of the virtual death of the International Coffee Organization in 1989 (Bates 1997). The oil boom had mixed effects on the Colombian economy, improving some economic indicators, such as GDP growth, increasing tax income and higher public spending, while deteriorating others, such as the trade balance and the external competitiveness of the non-oil economy (Echeverry et al. 2009). Against the background of this structural transformation of the economy, the simultaneous liberalization of the current and capital account in 1991 led to a rapid surge of capital inflows, especially foreign direct investment (see Figure 5.1 below). As a result, managing the rise of capital inflows became a major task for the economic authorities.

The 1991 Constitution provided the Board of Directors of the Central Bank with formal independence from the executive branch in terms of monetary, credit and exchange rate policies. The Constitution also committed the Central Bank to the sole objective of achieving price stability, albeit under consideration of economic growth concerns and in collaboration with the government. Active exchange rate management was relaxed and an exchange rate band with a width of 7.5 % above and below a mid-point rate was adopted in 1994, laying the foundation for the gradual introduction of a floating exchange rate regime (finally introduced in 1999).

In the period between 1991 and 1993, the Central Bank adopted a number of regulations eliminating its monopoly over foreign exchange transactions, the reduction of capital and exchange controls, and allowing the public to hold foreign currency. However, rather than including the full liberalization of all remaining restrictions on international capital movements in the so-called "first generation" package of reforms as done in Peru, Colombian capital account policy in the post-1990 period followed a different path, highlight-

90 Interview with Carlos Caballero, former executive director of the economic think-tank Fedesarrollo, May 2, 2007.

ing the critical role of pre-liberalization informal institutions for contemporary economic policymaking.

Figure 5.1 Private capital flows to Colombia, 1970–2004 (in millions of US$)

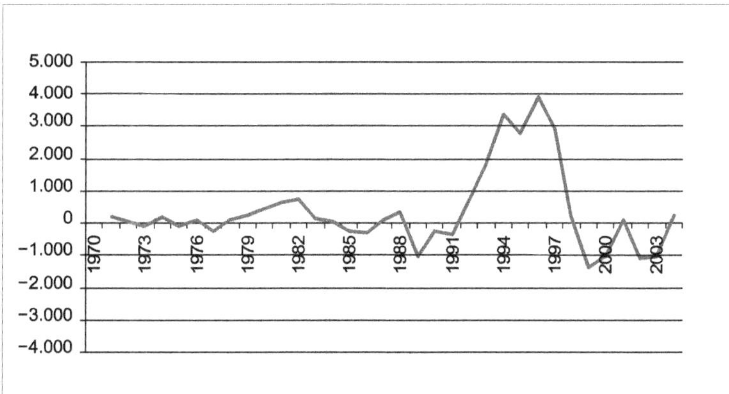

Source: Villar et al. 2005.

In the aftermath of the abolition of the *Estatuto Cambiario* and the introduction of a substantial import liberalization program, the country was faced with a strong appreciation of the real exchange rate (see Figure 5.2 below). From the last quarter of 1990 to the second quarter of 1997, the effective real exchange rate appreciated by around 40%, before depreciating sharply in the context of an economic crisis during the late 1990s (Kamas 2001: 136). The initial reaction of the Central Bank was a policy of aggressive sterilization of accumulated reserves in order to resist the appreciation pressure. The result, however, was an inconsistent policy which further contributed to appreciation and inflation by creating incentives for capital inflows and additional reserve accumulation. The failure of the initial approach to quell the surging peso gave rise to an alternative strategy to discourage short-term capital inflows: the *encaje* system (Urrutia 2002).

In September 1993 the Gaviria government, in close collaboration with the Central Bank and inspired by the Chilean model adopted in 1991, introduced the so-called *encaje* system or unremunerated reserve requirement (URR) – an implicit tax on foreign borrowing and portfolio inflows. Initially, the requirement was a deposit of non-interest bearing reserves of 47% to be held for one year against foreign loans with maturities of 18 months or less. The *encaje* system was frequently modified – with respect to the tax rate, the maturity of foreign borrowing subject to it, and the term limits of the deposits – over the course of the following seven years with the requirements ever more tightened in order to address the continued pressure of short-term capital to enter the country (Ocampo and Tovar 2003: 9–11).

Figure 5.2 Colombia bilateral real exchange rate with the US, 1980–2008, deflated by CPI indexes (Index 1 = average 1980–2008)

Source: Frenkel and Rapetti 2010.

The administration led by Ernesto Samper (1994–1998) went even further and introduced a Tobin tax-style measure restricting short-term capital movements across the board as part of an "economic emergency plan" in January 1997. Under this system, a tax was imposed on all foreign loans irrespective of maturity with rates between zero and 8 %, which would be levied in addition to the already existing URR. After the Constitutional Court overturned the declaration of "economic emergency" in March 1997, the government amended the *encaje* system by extending the maximum maturity of loans subject to the deposit requirement.[91]

With the onslaught of the Asian financial crisis in 1997/98, the global context for capital flows changed dramatically. Along with other emerging market countries, Colombia quickly lost its appeal as a lucrative investment location for foreign capital. As a result, the tax rate of the *encaje* was gradually reduced to zero and the holding period requirement waived in May 2000 in order to contain downward real exchange rate pressure.

However, the *encaje* system staged a comeback as soon as external circumstances changed yet again with the resumption of large capital inflows to emerging market countries during the first decade of the new century. Faced with a sharp and sustained appreciation of the national currency, the administration of President Álvaro Uribe decided to resurrect the *encaje* system in December 2004, albeit with only limited success (Concha and Galindo

91 The results of the *encaje* system in place during the 1990s have only partially vindicated its champions. While the URR did not reduce the overall amount of private capital inflows and did not alter the real exchange rate, it nevertheless enhanced the independence of monetary policy and led to a change in the composition of foreign capital toward long-term flows. The relative importance of short-term, highly liquid debt and private investment flows declined in favor of longer-term foreign direct investment flows (Cárdenas and Barrera 1997; Ocampo and Tovar 2003; Rincón and Villar 2003; David 2007).

2009; Clements and Kamil 2009; Coelho and Gallagher 2010).[92] With the beginning of the global financial crisis at the end of the decade and a depreciatory trend of the exchange rate, the government abolished all capital controls for foreign investment and external borrowing in October 2008.

The use of the *encaje* system by governments of different political orientations indicates its widespread acceptance among the policymaking elite, in particular during times of dramatic real exchange rate appreciation. Interestingly, the only partial success of the URR to deal with a surge in short-term capital inflows and currency appreciation during the 1990s has not prevented policymakers from reviving it in recent times. To be sure, the use of the *encaje* system has been justified as a *temporary,* strictly market-based measure in order to achieve a specific target in the short run, not as a permanent instrument for exchange-rate management. According to Colombian policymakers, capital controls are not considered an adequate instrument for achieving *long-term* macroeconomic goals.[93]

5.4 The Role of the IMF: The Limits of Persuasion

As pointed out earlier, economic reforms in Colombia at the beginning of the 1990s cannot be attributed to the specter of an economic crisis. Neither was coercion from international financial institutions responsible for this outcome.[94] The structural situation of the Colombian economy during the early 1990s and the traditionally autonomous economic course of the country confined the relationship between the government and the IMF to technical consultations until a Stand-by Agreement was signed in 1999 in the midst of a severe financial crisis.[95] For most of the 1990s and thereafter Colombia has enjoyed a favorable international investment grade which led to an investment boom and large inflows of foreign capital. These developments made the need for official capital flows, let alone IMF loans, virtually redundant.[96]

The direct influence of the IMF over economic policy decisions in Colombia was limited after the fall-out over exchange rate management during the Lleras Restrepo administration in the mid-1960s. Its principal instrument of leverage was confined to the annual policy dialogue as part of the Article IV consultations with the economic authorities. There was no financing arrangement between the Fund and the Colombian government after the expiration of the so-called "shadow program" in 1987.[97]

---

92 With a suspension between June 2006 and May 2007.

93 Interview with Mauricio Cárdenas, former executive director of the economic think-tank Fedesarrollo, September 28, 2004.

94 Estrada Álvarez argues that "the formulation of policies for trade liberalization, reforms of the capital market and of the productive sector, which were implemented during the Gaviria administration, were *under the control* of those institutions (IMF and World Bank)" (Estrada Álvarez 2005b: 285; my translation, emphasis added). However, he presents no empirical evidence to corroborate this assertion.

95 By which time, however, the *encaje* system was suspended and more importantly, the IMF had modified its view towards accepting controls on capital inflows at least as a temporary policy measure.

96 Interview with Salomón Kalmanovitz, former member of the Board of the Colombian Central Bank (1993–2005), August 30, 2004 and interview with Mauricio Cárdenas, September 28, 2004.

97 The term "shadow program" refers to an agreement concluded in July 1985 under which Colombia received the official 'seal of approval' for structural adjustment from the IMF but without signing a formal Stand-by

Judging from IMF staff reports for the Article IV consultations during the late 1980s and early 1990s, capital account liberalization did not form part of the policy discussions with the Colombian authorities until the government decided to introduce the URR in 1993 (IEO 2005: 30, 59). On the other hand, the Fund's position on the *encaje* system took an interesting, if somewhat counterintuitive, turn during the 1990s. Initially, the IMF country team was not opposed to the measure. According to the independent evaluation report on the Fund's approach to capital account liberalization, "this may have reflected the staff's understanding that the URR in Colombia was a tool to manage the transition from an administrative control regime to a liberal one" (IEO 2005, Annex 1: 69). The IMF's initial support for the *encaje* system may also have resulted from the simultaneous decision of the Colombian government to dismantle the remaining qualitative or administrative restrictions left over from the previous capital and exchange control regime.

Yet in 1994 the Fund's position on the URR suddenly turned negative. IMF staff tried to convince their Colombian counterparts during the policy discussions to get rid of the measure. For example, the staff report for the 1994 Article IV consultations stated that

> the authorities should move promptly away from external borrowing restrictions as a policy tool to slow down private capital inflows. Experience suggests that these regulations are increasingly circumvented. Furthermore, they could inhibit productive investment and be seen by the markets as inconsistent with the country's commitment to outward-looking policies (IMF 1994: 11).

After a strongly worded intervention defending the *encaje* system by the Colombian representative on the Fund's Board of Executive Directors prior to the discussion of the staff report in January 1995, the summary statement after the Board meeting noted that "a few speakers encouraged the authorities to remove the recent restrictions on external borrowing, but others considered that capital controls – despite their shortcomings – would be an acceptable temporary response to capital inflows" (IMF 1995: 2). After yet another change of heart, IMF staff praised the URR as an effective buffer against contagion resulting from the Mexican crisis in 1995 (IEO 2005: 68). The flip-flop course of the Fund during the mid-1990s clearly undermined the persuasiveness of its policy preferences on capital mobility and as a corollary significantly limited the IMF's influence over economic policymaking in Colombia. If anything, the largely positive experience with the URR in Colombia (and Chile) might have ultimately convinced the IMF staff of its utility in specific circumstances. As a result, a process of 'reverse learning' might have taken place where country experiences changed IMF views on particular economic policy issues (Gómez-Mera 2011).

Taken together, the IMF country team transmitted inconsistent, contradictory messages regarding the URR to the Colombian authorities during the 1990s. Apparently, different staff teams gave different assessments. This confirms recent findings about the heterogeneity of advice provided by IMF *operational* staff on capital account management during

Agreement as it is usually required, and without a request for money (Boughton 2001: 404). The program consisted of enhanced monitoring services by the IMF in exchange for signaling government creditworthiness to private investors and thereby obtaining a US$ 1 billion 'jumbo loan' from a consortium of private banks in order to finance large-scale investment projects (Junguito 1986; Garay et al. 1994: 25–69).

the 1990s, not only between countries – which would make some sense – but also between different mission teams to the same country (IEO 2005).[98] The credibility of policy suggestions made by the IMF vis-à-vis the Colombian authorities was severely tainted by these internal inconsistencies. As a result, the Colombian government felt little need to listen to the IMF's suggestions in terms of capital account management.[99] As the Fund's head of Article IV missions to Colombia during the second half of the 1990s put it,

> I think Fund staff took the view during the 1990s that other instruments or policies than the *encaje* might be used to help stem the capital inflows and take some pressure off monetary policy. In particular, the Fund recommended steps to reverse the burgeoning fiscal deficit in an effort to control the inflows, noting that it was the fiscal drift that was giving rise to the skewed policy mix. I think the Fund's position on the *encaje* was consistent, but the issue was not regarded as clear-cut in much of Latin America, as some pointed to the apparent usefulness of a similar arrangement in Chile (written communication, November 3, 2004).

His conclusion is that "I don't think the Fund mattered a great deal. What I think – or hope – is that we were able to help keep alive the debate on these issues". This statement highlights the limits of the Fund's strategy during the 1990s to persuade governments to adopt an open capital account policy. Internally inconsistent advice and economic conditions favoring an autonomous course of action of the country doomed the Fund's attempt to delegitimize the *encaje* system to failure.

5.5 Foreign-trained Economists' Views on Capital Account Policy

Given the long-standing involvement of technocrats in economic policymaking in Colombia, it could be expected that their increasing ideological commitment to unregulated markets – presumably acquired during their studies at 'neoliberal' universities abroad – would set Colombia unequivocally and permanently on the path towards capital account freedom (Flórez Enciso 2009). In contrast to other countries in Latin America, Colombia's polity has traditionally been fertile soil for technocrats who have enjoyed considerable autonomy vis-à-vis the particular interests of politicians and the private sector (Urrutia 1991; Botero 2005; Dargent 2011). As a result, the conventional cleavage between *'técnicos'* (technocrats) and *'políticos'* (politicians) has not been a feature of the Colombian political system. In fact, the two groups have little history of clashes and, as the metaphor of the 'revolving door' indicates, have tended to merge with one another, ensuring a constant stream of economic elite circulation (El Tiempo, August 11, 2002). Ever since the late 1960s, economists have frequently held high-ranking positions in government. 50 of the 55 people in top economic policy positions between 1974 and 1996 pursued graduate studies abroad, and 13 of them

98 In contrast, non-operational or policymaking staff at the Fund had a much more unified view on capital account policy during most of the 1990s, namely that it should be liberalized under basically all circumstances.

99 Analyzing a different region (Eastern Europe), a different sector (ethnic politics), and a different international actor (European Union), Kelley (2004b) comes to a similar conclusion regarding the limits of international institutions' influence over domestic policy choices.

held PhD degrees in economics from universities in the United States or Western Europe (Meisel 1996: 17).[100] What is the view on capital account management among this group of elite economists who have long enjoyed privileged access to policymaking?

In October and November 2004 I applied the same survey (see Appendix 3) that was used for the Peruvian sample to the recipients of the Colombian Central Bank scholarship for graduate studies abroad (which started in 1980). While this group is by no means a representative sample of the country's entire community of economists, it is nonetheless an indicative portion of all foreign-trained professional economists.[101] In addition, this group has a relatively high representation of senior positions within state institutions in charge of macroeconomic policymaking, i. e., the Central Bank, the Ministry of Finance, and the National Planning Department. Out of the total of 50 respondents of the survey, 28 alone were employed by the Central Bank. The rest mostly worked in academia or in international financial institutions.

While capital controls are traditionally thought of as an essential instrument for the preservation of national economic autonomy, 88 % of the respondents rejected this view. The same percentage agreed that market mechanisms – not government intervention – should determine capital flows. A slightly lower number of respondents (76 %) agreed that government restrictions of international capital movements should be abolished. For more than half of them, capital controls make no sense because alternative instruments are always more effective for achieving the same goals. 68 % agreed that capital controls can easily be circumvented, and for 70 % capital controls are redundant under a floating exchange rate regime.

The distribution of responses becomes somewhat more heterogeneous if one considers the details of capital account management. A clear majority (86 %) rejected restrictions on long-term capital movements, e. g., foreign direct investment and equity flows. However, the assessment becomes more nuanced concerning short-term capital flows. 56 % did not agree with price-based restrictions on capital movements such as the *encaje* system. On the other hand, a slight majority (60 %) agreed with the assertion that restrictions on short-term capital flows are essential to address international capital market volatility. It thus seems that only a narrow majority of Colombia's elite economists actually supports the URR. For comparison, 83 % of the Peruvian survey sample rejected such measures altogether.

Three-quarters of survey participants against restrictions on international capital movements, yet 60 % of them in agreement with limiting portfolio flows may sound like a contradiction. My interpretation is that most survey participants thought of traditional, administrative instruments of capital account management as applied under the ISI economic model when they responded to the first question. Their answers clearly reflect a rejection of those instruments. However, when asked about short-term capital flows, their responses reflect a moderate sympathy for quantitative capital controls – a crucial differentiation that

100 Included in this list are the positions of minister of finance, the president of the central bank, the director of the National Planning Department, the advisers to the Monetary Board (up to 1991), and the members of the Board of Directors of the Central Bank (since 1991).

101 The list of scholarship holders was provided by the Human Resources Department of the Central Bank. It contained a total of 114 names. However, email addresses existed for only 65 of them. 50 people completed the survey, which leads to a response rate of 44 %.

only became noticeable in mainstream economic theory after the 1990s Asian financial crisis.

Different types of capital flows pose different risks for the stability of the domestic financial system. The risks associated with short-term flows only received widespread attention after the Asian crisis. Apart from their volatile character, short-term flows have been blamed for the strong appreciation of the exchange rate in Colombia in recent years. On the other hand, the importance assigned to prudential regulations in the domestic financial sector is also a fairly recent phenomenon in mainstream economics. It is thus unlikely that before the Asian crisis such a high percentage of survey respondents (almost 90 %) would have agreed with the statement that prudential regulations are indispensable for the stability of the domestic financial system. In fact, when asked about their views on that question immediately after graduation from their studies abroad, 20 % did not think that prudential regulations were necessary at all. I thus interpret this specific survey result in the following way: the respondents associated the term 'capital controls' with the previous economic model – which an overwhelming majority strongly rejects – and interpreted the term 'prudential regulations' as referring to market-oriented policy instruments, which a majority approves of.

In order to assess the role that professional education abroad played for their views on capital account management, I asked survey participants to respond to the same policy propositions recollecting their position immediately after they finished graduate studies outside the country.[102] Generally speaking, there were no significant differences with their current views, with the important exception regarding controls on short-term capital flows, where their position became more supportive over time. In other words, strongly negative views on short-term capital controls somewhat softened after reinsertion into the domestic context. The acceptance of the proposition that the efficient market hypothesis (financial markets use information efficiently) applies to the international capital market stood at 75 % immediately after the respondents' graduation abroad. Asked about their current view, still 65 % supported the statement.

In terms of the role of professional education, the survey results demonstrate (i) overall support for (neo-)liberal capital account management, and (ii) a shift from strong to *qualified support* for capital account openness as more time is spent at the home front. This result highlights an interesting difference between Peru and Colombia: whereas the domestic context seems to boost neoliberal views among Peruvian economists, it has the opposite effect among their Colombian counterparts.

Asked about which factors determined their views on capital account policy, survey respondents pointed to a significant influence of the domestic economic context, the experience of other countries, current research findings, and their graduate studies abroad. Among those factors, professional training abroad played the most prominent role in terms of shaping policy preferences. In contrast, survey participants had little regard for the position of the international financial institutions or domestic business groups when forming their opinions on capital account management. The modest influence credited to the IMF as

102 66 % of the respondents studied in the United States, 21 % in the United Kingdom, and the rest in other Western European countries (France, Spain).

a source of individual preferences corresponds to the relatively low participation in Fund courses on capital account management. Only 11 % participated in such a course.

In sum, the survey results show that foreign-trained Colombian economists take a generally negative perspective on capital controls, at least in late 2005 when the survey was conducted. However, below the abstract level their views reveal important nuances compared with their Peruvian counterparts. Most importantly, they display a greater sympathy toward price-based, temporary controls on short-term capital flows as practiced by their own government, albeit their support for these measures can hardly be called overwhelming. Rather than ruling all forms of capital controls out on principal grounds as seems to be the case for Peruvian economists, a majority of foreign-trained Colombian economists believes that *temporary, market-oriented* capital controls are a legitimate and potentially useful instrument at the disposal of policymakers.

Consider the following statement by Andrés Felipe Arias, the young, foreign-educated[103] ex-minister of agriculture and former vice-minister of finance. In the context of the rising appreciation of the Colombian peso, Arias said in an interview in 2007 when asked about the application of capital controls to deal with this situation:

> It seems to me that it is an instrument that should be evaluated without any type of precaution or ideological prejudice. Such a measure will not stop the economy and could help a lot of sectors which are beginning to drown [...] At least I think that all these measures must be studied by the (Central) Bank (El Tiempo, May 6, 2007; my translation).

The domestic context of ideological moderation and his institutional affiliation as minister of agriculture defending a range of export-oriented sectors motivate Arias to assume a stance in favor of (limited) government intervention in financial markets for the sake of preserving exchange-rate stability (FitzGerald 2005).

In a similar vein, the doyen of economic neoliberalism in Colombia during the 1980s and 1990s, former minister of finance Rodrigo Botero declared in August 2011:

> The external sector must become the source of economic dynamism, in contrast to what happens today when the sector is negatively affecting GDP growth as a result of overvaluation. Thus, it is necessary to stop the excessive appreciation of the peso with all the instruments at the disposal of the authorities, including (...) the partial closing of the capital account in order to discourage the entry of short-term capital (Botero 2011; my translation).

The statements of Arias and Botero reflect the institutional context in which economic policymaking in Colombia is situated: the culture of pragmatism and the power of exporters.

103 Arias has a Ph. D. in economics from the University of California in Los Angeles.

5.6 State-Business Relations: The Culture of Pragmatism and the Power of Exporters

What lies behind the failed institutionalization of capital account openness in Colombia? What explains the frequent changes between openness and closedness in capital account policy after 1990? In order to provide an answer to these questions, let us go back to the *encaje* system.

The initial decision to introduce controls on short-term capital inflows was taken by the Gaviria administration in 1993. This fact seems to challenge conventional wisdom that interprets this government and the reformed, autonomous Central Bank as bastions of the neoliberal gospel in Colombia. To be sure, the *encaje* system was introduced under the most neoliberal government and Central Bank Board that the country arguably ever had. However, it did not need a change in economic doctrine related to a change in government, or the departure of free-market enthusiasts from high-ranking positions in the political bureaucracy in order to shift gears in capital account management away from the neoliberal orthodoxy. Essentially the same people who pushed for international financial liberalization at the start of the economic reform period were responsible for the introduction of – a new type of – capital controls.

This change in capital account policy coincides with the contemporary phase in the relationship between Colombian elite economists and policymakers as described by economic historian Marco Palacios. In his account, the period since the mid-1990s marks the return to 'business as usual'. The vitality of the traditional political system undermined the long-term sustainability and internal cohesion of the neoliberal project in Colombia. The traditionally high influence of economic interest groups combined with the need for a redistributive discourse on part of the political elite constituted a major obstacle for the enduring hegemony of the neoliberal discourse and its impact on economic policymaking (Palacios 2005: 203).

After the initial opening of the capital account in early 1991, 'business as usual' with a – now implicit but no less relevant – focus on exchange rate stability returned rather quickly. While the government's discourse justifying the neoliberal reforms was primarily focused on reducing inflation, it subsequently tried to balance the inflation target with the traditional exchange rate objective. I argue that this policy stance reflects the informal institution that defines economic policymaking in Colombia: *pragmatism*.

According to Palacios, three characteristics or core values define the Colombian economic policymaking process: (i) economic and business pragmatism ahead of doctrinal purity; (ii) collaboration and consensus between the private and the public sector instead of struggle and conflict; and (iii) priority for agreed-upon and limited state intervention in the economy in lieu of open competition among economic actors (Palacios 2005: 187).

According to former Central Bank head Miguel Urrutia, pragmatism in economic policymaking refers to the preservation of traditional solutions and approaches to current economic problems within a broadly defined orthodox framework.[104] As a result, governments cautiously pursued capital account liberalization mindful of its negative consequenc-

104 Interview with Miguel Urrutia, former head of the Colombian Central Bank Board (1993–2005), January 16, 2006.

es for important domestic constituencies. Policies have been pragmatically adjusted given changing external circumstances and based on a consensus-oriented strategy vis-à-vis the business community. Traditionally aware of the risks of large capital inflows, Colombian policymakers resisted the siren song coming from the outside world to pursue complete capital freedom. The *encaje* system represents an example of a pragmatic, market-based solution to a well-known problem of export-oriented countries in the aftermath of trade and financial liberalization.

The culture of pragmatism has permeated both the political and economic structures of Colombia ever since the country gained independence in the early nineteenth century (Safford 1976; Safford and Palacios 2001). It was reinforced and politically institutionalized during the era of the *Frente Nacional* (National Front), a unique coalition government arrangement inaugurated in 1958 after the end of a civil war *(La Violencia)*. Under the *Frente Nacional* the conservative and liberal parties shared political power, alternating the presidency between them every four years (Hartlyn 1988). The *Frente Nacional* initially operated until 1974, but continued unofficially with the inclusion of ministers from the defeated political party in the government until 1986. However, the informal practices or socially acceptable rules of behavior rehearsed during the *Frente Nacional* have shaped economic policymaking beyond its formal end.[105]

The absence of populist movements during the twentieth century in Colombia was accompanied by distaste for political and economic ideologies among the country's elite. Instead the elite revealed a clear penchant for gradualism in political and economic affairs beyond the fashionable doctrines of the time combined with a "relative sophistication and health of the short-term economic management system (...) backed by impressive resources in terms of academic and technical skills" (Thorp 1991: xvi). The result was a unique pattern of economic policymaking in Colombia that reflects "a tendency toward market opening and restrictions on the role of government, but usually with a rhythm of two steps forward and one step back [...] The two steps forward usually occur during normal times, whereas the step back is almost invariably related with a crisis" (Lora 2005: 46–7; my translation). In other words, whereas economic actors in other Latin American countries perceive economic crises as a window of opportunity in order to introduce reforms in line with their material self-interest, major reforms in Colombia tend to occur during 'good times' when consensus and cooperation can be more easily achieved. The sustainability of economic policies then depends on how effectively the specific policy or instrument can withstand stress tests during 'bad times'. Policies that do not perform satisfactorily are usually not buried altogether but rather – pragmatically – adjusted.

Closely related to the culture of pragmatism in economic policymaking are congenial relations between government and business (Schneider 2004: 128). Informal agreements rather than fierce power battles have long characterized this relationship. While rationalist-material political economy approaches postulate irreconcilable differences between economic groups along class or sectoral lines, the behavior of business actors in Colombia instead reflects a tradition of collaboration and consensus-building through negotiations

105 Similarly, the informal institution of clientelism that dominated the Colombian political system during the *Frente Nacional* has survived its formal end (Leal Buitrago and Dávila Ladrón de Guevara 2009).

among themselves and with the government (Thorp and Durand 1997). Starting in the 1920s with the formation of the coffee growers' association, state actors have tried to organize domestic business by providing their associations *(gremios)* with significant benefits – from privileged access to material resources – encouraging companies to join them. As a result, the *gremios* became important interlocutors between the government and private sector interests (Urrutia 1983; Hartlyn 1985; Losada 2000; Jaramillo et al. 2001). For example, the president regularly invites the leaders of the major *gremios* for consultations in which government initiatives and specific proposals for economic and sectoral policies are discussed and political decisions agreed upon. It is not uncommon during those meetings for the representatives of the *gremios* to agree to economic measures that hurt the short-term interests of their own constituency but contribute to the solution of economic problems facing the majority of the business community and the country as a whole.

Unlike other governments in Latin America during the 1990s that pursued the rapid reduction of inflation as their top economic priority while accepting exchange-rate appreciation as a necessary complement, the Colombian government was unable to take such an orthodox position. Preventing real exchange-rate volatility has remained an important imperative from previous times and has shaped the country's approach to capital account management also during the economic liberalization period.

As soon as the strong appreciation of the exchange rate started to undermine their external competitiveness, the export and import-competing sectors of the economy made their voices heard. In contrast to their Peruvian counterparts, though, the government proved receptive to their concerns. As Edwards explains, "maintaining a highly depreciated real exchange rate – and even further depreciating it – was the key compensation mechanism offered to most of the influential private sector *gremios,* in order to obtain their support for the trade liberalization reform" (Edwards 2001: 67). Having surprised the country with the bold move to open the capital account in 1991, the Gaviria administration had to partially retract from it in order to safeguard the support of the business community for its economic reform agenda. The initial introduction of the *encaje* system can thus be interpreted as a pragmatic move on part of the government to placate the influential export sector.[106]

A vivid example of the essence and operation of pragmatism and consensual state-business relations is the decision-making process leading up to the government's ruling in December 2004 to require a minimum one-year stay for nonresident portfolio inflows, in order to halt the rapid appreciation of the peso against the US dollar. Formally a government prerogative, the decision was preceded by an emergency meeting of the president, his economic advisers, the head of the Central Bank, the presidents of the two most important commercial banks, and the leaders of the major business associations. In light of the accelerating appreciation of the real exchange rate (see Figure 5.2 above), at the beginning of the meeting President Uribe stated his intention to declare an "economic emergency" allowing the government to impose extraordinary measures, including capital controls. Seeking

106 Even though some observers have diagnosed a fall from grace for the *gremios* as the preferred interlocutor for the state in its dealings with the private sector (Revéiz 1997; Rettberg 2003, 2006), the influence of the organized business community over economic policymaking in Colombia is still substantial when compared to other countries in Latin America rather than to its own 'golden past' (Giacalone 1997; Schneider 2004).

to mitigate this threat, the president of the second-largest commercial bank in Colombia proposed to restrict portfolio inflows as a solution to quell the peso's appreciation.[107] His suggestion ended up generating the least resistance among the participants of the meeting and was subsequently adopted by the Ministry of Finance (El Tiempo, December 15, 2004).

5.7 Conclusion

Three broad conclusions emerge from the analysis of Colombia's capital account policy during the past twenty years. First, the ineffectiveness of IMF 'soft power' in the presence of favorable economic conditions of the country and internal contradictions in the policy advice given to the domestic authorities. As a result, the Fund's strategy to persuade Colombian policymakers to maintain or expand capital account openness fell on deaf ears. Despite having a coherent economic team embracing the free-market agenda during the Gaviria administration, the policy dialogue with the IMF did not produce a convergence of views on capital account management. Instead, one could argue that a reverse socialization effect occurred after several rounds of discussion when the IMF country team finally came around to accept the legitimacy and potential usefulness of the *encaje* system.

Second, the existence of a foreign-trained cadre of elite economists with prominent positions in the state bureaucracy constitutes no guarantee that neoliberal ideas about capital account management – presumably acquired during professional training abroad – become embedded in domestic policy outcomes. Survey data show a moderation in the pro-capital account freedom beliefs of this group upon reintegration into the domestic context. As a result, the effect of professional training on capital account policy is conditional on the domestic social context which may either enhance (Peru) or reduce (Colombia) the preference of foreign-trained economists for capital account openness.

Third, the domestic social context that has prevented the institutionalization of capital account openness in Colombia is characterized by an engrained sense of pragmatism among the country's elites as well as the political influence of exporters' interests. The behavior of government and business actors is fundamentally shaped by the search for pragmatic solutions to economic challenges, rather than being driven by irreconcilable differences based on sectoral cleavages. However, interest-group politics is salient for capital account policy in Colombia, too. Given the traditionally powerful position of export-oriented sectors vis-à-vis the government and other members of the business community, maintaining an open capital account against the threat of substantial exchange-rate appreciation ultimately proved to be a bridge too far in Colombia. Pragmatism is first and foremost guided by exporters' interest in maintaining macroeconomic stability in general, and preventing exchange-rate appreciation in particular. As a result, outlawing capital controls goes against the social purpose of Colombian national economic identity as defined by the material interests of politically powerful business actors.

107 Interview with María Angélica Arbeláez, deputy head of the Colombian Bankers Association (Asobancaria), December 20, 2004.

Chapter 6: Conclusions

> The world economy is full of all manner of fascinating, important social constructs, identities, norms, and collectively held beliefs, and they should be incorporated into our explanations along with the obviously important material facts of the world (Abdelal 2009: 76).

> A rigorous political science needs to be built on the foundation of contextual and comparative historical studies, which helps us to uncover tacit knowledge. Within particular parameters, we can arrive at historically bounded generalizations that identify material and ideational structures and the agents that move within and between them to create, over time, both choice and change (Katzenstein 2010: 20).

Economic policies are the result of both domestic and international factors, even more so in developing countries. In order to explain the evolution of capital account policy scholars must first consider political and ideational changes at the international level before proceeding to analyze their (lasting) impact at the domestic level. As the proponents of the policy diffusion literature have pointed out, it is unlikely that national policymakers made the decision to liberalize their economies for purely domestic reasons. Instead, their choices were influenced by events and actors at the international level. The fact that capital account openness simultaneously increased in several regions of the developing world illustrates the importance of taking global factors and actors – especially in terms of ideational changes – into account.

International institutions such as the International Monetary Fund came to embrace a policy of open capital accounts during the late 1980s and early 1990s. Having adopted it internally, the IMF tried to spread the norm of capital account openness to its member-states, in particular to developing countries. The organization sought to acquire the legal mandate over national capital account policies through an amendment of its Articles of Agreement in 1997. However, the Asian financial crisis in 1997–98 derailed this plan and led to a reconsideration of the costs and benefits of international capital mobility inside and outside the IMF. Subsequently, the organization has refrained from promoting capital account liberalization as an international norm. In the context of the current global economic crisis, the IMF has given up its principled opposition to the introduction of capital controls in developing countries, now considering them a useful, albeit temporary instrument of last resort to ensure macroeconomic stability. However, until the present day the Fund has not given up its principal conviction that the free movement of international capital is a desirable policy for all countries in the long run.

Global forces are important for domestic economic policy choices, but they do not determine their durability over time. Internal factors play a crucial role in ensuring whether capital account openness is sustained or not. For example, Peru's commitment to an open capital account has been largely unaffected by the global discussion about the costs and benefits of capital mobility in the aftermath of the Asian financial crisis during the late 1990s and also during the most recent global financial crisis. Peru's policymaking and business elites show unwavering support for the free movement of capital into and out of the country. Conversely, Colombia's elites did not subscribe wholesale to the capital freedom discourse emanating from Washington, D.C. in the early to mid-1990s. Despite outside pressure, the country has remained committed to an independent course on capital account management, most visibly in the context of the *encaje* system to limit capital inflows.

In a similar vein, global market forces pressuring countries to adopt a specific economic policy are insufficient to account for national policy variation. While international financial markets exerted a constant pressure on countries to liberalize their capital account during the last two decades, the question remains why countries have reacted in different ways to this uniform pressure from markets. Put more generally, the focus on structural forces – be they of a material or of an ideational nature – affecting all countries in a similar fashion is ill-suited in order to understand why capital account openness has become a lasting feature in only a few countries in Latin America during the last twenty years. International factors such as the IMF or financial markets play an important role to understand the uniform and simultaneous trend towards capital account liberalization in the developing world during the early 1990s. However, their power to explain the cross-country variation of capital account policy after the initial liberalization has clear limits.

While the general trend during the last twenty years towards greater capital account openness is unquestionable, the durability of capital account liberalization in developing countries generally, and Latin America specifically, shows considerable variation – both cross-nationally and longitudinally. Contemporary political economies in Latin America reflect the difference between an 'embedded' and an 'orthodox' path toward neoliberalism. While the latter version is wedded to the concept and practice of the minimal state, in the former version "the state becomes a promoter of economic production through active *supply-side* interventions" (Kurtz and Brooks 2008: 233). What then explains why some countries – in line with orthodox thinking – enthusiastically embrace capital mobility, while others – in line with the concept of "embedded neoliberalism" – show a more ambivalent approach toward capital account openness?

I have argued that national economic identity, understood as informal institutions at the domestic level in combination with specific state-business relations, is key to understanding this variation. Domestically shared beliefs about legitimate economic policies and policy instruments on the one hand, and changing or continuing state-business relations on the other hand, constitute a prism through which (emerging) international norms are refracted. Domestic informal institutions either reinforce or constrain the impact of the capital freedom discourse at the international level, thus leading to the diversity of capital account policy amidst global and regional convergence around higher levels of capital account openness. More precisely, whether capital account openness is sustained over time depends on the extent of agreement among the national policymaking and business elites that capital controls continue to be effective and legitimate, or else that they have lost their effectiveness and legitimacy as instruments of macroeconomic policymaking.

In order for capital account openness to last over time, state-business relations need to undergo an important transformation. If business actors largely unaffected by exchange-rate fluctuations but with vested interests in unfettered capital movements are able to co-opt government decision-making on economic policy, capital account liberalization is based on a sustainable material fundament. Conversely, if export-oriented sectors concerned about exchange-rate volatility and external competitiveness remain influential players for government decisions on capital account policy, capital controls will be considered legitimate instruments for the defense of national economic stability and autonomy.

This concluding chapter is structured as follows. First, I assess the power of alternative accounts in explaining the variation of capital account policy in Peru and Colombia in the time period after 1990. I focus on two 'outside-in' explanations: (i) the role of the International Monetary Fund, and (ii) the epistemic community of foreign-trained elite economists. Second, I summarize the novel argument of this book, emphasizing the importance of socially shared understandings about legitimate policies and instruments of macroeconomic management in combination with their material counterpart, state-business relations. Finally, I elaborate on the relationship between international norms, the domestic social and material context, and economic policies. I highlight how domestic informal institutions act as filters for global norms and ideas, reinforcing or reducing their impact on economic policy choices, thereby determining the durability or fragility of free-market economic reforms.

6.1 The International Monetary Fund and Capital Account Policy

The global trend toward more open capital accounts is inextricably linked to a normative change at the international level. During the 1980s, international financial institutions, in particular the International Monetary Fund, began to change their position on the desirability of capital controls in developing countries. Primarily related to internal organizational dynamics, the IMF started to promote the removal of all remaining obstacles to unfettered capital flows across borders (Abdelal 2007, Chwieroth 2010a, Moschella 2010, 2012). During the 1990s, IMF staff began to actively advocate capital account liberalization in their interactions with authorities from developing countries, albeit with significant (i) country-to-country, (ii) region-to-region, and (iii) up to mission-to-mission variation (IEO 2005). The attempt to transform capital account openness into an international norm culminated in the 1998 proposal to change the Fund's Articles of Agreement to give the organization the legal mandate to promote and supervise capital account liberalization in its member states. After most countries had closed their capital accounts in the aftermath of the 1980s debt crisis, Latin America became one of the prime targets for the IMF's capital account freedom campaign.

Yet capital account openness was not institutionalized as an international norm after all. The proposal to amend the IMF's Articles of Agreement failed. The critical juncture that derailed the norm's institutionalization was the Asian financial crisis of the late 1990s. The advocates for embedding capital account liberalization within the Fund's charter did not succeed in convincing the internal and external constituencies of the IMF of their interpretation of the causes of the crisis and its consequences for the Fund's mandate and policies. Most members of the IMF's Executive Board and influential outside observers interpreted the causes of the crisis as inconsistent with the glorification of capital account openness. As a result, the IMF's official position after 1998 has reflected a more accommodating view on restricting international capital movements, notably regarding short-term capital inflows. In turn, the organization has refrained from actively promoting rapid, unconditional capital account liberalization. Instead it has expressed qualified support for temporary, market-based capital account management techniques given a number of institutional requirements. As a result, capital controls constitute a "legitimate part of the toolkit to manage capital inflows in certain circumstances" (Ostry et al. 2010: 15; emphasis added). However, the Fund's principled support for the goal of capital freedom has remained unchanged. In contrast to previous arguments emphasizing a direct positive relationship between capital account openness and economic growth, the IMF now points to indirect, collateral economic benefits in order to make the case for capital account liberalization (Kose et al. 2006).

The 1998 watershed also affected the interaction between the IMF and its member states. Before the Asian crisis, the Fund was a significant push factor for capital account liberalization in developing countries. Its role can perhaps best be described as the *intellectual cheerleader* for the cause of capital freedom, helping to push governments over the brink towards the adoption of capital account liberalization, given specific domestic conditions and like-minded government interlocutors (Chwieroth 2006).[108] Given that capital account liberalization could not openly be included in the conditionality part of lending agreements, the IMF was forced to resort to 'soft' or discursive power to persuade developing country governments of the advantages of capital account openness.

Yet as the two case studies on Peru and Colombia show, the impact of IMF 'soft power' on domestic capital account policy decisions was marginal at best, even in the Peruvian context of profound economic dire straits. On the one hand, the effectiveness of 'soft power' in institutionalizing specific international norms into domestic politics is closely linked to the simultaneous availability of 'hard power' instruments (Kelley 2004a). The power of the IMF to influence domestic policy outcomes is severely constrained by the absence of lending agreements, and even more importantly by the impossibility of formally including capital account liberalization in the accompanying conditionality package. As a result, countries that did not depend on the Fund for financial assistance due to favorable economic conditions could ignore the siren song for capital account openness coming out of Washington, D.C. In short, even the full display of 'soft power' to convince recalcitrant governments to pursue capital account liberalization is ineffective in the absence of accompanying 'hard power' instruments related to the material incentives of conditionality.

However, even the co-existence of coercive and persuasive power instruments on part of the IMF does not ensure that domestic policy results reflect Fund prescriptions. Rather, the impact of the IMF on domestic policies requires a particular social context that establishes the match between the norms promoted by international institutions and domestic policy outcomes. Three distinct characteristics define the social context and thus condition states' compliance with the policy prescriptions of international institutions (Epstein 2006).

108 According to Woods (2006: 65–83), an 'ideal' setup for the IMF and the World Bank to persuade states to adopt certain economic policies would have the following three characteristics: (i) the occurrence of an economic crisis and the resulting resource constraint on governments; (ii) a like-minded technocratic epistemic community pulling the levers of policy clear of any pressure from recalcitrant societal groups; and (iii) a centralized policymaking process with strong powers for the executive.

The first scope condition refers to the international level: a normative consensus in the international community about the technical correctness or political desirability of the policy prescription. Elsewhere I have argued that such a normative consensus on capital account liberalization existed in the international community up until the outbreak of the Asian financial crisis (Leiteritz and Moschella 2010). Most international institutions, academic experts, private sector representatives, policymakers, and states agreed during the 1990s that capital controls were on their way out of the international monetary system. The debate at the time was how soon that would and should happen and whether the domestic liberalization processes needed to be supervised or controlled at the international level. The general commitment to capital freedom was conventional wisdom at the international level, eliciting a low level of normative contestation during the 1990s. The international community debated the appropriate strategy needed to achieve the goal of unfettered international capital flows but did not question the legitimacy of the goal in itself.

In the context of the Asian financial crisis, doubts increasingly clouded the previously existing consensus and unraveled the united front of capital freedom supporters. The prescription to liberalize the capital account rapidly and under virtually all possible circumstances quickly lost credibility and subsequently disappeared from the agenda of the Fund. From then on, IMF research staff has become immersed in the search to justify why and under what conditions capital account openness is an optimal policy. The hitherto existing assertiveness and principled conviction that capital account liberalization was the appropriate path towards economic development was gone. An ever increasing host of institutional and policy conditions was identified before capital account openness could become an economically beneficial policy. Yet an organization debating the effectiveness of a policy prescription can hardly be a convincing advocate for its worldwide adoption or maintenance.

The second scope condition for the power of international organizations over domestic policy outcomes requires a discontinuity in the economic sector under consideration. The traditional pattern of operation must become unviable in the context of policy failure. This was clearly the case in Peru in the aftermath of the economic crisis in the late 1980s. The imposition or tightening of capital and exchange controls during the García administration was widely held responsible for the worsening of the crisis. As a result, restrictive forms of capital account management lost domestic legitimacy. In contrast, Colombia's capital and exchange control regime worked rather well until its abrupt end in 1991. Certainly it could not be held responsible for causing or worsening an economic crisis.

The third scope condition refers to the need of a country to receive social recognition from the international community. Governments in urgent need of such recognition are more susceptible to give in to the policy demands of international institutions. Again, this was the case of Peru during the early 1990s: a small country with a terrible reputation trying desperately to shed its image as a pariah in the international community in order to attract fresh capital. In contrast, Colombia was in a rather comfortable economic position during the same period, receiving large amounts of private capital. Obtaining social recognition from international institutions or investors was not a priority for Colombian policymakers at the time.

Taken together, the IMF faced distinct social contexts in Peru and Colombia during the 1990s. As a result, its impact on domestic policy decisions theoretically carried a better chance in Peru than in Colombia. However, in neither case was the IMF the decisive factor for decisions on capital account policy. Put briefly, whether capital account openness becomes an institutionalized domestic policy has little to do with the IMF. At best, the organization can use its intellectual leadership to promote the maintenance of capital account openness, but only if the policies and policy instruments associated with previous or alternative development strategies have been removed from legitimate macroeconomic management.

6.2 Epistemic Communities of Foreign-Trained Economists and Capital Account Policy

An alternative explanation for the introduction and sustainability of capital account openness in developing countries emphasizes the role of epistemic communities of foreign-trained economists. This theory posits a direct relationship between individual professional training and preferences over economic policies. As intellectual norms within a specific profession change, so will the policy-relevant beliefs of people trained in this profession. Put simply, as the neoclassical orthodoxy became hegemonic in (most) US and UK graduate programs in economics and more future policymakers from Latin America obtained professional degrees at universities in the United States or Great Britain, their economic policy preferences became aligned with the free-market gospel.

Several scholars have pointed out that the liberalizing trend in capital account policy was preceded by the rise of a new elite of policymakers in Latin America. The central characteristic of these technocrats or "technopols" was their professional training abroad (Domínguez 1997; Centeno and Silva 1998). As the mainstream discourse in the economics profession moved towards neoclassical orthodoxy during the 1970s and 1980s, the previously dominant Keynesian perspective on capital account management gradually went out of fashion and was removed from the curricula of graduate programs in economics at most universities. As a result, graduate students, including an increasing number of students from developing countries (Aslanbeigui and Montecinos 1998), were subjected to a negative outlook on capital controls. Subsequently occupying prominent positions in the policymaking arena in their home countries, those economists-turned-politicians acted upon their beliefs acquired during professional training, formed "coherent policy teams" and introduced and institutionalized capital account openness (Chwieroth 2007).

The empirical evidence presented in the two case studies casts doubts on the explanatory power of this theory. In short, professional training at foreign universities does not account for the variation of capital account policy between Peru and Colombia. On the one hand, despite a relative lack of professional training abroad, Peruvian economists implemented drastic neoliberal reforms, including capital account liberalization, during the administration of President Fujimori in the early 1990s. On the other hand, Colombian economists who have traditionally held professional degrees from US or UK universities have not followed the pure tenets of neoliberalism in terms of capital account management. The same technocrats who rose to political power during the early 1990s and introduced capital account liberalization were later responsible for the re-vitalization of capital controls in form of the *encaje* system.

To be sure, foreign-trained elite economists in both countries share a negative assessment of capital controls. The empirical evidence thus supports the epistemic community theory. It suggests that professional training abroad forms the views of economists on capital account policy. However, beyond the overall rejection of capital controls as useful instruments of macroeconomic management, important nuances emerge. Peruvian economists reject restrictions on all forms of international capital flows, including short-term portfolio flows, while a majority of their Colombian counterparts have a favorable view of them.

These differences cannot be deduced from differences in professional training between economists from both countries. Colombian economists 'see a world' where temporary, market-based controls on capital inflows fulfill an important macroeconomic function, which justifies their use under specific circumstances. In contrast, Peruvian economists 'see a world' where all forms of restrictions on international capital movements have been relegated to the history books. According to their view, capital controls writ large have not only lost their effectiveness but more importantly their overall legitimacy in today's world.[109] They do not belong to the inventory of a 'modern' nation. I argue that these important nuances in capital account policy amidst a general convergence in favor of capital account openness have their origin in distinct shared understandings about legitimate economic policies and instruments among Peruvian and Colombian economists.

In conclusion, the epistemic community theory overstates the link between professional training and policy preferences of domestic policymakers. Following Chwieroth (2010a), such a socialization mechanism might indeed be substantial for staff of international organizations such as the IMF or economists working at universities or think-tanks, where a detached, technical discourse and ideological consistency from academic training to professional practice are highly esteemed and thus relatively easy to maintain. However, maintaining the consistency of beliefs about 'appropriate' capital account policy is much less likely for policymakers whose actions are subject to a significantly greater variety of factors beyond the impact of professional norms acquired during studies abroad.

As a result, the epistemic community theory overestimates the unity of the "neoliberal thought collective" (Estrada Álvarez 2004, 2005a; Mirowski and Plehwe 2009). Beyond a general consensus on free market principles, country-specific nuances on economic policies prevail among the members of the community of foreign-trained economists in Latin America. In other words, despite having been taught similar professional principles and norms, elite economists in Peru and Colombia have been responsible for rather different capital account policies. Apparently, the neoliberal core of economic thought allows for a variety of capital account management techniques. I have highlighted the crucial role of the domestic social and material context as the intermediary factor between international norms and national policy outcomes.

109 The metaphor of 'seeing the world' is inspired by James C. Scott (1998). Scott emphasizes how the creation of technical knowledge requires a "narrowing of vision" (Scott 1998: 78), a process of abstraction and simplification that by increasing the legibility of a society increases the capacity of policymakers to design formal institutions to shape social behavior. As a result, how a specific epistemic community of economists 'sees' its domestic society will shape its economic policy preferences and recommendations.

6.3 Domestic Informal Institutions, State-Business Relations, and Capital Account Policy

Both material and ideational factors at the international level drive countries in the direction of capital account openness. However, global forces fail to account for the variation of capital account policy after the initial liberalization. Domestic-level factors lie behind the fact that – seen over time – some countries are capital mobility enthusiasts, while others are laggards. I have argued that national economic identity, composed of informal institutions and state-business relations, act as a prism through which emerging international norms on economic policies are refracted. Depending on a specific content of socially shared rules and understandings underpinning and legitimizing economic policies and a specific set of state-business relations, an open capital account becomes institutionalized in the domestic political economy. In other words, national economic identity minimizes or maximizes external forces pushing and pulling toward capital account liberalization.

Informal institutions do not exist on their own volition. Rather their function to legitimize and delegitimize the use of certain policies or instruments in the national arena is linked to specific actors with specific interests that bring them into being and underwrite their continued existence. Put differently, for socially shared understandings about legitimate and illegitimate economic policies to emerge and survive, they need powerful sponsors. Given that capital account liberalization has not received unequivocal support as an optimal policy choice for developing countries in the academic literature, policymakers and society at large are not given clear instructions on what is best in terms of capital account policy (Blyth 2002). However, specific business actors are keen to overcome this uncertainty based on their material interests vis-à-vis the flow of international capital. Assuming that these actors are able to dominate state-business relations and their interests resonate with the informal institutions governing economic policymaking in the country, the long-term direction of capital account policy has both a solid social *and* material fundament.

The factors highlighted in the literature as causes of capital account policy are associated with rather different outcomes. The variation of capital account policy in contemporary Latin America goes beyond the variation in structural economic strength, the dependence on foreign capital, the fragmentation of the legislature, or the political orientation of the government. Peru and Colombia have comparable sizes and characteristics in their economies, in addition to similar political and economic institutions, and ideologically like-minded governments during the past two decades. In addition, both countries have confronted similar macroeconomic challenges and a constant interest and pressure from international financial markets in the post-1990 era. In light of the overall congruence of causal factors identified in existing explanations and the divergent path of capital account policy in Peru and Colombia, I have focused my attention on a variable that is conspicuously absent in the literature to explain capital account policy: informal institutions underpinning and legitimizing economic policies in both countries.

Whether domestically shared rules and understandings act as catalysts or brakes for the impact of international norms is closely related to (i) the context in which capital account liberalization was initially adopted, and (ii) the nature of state-business relations. First, the specific context in which capital account liberalization was introduced shapes the likelihood of it being sustained over time. The capital account has the high probability of remaining open if its initial liberalization occurred in the context of a profound economic crisis, as a result of which the previous economic development model associated with the use of capital controls was discredited. Second, capital account openness is a durable policy if economic actors materially benefitting from capital mobility are able to dominate state-business relations.

The formation process of actor interests vis-à-vis capital account policy tends to be overly static in the existing literature. According to interest-based accounts, actor preferences over economic policy outcomes are cast in stone and essentially unmovable after the initial adoption of capital account liberalization. However, the domestic interest group coalition supporting the initial opening of the national economy to international capital flows is not automatically stable over the medium and long term. Within the export-oriented sector, a cleavage emerges between multinational corporations and domestic economic conglomerates on the one hand, and small and medium-sized firms on the other. The former group maintains its support or demand for capital account openness beyond the initial liberalization period. In fact, domestic economic conglomerates largely absorb the financial industry and due to its multisectoral business activities are less susceptible to exchange-rate fluctuations. In contrast, small and medium-sized export companies focused on only one product or industry, usually in the non-traditional sector, remain highly concerned about exchange-rate volatility. They rather quickly realize that capital account openness in combination with trade liberalization and a floating exchange-rate regime leads to exchange-rate appreciation and thus negatively affects their external competitiveness. As a result, the initial support for capital account liberalization among them, based on short-term gains such as access to foreign capital sources, rapidly dwindles and gives rise to demands for limits on capital inflows in order to stop the appreciation of the exchange rate. In turn, the pro-capital mobility coalition from the beginning of the economic liberalization process unravels and the sustainability of capital account openness is put at risk.

The case of Peru illustrates the durability of capital account liberalization in the context of its introduction during a deep economic crisis and the transformation of state-business relations privileging the interests of economic sectors benefitting from capital mobility over the long run. The deep economic crisis that affected the country at the end of the 1980s profoundly changed the institutional landscape. The Fujimori government succeeded in its discursive strategy to link the causes of the crisis with government interventions in the economy per se, including the existence of capital controls. As a result, the initiation and maintenance of capital account openness has been based on a changing interpretation in terms of the legitimacy of capital controls in the aftermath of the crisis. An agreement among Peru's policymaking and business elites regarding the illegitimacy of capital controls emerged and was formally codified in the 1993 Constitution.

In addition, the economic liberalization process during the early 1990s fundamentally changed the balance of power between the economic interest groups and thus the nature of state-business relations. The winners of the country's economic opening were primarily composed of large players (big business) in the financial and mining industries. Their representatives have constituted important allies for the state within the business community. In return, the influence of these actors – who are largely unaffected by exchange-rate volatility in terms of their income – on government decisions has eclipsed those of other economic groups, notably smaller-sized industrialists and non-traditional exporters. The business associations representing the financial and mining industries have become the preferred interlocutor for the state-business dialogue on economic policy issues. Given this constellation, the focus on exchange-rate stability and competitiveness, including the contemplation of capital controls as a possible instrument to reduce the appreciation of the local currency, became largely a non-issue for state-business interactions in Peru.

In contrast, capital account openness faces a low probability of being sustained over time if its initial adoption occurred in the absence of a dire economic situation and if encompassing business associations give pride of place to the interests of all economic sectors, including small and medium-sized exporters, in their interactions with the government. Colombia's trajectory after 1990 illustrates the fragility of capital account openness given the survival of the pre-liberalization national economic identity that largely remained unchallenged by an economic crisis.

The culture of pragmatism and consensus-seeking in state-business relations was traditionally associated with the prudence and stability of economic policy in Colombia. The engrained sense of pragmatism survived the liberalization of the economy during the early 1990s and continues to permeate the business and policymaking elites of the country, tilting their behavior and actions toward compromise-building and the pursuit of national – not particularistic – macroeconomic goals. Pragmatism and the prominent position of smaller-sized exporters' interests in state-business relations ensure that exchange-rate stability and external competitiveness remain a central concern for Colombian policymakers in the context of a liberalized economy.

In addition, the domestic business coalition actively supporting or at least acquiescing to the initial adoption of capital account liberalization unraveled as soon as its negative consequences became visible, in particular in terms of a rapid appreciation of the nominal exchange rate. Concerned about their diminished income, exporters exploited their traditionally close connections to the Colombian government in order to impress upon it the need to take policy measures to get the appreciation under control. Given the Central Bank's exclusive control over monetary and exchange-rate policy, the executive followed suit with the introduction of the *encaje* system, administratively and temporarily restricting the inflow of foreign capital.

The *encaje* system also survived the adoption of a (managed) floating exchange rate regime by the Central Bank in 1999. Contrary to conventional wisdom, the Colombian case shows that a floating exchange rate regime can co-exist with capital controls. The post-1999 governments have utilized the *encaje* system in comparable proportions to their predecessors during the fixed exchange-rate period in Colombia. As a result, the formal economic institution of a floating exchange-rate regime is not a structural impediment for restrictions on international capital flows.

To be sure, the focus on pragmatism and consensus-seeking as an informal institution underpinning economic policymaking in Colombia does not deny or downplay the relevance of distributive preferences on actor behavior. Clearly, the influence of small and medium-sized exporters in state-business relations is crucial in order to understand the fragility of capital account openness in Colombia. However, traditional interest-based approaches overestimate the intensity or cohesive force to which these preferences are held among economic actors. In the case of Colombia, the informal institution of pragmatism leads the business community as a whole to interpret their interests in line with overall macroeconomic goals focused on the stability and autonomy of the economy. As such, pragmatism–supported by the prominent role of exporters in state-business relations–has worked against entrenching capital account openness in the Colombian political economy. Traditional interest-based approaches to explain capital account policy built on an ontological edifice of rationalism and materialism fail to recognize that actors' material incentives are socially mediated, i. e., that for their emergence and realization they must resonate with pre-existing formal and informal institutions governing economic policymaking (Kingstone 2001; Crystal 2003).

At any rate, the consideration of state-business relations highlights the contribution of interest-based approaches for an adequate understanding of capital account policy. Yet it is not the level of business organization or the extent of government autonomy from economic interest groups per se that is related to specific economic policies. Both Colombia and Peru have highly organized business communities dominated by peak associations, providing economic interest groups with multiple entry points into politics. In both countries, the government is highly dependent on private sector support and hence susceptible to the interests of the business community. Yet despite these similarities between Colombia and Peru in terms of state-business relations, the approach of both countries towards capital account management is rather different. The crucial point is what kind of coalition is able to dominate the business community and thus able to enjoy privileged political access and veto-power over economic policy decisions. Capital account openness could be sustained in Peru based on the effective exclusion of actors concerned about exchange-rate volatility and external competitiveness from state-business interactions.

Taken together, political decisions on capital account policy are inextricably linked to collectively held understandings among a country's policymaking and business elites. Intersubjectively shared beliefs about legitimate economic policies shape actors' perceptions of their interests and inform their behavior above and beyond their material self-interest. Domestic informal institutions supported by specific state-business relations demarcate the limits of legitimate thinking and possible actions in terms of economic policies and instruments.

Collectively shared understandings mold how economic agents perceive and pursue their interests, thereby defining the range of socially acceptable forms of macroeconomic management. Intersubjective rules and beliefs lead societies "to their own interpretations of the purposes of economic activity, the legitimacy of certain economic institutions, and the meaning of their economic interdependence with others" (Abdelal 2009: 72). As a result, the social purpose of the national economic identity can advance or restrict the international campaign for open capital accounts.

6.4 International Norms, the Domestic Social Context, and Economic Policies

The analysis of domestically shared beliefs and understandings about legitimate economic policies is a lacuna in the extant literature on capital account policy that I have set out to fill. Scholars interested in explaining the sustainability of neoliberal economic reforms and the impact of international norms and ideas on domestic policy choices ignore the role of domestic informal institutions at their peril. Traditional approaches focused on material interests, formal political and economic institutions, and global norms and ideas fail to account for the variation of capital account policy in an age of financial globalization. Paying heed to the change and continuity of shared understandings about legitimate economic policies is key to understanding both the influence of international norms on domestic policy, and the durability or fragility of economic reforms. In order to become institutionalized in the domestic political economy, international norms setting out to diffuse free-market policies must encounter a social and material context in which alternative development strategies have lost their legitimacy.

My focus on domestic informal institutions is situated within the constructivist research program in comparative and international political economy (Blyth 2009; Abdelal et al. 2010). However, constructivist scholarship has not paid sufficient attention to how shared understandings emerge, operate, and change at the *domestic* level – independent from global norms and ideas.[110] Rather than merely norms and ideas held by a specific group of actors such as epistemic communities, shared rules and beliefs among a country's policymaking and business community assume the status of social institutions within the domestic context. These informal institutions, in turn, define how states and societies react to (emerging) international norms. Policy outcomes are thus the result of the dynamic interaction between domestically and internationally shared rules and understandings.

Collectively shared beliefs about 'appropriate' economic policies have unique national-historic roots and manifestations which to a certain degree overlap with, but are not reducible to universal economic ideologies and their concomitant norms, such as Keynesianism or neoclassical economics (FitzGerald 2005). Given their focus on the level of the international system, structural constructivists such as Martha Finnemore, Kathryn Sikkink, and Alexander Wendt tend to overstate the domestic impact of international norms and ideas (Finnemore and Sikkink 1999; Wendt 1999).[111] Global norms and ideas interact with pre-existing national social orders. The result of the dynamic interaction between foreign and domestic norms and ideas are contingent policy outcomes. Going beyond the dichotomous results of wholesale adoption or outright rejection of global norms and ideas, *norm localization* describes "a complex process and outcome by which norm-takers build congruence between transnational norms (...) and local beliefs and practices. [...] The success of norm diffusion strategies and processes depends on the extent to which they provide opportunities for localization" (Acharya 2004: 241).

---

110 Exceptions are Abdelal (2001) and Darden (2009).

111 See Checkel (1998) for the difference between structural and agent-focused approaches in constructivist scholarship in international relations.

The process of norm localization builds on Peter Hall's crucial insight that the domestic impact of economic ideas critically hinges on their fit with the existing "structure of political discourse" in a country (Hall 1989: 383).[112] Agency-oriented constructivists such as Jeffrey Checkel speak of a *cultural match* between international norms and historically constructed domestic institutions leading to

> a situation where the prescriptions embodied in an international norm are convergent with domestic norms, as reflected in discourse, the legal system (constitutions, judicial codes, laws), and bureaucratic agencies (organizational ethos and administrative agencies). (Checkel 1999: 87)

However, *matchmaking* is a dynamic process that defies the notion of a primordial, existential match between foreign and domestic norms, in addition to recognizing the essential role of domestic actors for norm localization and congruence-building between domestic and international ideas (Acharya 2004; Chwieroth 2010b). I have argued that the sustainability of neoliberal reforms over time depends on the change of the national economic identity that provided both the ideational and the material fundament for the previous development model. Policy instruments associated with alternative strategies of economic development must become illegitimate in the eyes of the national policymaking and business community. The attempt of ideationally or materially motivated entrepreneurs to reconfigure the social rules and understandings underpinning and legitimizing economic policies toward free-market solutions is made easier by the existence of a profound economic crisis that can be blamed on previously dominating development models, associating the use of alternative policy instruments such as capital controls with the specter of economic mismanagement, corruption, and chaos (Hall 2003).[113]

Economic crises thus serve as critical junctures for the redefinition of collectively shared beliefs about legitimate economic policies and policy instruments.[114] New ideas about economic management are able to fill the intellectual void left by the failure of the previous development model and its concomitant economic policies and instruments (Blyth 2002). As a result, crises provide an ideal launching pad for alternative norms and ideas for policymaking (Widmaier et al. 2007).

However, a crisis – even a profound one of the magnitude we have recently experienced – in combination with new ideas about economic management is not sufficient to engender large-scale political and economic change on its own. Rather, the widely shared perception of a crisis or a lack of legitimacy of the existing economic order must encounter favorable institutional conditions at the domestic level in order to become an effective catalyst for a "great transformation" (Polanyi 1944). The varied reaction within the developing

112 According to Hall, the political discourse of a nation includes "shared conceptions about the nature of society and the economy, various ideas about the appropriate role of government, a number of common political ideals, and collective memories of past policy experiences" (Hall 1989: 383).

113 Note, though, that an economic crisis is not a prerequisite for the initial *adoption* of capital account liberalization (Pepinsky 2012). In fact, it was introduced in Colombia in the absence of an economic crisis.

114 Critical junctures can loosely be defined as a "*relatively* short period of time during which there is a *substantially* heightened probability that agents' choices will affect the outcome of interest" (Capoccia and Kelemen 2007: 348). Put differently, agents' choices made during critical junctures close off alternative options and lead to the establishment of institutions that generate self-reinforcing path-dependent processes.

world to current proposals for a more restrictive regulation of international capital movements, including the possible introduction of a financial transactions tax, comes thus not as a surprise. Beyond the "usual suspects" among the developed countries such as the United States and Great Britain, there is quite a large number of emerging market countries who reject these proposals. I submit that their rejection may at least partially be based on a national economic identity that defines international capital mobility as a sacrosanct goal. In other words, when internal beliefs and understandings about legitimate economic policies clash with internationally held ones, a global economic crisis in and of itself does not lead to changing preferences or policies at the domestic level. If, however, an economic crisis challenges domestically shared beliefs and understandings about appropriate polices *and* is accompanied by a transformation of the existing state-business relations that, in turn, provide the material foundation for informal institutions governing economic policymaking, a profound change of economic policies can be expected.

Finally, a methodological caveat is in order. Informal institutions do not lend themselves to simplistic forms of causality and consequences, suitable for the testing of explanatory variables where a preexisting cause is linked to a subsequent effect in a more or less mechanistic way. As shared ideas, informal institutions rely on a *constitutive* notion of explanation (Wendt 1998). According to this perspective, the researcher seeks to establish conditions of possibility (or impossibility) for certain actions and policy outcomes. As such, a specific economic policy is an 'effect' of the conditions that make it possible in the first place. In other words, intersubjective beliefs and rules – social facts (Searle 1995) – cannot be pressed into the straightjacket of causal theorizing precisely because of the depth and complexity of context-specific institutional forces that permeate social and economic life. As Marion Fourcade puts it, "(t)he explanatory factor (…) is no less dense than the object to be explained" (Fourcade 2009: 16).

Put differently, national economic identity based on a specific set of domestically shared rules and beliefs and state-business relations makes it possible (or impossible) to sustain capital account openness, even though national economic identity does not 'cause' policy outcomes in any direct or linear way required by the traditional notion of causality.[115] Rather, the unfettered flow of international capital is nationally viable because alternative courses of action have become virtually unthinkable among the domestic elites.

In conclusion, the major contribution of this book to a better understanding of capital account policy lies in its insight that national economic identity defines the range of socially acceptable economic policies and policy instruments, thus sealing the fate of economic reforms over time. The sustainability of economic reforms is based on the shared belief among domestic elites that alternative policies and instruments no longer represent a legitimate part of macroeconomic management. As a result, scholars need to pay greater attention to the interaction of norms and ideas located at the global and the national level, leading to contingent policy outcomes. Despite living in an age of financial globalization, the potential

115 Friedrich Kratochwil and John Ruggie have coined the useful analogy that social facts such as ideas, norms, or identities "do not effect cause in the sense that a bullet through the heart causes death or an uncontrolled surge in the money supply causes price inflation" (Kratochwil and Ruggie 1986: 767).

for and practice of state interventionism and policy divergence including among developing countries exist unabated.

Appendix 1: The Economics of Capital Account Policy

A short discussion of the technical foundations of capital account management is in order. In this appendix, I provide brief introductions to: (i) the capital account and its transactions; (ii) restrictions or controls on capital account transactions; (iii) capital account liberalization; and (iv) measuring capital account openness.

What is the Capital Account and What are Capital Account Transactions?

The capital account refers to a country's international investment flows and is the part of a nation's balance of payments used to register international capital flows. International capital flows are all transnational transactions with assets other than official reserves – the latter being the prerogative of governments for the sole purpose of bringing the country's payments position into balance. Capital account transactions or trade in assets are thus undertaken by residents of a country for normal business purposes.

There are three ways to distinguish international capital flows: (i) between inflows and outflows; (ii) by type of capital; and (iii) by intended purpose. Capital inflows entail foreign purchases of domestic assets – such as stocks, government bonds, land, or factories – or foreign loans to domestic residents. Conversely, capital outflows entail domestic purchases of foreign assets or loans to foreign residents by domestic residents. A country experiencing capital outflow or a capital account deficit is accumulating net claims on the rest of the world by purchasing more assets and/or making more loans to the rest of the world than it is receiving.

Net capital inflows appear in the fundamental identity of a country's balance of payments: net capital inflows + current account surplus + official reserves = 0. As a result, a current account deficit, i. e., savings lower than investments, can be financed either by capital inflows or by a reduction in official reserves.

Capital account transactions refer to the purchase or sale of financial assets. An asset – real or financial – is simply a means to hold wealth, such as money, stocks, bonds, production facilities, public debt, or real estate (Krugman and Obstfeld 2009: 302). Three types of financial assets or capital can be distinguished: (a) direct *investments;* (b) *securities;* and (c) *debt* flows. Each type can be considered as an inflow or outflow of capital for a specific country. In addition, the three types of capital have different duration periods or volatility profiles. Direct investments refer to the purchase or sale of shares or some equivalent title of ownership sufficient to exercise managerial control over an enterprise, the purchase or sale of real estate, or substantial equity investment.[1] Direct investment transactions are usually considered long-term (over a year) capital flows, less subject to volatility risks given that selling real assets such as production facilities is more difficult than securities. The sale or purchase of securities, such as stocks, bonds and equities in amounts that do not confer managerial control – also known as portfolio investments – are considered medium-term capital flows. Purchases of foreign securities by local residents involve outward movements of capital. Lastly, the purchase or sale of debt instruments, e. g., bank loans, derivatives, and various forms of credit (commercial, financial, guarantees) across countries is considered the most volatile or short-term form of capital flows. Borrowing by national residents from foreign financial entities involves an inflow of capital; lending, an outflow.

Finally, it is important to distinguish between the uses of capital transactions. One form of financial transactions is related to the import and export of goods and services. Payments made or received for these transactions are registered in the current account of the balance of payments. On the other hand, all other not trade or service-related financial transactions, i. e., for investment or speculation, are registered in the capital account. As a result, liberalizing controls on current-account transactions allows increased ability of local residents to convert domestic currency into foreign exchange in order to import, or vice versa for the export of goods and services. In other words, current-account convertibility allows residents to make and receive trade-related payments receive dollars (or any other foreign currency) for the export of goods and services and pay dollars for the import of goods and services, make remittances, access foreign currency for travel, studies abroad, medical treatment and gifts, etc. Lifting restrictions on all other forms of financial transactions, in particular transactions such as investment and loans, refers to capital account convertibility.

What are Capital Controls?

In the context of 'embedded liberalism' in Western countries after the Second World War, governments maintained a host of restrictions on international capital movements. Having learned the lessons from the two decades of the interwar period and in line with the then dominating Keynesian thinking, controls were intended to shield national economies from the distortionary effects of volatile capital flows. In fact, capital controls worked rather well in the context of the Bretton Woods System (Eichengreen 2008: 92). They provided governments with enough breathing space for the application of independent monetary policy during the Bretton Woods era of fixed-exchange rates. They could cope with balance-of-payments difficulties without the need to apply expenditure-switching policies or undermining fundamental policy goals such as full employment and economic growth. Capital controls fulfilled an essential function for the overall stability of the Bretton Woods System.

Seeking to promote international trade, in 1959 IMF member states committed themselves to lifting restrictions on current-account convertibility under Article VIII of the Articles of Agreement. As mentioned earlier, current account convertibility allows free capital

1 Equity investment is considered direct investments when it exceeds ten percent of the market capitalization of a firm.

inflows and outflows for the import and export of goods and services. Yet while countries progressively relaxed their national restrictions on current-account transactions in line with IMF obligations, they maintained their statutory restrictions on the majority of capital account transactions.

Governments pursue various purposes with different forms of capital controls (Johnston and Tamirisa 1998). As with international trade flows, there have historically been few limits to the ingenuity of governments to invent and impose restrictions on capital flows, both on inflows and outflows. In most developing countries, controls on capital outflows have been used to generate revenue for governments or to permit them to allocate credit domestically without risking capital flight. Typical examples of restrictions on capital-account convertibility still in use today include:

- Limits on the possession and availability of foreign exchange;
- Limitations on the external asset and liability positions of domestic financial institutions;
- Limitations on residents firms' and individuals' foreign portfolio assets, real estate holdings, and direct investment;
- Reserve requirements for short-term capital inflows.

In general terms, controls have taken the form of (a) *price* or market-based mechanisms, and (b) *quantity* limits. Both types of controls can be applied to capital inflows and outflows. Outright bans on long-term capital flows often reflect political sensitivity to foreign ownership of domestic assets. An example is Article 27 of the Mexican Constitution limiting foreign investment in Mexican domestic assets, especially natural resources. As a result, the article prevents the government from authorizing concessions and contracts to foreign residents or companies for the exploitation of Mexican petroleum.

Price controls may take the form of special taxes on returns to international investment, taxes on certain types of transactions – such as the 'Tobin tax' on short-term capital flows – or a mandatory reserve requirement that functions as a graduated tax, as used for short-term capital inflows in Chile and Colombia during the 1990s. Quantity restrictions on capital flows may include rules mandating ceilings or requiring special authorization for new or existing borrowing from foreign residents. Other forms are administrative controls on cross-border capital movements in which a government agency must approve transactions for certain types of assets. In terms of quantitatively restricting capital outflows, forbidding or requiring special permission for the repatriation of profits by foreign enterprises operating domestically used to be a popular policy instrument in many developing countries.

Finally, it is important to distinguish capital controls from prudential regulations, even though sometimes the exact difference lies in the eye of the beholder. Measures of prudential supervision and regulation of the domestic financial system are designed to limit the scope and incentives of financial market participants to take on excessive risk, in particular regarding the dependence on short-term foreign currency debts. A variety of capital, liquidity, reserve, and open position requirements have been devised in order to deal with the systemic-risk implications of the assets and liabilities of bank and nonbank firms' balance sheets (Eichengreen et al. 1998: 23–28). The imposition of prudential regulations and controls on capital inflows have often been justified with the same arguments. Some price-based controls on inflows indeed have a prudential objective. However, one cannot conclude that all or even most capital controls have been imposed due to prudential reasons. In fact, many of them have traditionally been imposed for other reasons, usually related to political expediency or in order to reconcile otherwise incompatible internal and external macroeconomic objectives.[2]

What is Capital Account Liberalization?

The freeing of international capital flows, also known as international financial liberalization, capital-account convertibility or capital account openness, is a subset of financial liberalization. As a whole it refers to the "process of giving the market the authority to determine who gets and grants credit and at what price" (Williamson and Mahar 1998: 2).

According to Williamson and Mahar (1998), financial liberalization encompasses six dimensions:

1. The elimination of credit controls;
2. The deregulation of interest rates;
3. The free entry into the banking sector or financial-service industry;
4. Bank autonomy;
5. The private ownership of banks; and
6. The liberalization of international capital flows.

Unfortunately, no positive or precise definition of capital mobility is readily available. Capital account convertibility is usually defined through its opposite – the existence of restrictions on international capital movements. In general terms, capital account convertibility refers to the freedom to convert local financial assets into foreign financial assets and vice versa. Put simply, it allows firms and households to freely convert domestic currency into foreign exchange and back, regardless of the duration or purpose of the underlying financial transaction. As the result of full capital account convertibility, capital can enter and leave the country at will. The liberalization of international capital flows is distinct from the other five types of financial liberalization, even though they often occur in conjunction. For example, the permission for foreign banks or other financial intermediaries to enter the domestic financial industry does not count as part of capital account liberalization. Both processes follow a separate, albeit somewhat connected economic logic. Allowing capital

2 The question of what counts as prudential regulation or as capital control still occupies the economic literature. For example, Mishkin (2006) argues that the risks associated with capital account liberalization need to be dealt with through prior appropriate prudential regulation of the financial system and other policy reforms. In other words, prudential regulation is the prerequisite for capital account liberalization. The corollary is that there should be no capital controls beyond their justification as prudential regulations. However, the devil lies in the details: exactly which measures prevent excessive – however defined – risk-taking by domestic financial intermediaries and which serve other purposes? As a result, what some observers call – usually pejoratively – capital controls, others consider appropriate prudential regulations in a world of global finance.

to freely move in and out of the country does not require the free establishment of financial firms. In fact, domestic financial intermediaries might support capital account openness on the condition that certain legal regulations limit the free entry of foreign banks into the domestic financial sector (Pepinsky 2009).

How to Measure Capital Account Openness?

Since there is no formal definition of capital-account convertibility, measuring the removal of national restrictions on international capital movements is not a straightforward empirical exercise. In fact, the search for better, i. e., more detailed or precise indexes of capital account restrictions has been a long-standing occupation for macroeconomists (Eichengreen 2001). Miniane states the fundamental problem for the construction of comparable cross-country indexes of capital account openness:

> Capital controls can take many different forms, making it time-consuming to track all changes in restrictions within a single country. Moreover, the construction of any capital controls index raises the problem of aggregation. By how much should a measure drop if a country relaxes one of its many restrictions? Last but not least, the effectiveness of capital controls depends crucially on the government's willingness and ability to enforce them. Assuming one has qualitative evidence on enforceability, how should it be weighted in the index? (Miniane 2004: 277)

Researchers have constructed two different categories of time-series analyses of capital account openness: (a) rules-based, qualitative or *de jure* and (b) quantitative or *de facto* indicators.[3] Various indices have been constructed in order to directly measure global capital mobility. They use a variety of indicators such as the ratio of total market capitalization of equities available for purchase by foreign investors over total market capitalization (Edison and Warnock 2003), the ratio of a country's external capital stock, i. e., portfolio and direct investment assets and liabilities, as a share of GDP (Lane and Milesi-Feretti 2007), the national savings rate over the national investment rate with the correlation between the two series taken as an indicator of impediments to capital mobility (Feldstein and Horioka 1980), or the estimated stocks of gross foreign assets and liabilities as a ratio of GDP (Edison et al. 2004).

Qualitative or *de jure* measures of capital account openness take a political-legalistic view. They focus on statutory country regulations reported in government publications and are indexed annually in the IMF's *Annual Report on Exchange Arrangements and Exchange Restrictions* (AREAER). From 1967 until 1996, the AREAER used a 0–1 single dummy variable in order to measure restrictions on capital account transactions. Since 1996, the

3 A similar distinction between *de jure* and *de facto* regimes exists for exchange rates. The first is based on official data reported by governments to the IMF and the latter is inferred from the actual behavior of the currency and policies towards it. Similar to the comparison for capital account openness, Reinhart and Rogoff (2004) find substantial differences between the measures for each regime type.

AREAER uses a disaggregated, binary coding scheme based on a wide range of subcategories of capital account transactions:

- Capital market securities
- Money market instruments
- Collective investment securities
- Derivatives and other instruments
- Commercial credits
- Financial credits
- Guarantees, sureties, and financial backup facilities
- Direct investment
- Liquidation of direct investment
- Real estate transactions
- Personal capital movements

While being a substantial improvement over its earlier, cruder, measure of capital account openness, the revised AREAER index still has some inherent limits. It records the mere existence of controls in several sub-categories of the capital account but not their intensity, type (direct versus portfolio investments or capital inflows versus outflows), or relative effectiveness. As a result, misleading assessments based on the IMF coding scheme have been rather frequent. For example, Chile, Mexico and Brazil were coded as having a closed capital account between 1992 and 1994 despite the fact that the three cases are very different. While Chile had restrictions only on short-term inflows, Brazil maintained a wide array of restrictions on inflows and outflows, and Mexico was virtually open to all types of capital flows (Edwards 2007: 78).

The fundamental trade-off involved in the construction of *de jure* indices of capital account openness is between fine-grained measures of capital account transactions and the coverage in terms of years and countries. In other words, most comprehensive measures of capital account restrictions are only available for a handful of – usually developed – countries and limited time periods (Quinn 1997; Miniane 2004; Schindler 2009). The most recent attempts to develop fine-grained indices of *de jure* capital account openness are all based on IMF original data but seek to widen their measurement precision, above all in terms of the intensity of capital account restrictions, in the context of a substantially improved coverage across time and countries (Brune 2006; Edwards 2007).

De facto indexes tend to find a substantially higher level of capital account openness compared to the ones reported in *de jure* indexes. In other words, capital is actually more mobile across borders as stipulated in legal regulations. This is especially the case in countries with severe legal impediments to capital mobility, including banning international capital movements altogether. Ample historical evidence suggests that the private sector has traditionally resorted to over-invoicing of imports and under-invoicing of exports, i. e., channelling capital transactions through the current account, in order to sidestep legal controls on capital flows (Eichengreen 2008: 92). However, the limitation of *de facto* indices of capital account openness is that these measures may be correlated with other factors that trended together during the same period of analysis, but which have nothing to do with capital account openness. In other words, high capital mobility might indicate volatility in the investment climate rather than openness to cross-border movements (Frankel 1993).

The most commonly used measure of *de jure* capital account openness was developed by Chinn and Ito using information gleaned from the AREAER.[4] The latest version of their Financial Openness Index (KAOPEN) covers 182 countries between 1970 and 2007 (Chinn and Ito 2008). Their index includes four major categories of restrictions on external accounts, for all of which binary dummy variables exist: (i) existence of multiple exchange rates, (ii) restrictions on capital and (iii) current account transactions, and (iv) requirements of surrender of export proceeds. In addition, for capital account transactions after 1997 they use the sub-categories introduced in the 1996 AREAER. For each of the four categories Chinn and Ito consider the average measure of the first standardized principal component. The index is constructed such that the series has a mean of zero. The index has a higher value for countries that are more open to cross-border financial transactions. Country values range from 2.603 to −1.767.

However, there are several problems with the Chinn-Ito index that render its usefulness as a measure of the dependent variable in quantitative or regression studies on the causes of capital account policy rather problematic. First, the inclusion of information on capital account policies over the past five years overstates the causal effects of variables that change in response to capital account policy and underestimates the importance of variables that contribute to large changes in capital account policy (Karcher and Steinberg 2010). Second, the Chinn-Ito index does not distinguish between controls on inflows and outflows of capital. Third, the index contains measures of *other,* i. e., not capital account-related, policy choices that governments make. In other words, the index measures the *extensity* of capital controls since it analyzes the existence of different types of restrictions, but it does not directly refer to the stringency of capital movement restrictions. As a result, the Chinn-Ito index is problematic because of the high risk of endogeneity between financial liberalization and other policy measures (Brune and Guisinger 2007).

Notwithstanding its inherent problems as an adequate measure of capital account openness, the Chinn-Ito index has become the standard reference point for measuring capital account openness in the political science literature. While being aware of the significant limits of the index, I have used it in order to describe the global and regional trends of capital account policy after the end of the Bretton Woods System in Chapter 1. I have done so for purely illustrative purposes, not with the intention to employ the index within a quantitative analysis of the causes of capital account policy.

4 A newer and more fine-grained index using the AREAER was developed by Brune (2006). It reports IMF country data on twelve different categories of capital flows. The dataset is based on a 0–9 index, where higher numbers denote a greater level of financial openness. It covers 187 countries between 1965 and 2003. It is constructed as the sum of all 0–1 dummies over the different categories of capital flows.

Appendix 2: List of Interviewees

For IMF case study (all in Washington, D. C.)

Manish Bapna and Bruce Jenkins, Executive Director and Policy Director, Bank Information Center, August 4, 2003

Andrew Baukol, former assistant to Timothy Geither in US Treasury, later adviser to the US Executive Director at the IMF, August 5, 2003

Onno de Beaufort Wijnholds, Permanent Representative of the European Central Bank at the IMF, former Dutch Executive Director at the IMF, November 11, 2003

Amar Bhattacharya, Adviser, PREM Vice-Presidency, World Bank, August 5, 2003

Karl Bischofberger, Executive Director for Germany at the IMF, August 7, 2003

James Boughton, Assistant Director, Policy Development and Review Department, IMF, August 7, 2003

Ariel Buría, Executive Director, Group of 24 (G-24) Secretariat, July 31, 2003

Randall Dodd, Director, Financial Policy Forum, August 12, 2003

Jessica Einhorn, former World Bank Managing Director, Dean of the Paul H. Nitze School for Advanced International Studies, July 31, 2003

Bernd Esdar, former German Executive Director at the IMF (1995–2001), August 5, 2003

Guillermo Le Fort, Executive Director for Southern Cone Countries, November 13, 2003

Gerd Häusler, Head of International Capital Markets Division, IMF, November 10, 2003

Yusuke Horiguchi, Institute of International Finance, August 13, 2003

David Mathieson, IMF Research Department, August 6, 2008

Michael Mussa, former Chief Economist of the IMF (1991–2001), Senior Fellow, Peterson Institute for International Economics, August 4, 2003

Lorraine Ocampos, Country Data Review Division, Statistics Department, IMF, November 14, 2003

Jacques J. Polak, former IMF Chief Economist and Executive Director, President of the Per Jacobsson Foundation, August 11, 2003

Murrillo Portugal and Alexandre Tombini, Brazilian Executive Director and Adviser to Executive Director, respectively, November 14, 2003

Mark Sobel, US Treasury, Office for International Affairs, August 8, 2003

Marianne Schulze-Ghattas, Surveillance Operations, Policy Development and Review Department, IMF, August 13, 2003

John Williamson, Senior Fellow, Peterson Institute for International Economics, August 4, 2003

Jeromin Zettelmeyer, IMF Research Department, August 8, 2003

For Peru case study (all in Lima)

Javier Abugattás, Professor, Department of Political Science and Public Policies, Pontificia Universidad Católica del Perú, former functionary in the Ministry of Economy and Finance, October 12, 2009

Roberto Abusada, Chief Adviser, Ministry of Economy and Finance (1993–1998), June 7, 2005 and October 16, 2009

Adrian Armas, Chief Economist, Central Bank, June 8, 2005

Gianfranco Castagnola, Head, APOYO Consultoria, June 8, 2005

Elmer Cuba, Chief Economist, Macroconsult, June 8, 2005

Oscar Dancourt, Professor, Department of Economics, Pontificia Unversidad Católica del Perú, former member and president of the Board of Directors of the Central Bank (2004–2006), October 2, 2007 and October 12, 2009

Luis Duran-Downing, Mission Chief for Peru and Head of Pacific Division (1991–1996), International Monetary Fund, written communication, August 3, 2007

César A. Ferrari, Professor, Department of Economics, Pontificia Universidad Javeriana Bogotá, former Member and General Manager of the Board of Directors of the Central Bank (1987–88), April 19, 2007

Carlos González, Chief Economist, Association of Exporters (ADEX), October 15, 2009

Jorge Gonzalez, Professor, Department of Economics, Universidad del Pacífico, June 9, 2005

Esteban Hnyilicza, former functionary of Central Bank (1990–2003), June 8, 2005

Eduardo Morón, Professor, Department of Economics, Universidad del Pacífico, ex-Vice Minister of Economy and Finance (2008–2009), October 1, 2007

Felipe Ortiz de Zevallos, Head of APOYO Group, June 8, 2005

Hugo Perea, Chief Economist, BBVA Banco Continental (October 14, 2009)

David Rivera, Editor, PODER 360°, October 16, 2009

Martha Rodriguez, Department of Economics, Universidad del Pacifico, June 9, 2005

Hugo Santa María, Chief Economist, APOYO Consultoria, October 13, 2009

Jürgen Schuldt, Professor, Department of Economics, Universidad del Pacífico, October 1, 2007

Germán Suarez, former president of Central Bank (1990–1992), June 9, 2005

Martin Tanaka, Director, Instituto de Estudios Peruanos, June 9, 2005

Gilbert Terrier, former member of Peru country team during the 1990s, International Monetary Fund, personal communication, July 5, 2007

Richard Webb, former president of the Central Bank (1981–1985), June 8, 2005

For Colombia case study (all in Bogotá)

María Angélica Arbeláez, Vice-president of Colombian Bankers' Association (Asobancaria), December 20, 2004

Carlos Caballero, Head of the School of Government at the Universidad de los Andes, May 2, 2007

Mauricio Cárdenas, Head of the Colombian economic think-tank Fedesarrollo, September 28, 2004

María Mercedes Cuellar, President of Colombian Bankers' Association (Asobancaria), March 13, 2007

Juan Carlos Echeverry, former Minister of National Planning (1998–2000), August 12, 2004

Olav Gronlie, Member of IMF Mission team for Colombia during the 1990s, written communication, November 3, 2004

Roberto Junguito, former Colombian Minister of Finance (1982–1984 and 2002–2003), October 1, 2004

Salomón Kalmanovitz, Member of Colombian Central Bank Board (1993–2005), August 30, 2004

Marco Palacios, President of the National University of Colombia, November 29, 2004

Guillermo Perry, former Colombian Finance Minister (1994–1996) and World Bank Chief Economist for Latin America (1996–2005), September 21, 2004

Leonardo Villar, Member of Colombian Central Bank Board (1997–2009), September 7, 2004

Fabio Villegas, Head of the Colombian National Association of Financial Institutions (ANIF), September 15, 2004

Miguel Urrutia, former Head of Colombian Central Bank (1993–2005), January 16, 2006

Appendix 3: Survey Questions for Foreign-trained Elite Economists in Colombia and Peru

1 Introduction

Thank you for your time and interest in completing this survey on economists' views on capital controls. In particular, I want to gauge the role that professional education abroad has on your view today.

This survey is part of a broader study on capital account liberalization in Latin America in the 1990s.

The online survey will take approximately 15 minutes to complete.

Do not hesitate to contact me at r.j.leiteritz@lse.ac.uk should you have any questions or need further information regarding this study. Thank you again for your time and participation.

Ralf Leiteritz

2 Current view on capital controls

This section asks for your view on capital controls TODAY.

Please use COLOMBIA (PERU) as your point of reference when making your judgments. Please click on the option (strongly agree, mostly agree, etc) that best corresponds to your opinion on each of statements provided below.

	Strongly agree	Mostly agree	Mostly disagree	Strongly disagree	Not sure/ No position
The efficient market hypothesis (i. e., prices can be regarded as optimal estimates of true investment value at all times) applies to the international capital market.					
Government restrictions of international capital movements should be abolished.					
Capital controls make no sense because alternative instruments are always more effective for achieving the same goals.					
Capital controls make no sense because they can be easily circumvented by financial agents.					
Capital controls are essential for the preservation of national economic autonomy.					
Market mechanisms, not government intervention, should determine capital flows.					
Capital controls are redundant under a floating exchange rate system.					
Restrictions on short-term portfolio capital flows are essential to address international capital market volatility.					
Restrictions on long-term capital flows (FDI, equity) are essential to foster domestic welfare.					
Quantitative restrictions, e. g., caps on foreign investment, are essential for the stabilization of the domestic economy.					
Price-based restrictions, e. g., an implicit tax on capital inflows, are essential for the stabilization of the domestic economy.					
Prudential regulations are indispensable for the stability of the domestic financial system.					
Capital controls can be easily disguised as prudential regulations.					

3 View on capital controls immediately after graduation abroad

This section asks for your view on capital controls at the time when you received your professional degree ABROAD.

Please use COLOMBIA (PERU) as your point of reference when making your judgments. Please click on the option (strongly agreed, mostly agreed, etc.) that best corresponded to your opinion on each of the statements provided below at the time of receiving your professional degree abroad.

	Strongly agree	Mostly agree	Mostly disagree	Strongly disagree	Not sure/ No position
The efficient market hypothesis (i. e., prices can be regarded as optimal estimates of true investment value at all times) applies to the international capital market.					
Government restrictions of international capital movements should be abolished.					
Capital controls make no sense because alternative instruments are always more effective for achieving the same goals.					
Capital controls make no sense because they can be easily circumvented by financial agents.					
Capital controls are essential for the preservation of national economic autonomy.					
Market mechanisms, not government intervention, should determine capital flows.					
Capital controls are redundant under a floating exchange rate system.					
Restrictions on short-term portfolio capital flows are essential to address international capital market volatility.					
Restrictions on long-term capital flows (FDI, equity) are essential to foster domestic welfare.					
Quantitative restrictions, e. g., caps on foreign investment, are essential for the stabilization of the domestic economy.					
Price-based restrictions, e. g., an implicit tax on capital inflows, are essential for the stabilization of the domestic economy.					
Prudential regulations are indispensable for the stability of the domestic financial system.					
Capital controls can be easily disguised as prudential regulations.					

4 Determinants of your view on capital controls

This section asks for the origins of your view on capital controls TODAY. Please click on the option (strong influence, moderate influence, etc.) that best describes the influence of the factors listed below on your view on capital controls today.

	Strong influence	Moderate influence	Little influence	No influence
University studies abroad				
View of the IMF				
Current state of research				
Domestic economic context				
Experiences of other countries				
Position of domestic business groups				
Other				

If 'Other', please explain.

5 Influence on political decision-making process

This section asks for the positions from where you influence or influenced capital account policy in Colombia (Peru). Please click on the option/s (you can choose more than one) that best describe the position/s from which you are/were able to shape capital account policy in Colombia (Peru).

- Political executive (government, Central Bank)
- Political legislature (Congress, Senate)
- Advisory position (think tank, business group)
- Academia
- Political commentator in media
- No position of influence
- Other (please specify)

Have you attended courses on Capital Account Management?

- No
- Yes, offered by the IMF (in Washington or elsewhere)
- Yes, offered by: (Please indicate course provider)

References

Abdelal, Rawi (2001) *National Purpose in the World Economy: Post-Soviet States in Comparative Perspective*. Ithaca and London: Cornell University Press.

Abdelal, Rawi (2007) *Capital Rules. The Construction of Global Finance*. Cambridge, MA and London: Harvard University Press.

Abdelal, Rawi (2009) "Constructivism as an approach to international political economy", in: Mark Blyth, ed., *Routledge Handbook of International Political Economy (IPE). IPE as a Global Conversation*. Abingdon and New York: Routledge, pp. 62–76.

Abdelal, Rawi, Yoshiko M. Herrera, Alastair Ian Johnston, and Rose McDermott (2006) "Identity as a Variable". *Perspectives on Politics* 4(4): 695–711.

Abdelal, Rawi, Mark Blyth, and Craig Parsons (2010) *Constructing the International Economy*. Ithaca and London: Cornell University Press.

Abugattás, Luis A. (1999) *Estabilización macroeconómica, reforma structural y comportamiento industrial: la experiencia peruana*. Serie Reformas Económicas no. 48, Santiago de Chile: Naciones Unidas, CEPAL.

Abusada, Roberto (2000) "La reincorporación del Perú a la comunidad financiera internacional", in: Roberto Abusada, Fritz Du Bois, Eduardo Morón, and José Valderrama, eds., *La Reforma Incompleta: Rescatando los Noventa*. Lima: Universidad del Pacifico and Instituto Peruano de Economía, pp. 121–161.

Abusada, Roberto, Fritz Du Bois, Eduardo Morón, and José Valderrama (2000), eds., *La Reforma Incompleta: Rescatando los Noventa*. Lima: Universidad del Pacifico and Instituto Peruano de Economía.

Acharya, Amitav (2004) "How Ideas Spread: Whose Norms Matter? Norm Localization and Institutional Change in Asian Regionalism". *International Organization* 58(2): 239–275.

Akerlof, George A. and Robert J. Shiller (2009) *Animal Spirits: How Human Psychology Drives the Economy, and Why It Matters for Global Capitalism*. Princeton: Princeton University Press.

Akerlof, George A. and Rachel E. Kranton (2010) *Identity Economics: How Our Identities Shape Our Work, Wages, and Well-Being*. Princeton: Princeton University Press.

Alesina, Alberto, Vittorio Grilli, and Gian Maria Milesi-Ferretti (1994) "The Political Economy of Capital Controls", in: Leonardo Leiderman and Assaf Razin, eds., *Capital Mobility. The Impact on Consumption, Investment and Growth*. Cambridge: Cambridge University Press, pp. 289–321.

Andrews, David (1994) "Capital Mobility and State Autonomy: Toward a Structural Theory of International Monetary Relations". *International Studies Quarterly* 38(2): 193–218.

Arango, Gilberto (2005) *Estructura Económica Colombiana*, 10th ed., Bogotá: McGraw-Hill.

Arce, Moisés (2003) "The Sustainability of Economic Reform in a Most Likely Case: Peru". *Comparative Politics*, Vol. 35, No. 3, pp. 335–354.

Arce, Moisés (2005) *Market Reform in Society. Post-Crisis Politics and Economic Change in Authoritarian Peru*. University Park: Pennsylvania State University Press.

Aslanbeigui, Nahid and Verónica Montecinos (1998) "Foreign Students in US Doctoral Programs". *Journal of Economic Perspectives* 12(3): 171–182.

Babb, Sarah L. (2001) *Managing Mexico: Economists from Nationalism to Neoliberalism*. Princeton: Princeton University Press.

Bhagwati, Jagdish (1998) "The Capital Myth: The Difference between Trade in Widgets and Dollars". *Foreign Affairs* 77(3): 7–12.

Bhagwati, Jagdish and Daniel Tarullo (2003) "A Ban on Capital Controls Is a Bad Trade-off", *Financial Times*, March 17.

Barnett, Michael and Martha Finnemore (2004) *Rules for the World: International Organizations in Global Politics*. Ithaca and London: Cornell University Press.

Bartolini, Leonardo and Allan Drazen (1997) "Capital-Account Liberalization as a Signal". *American Economic Review* 87(1): 138–154.

Bates, Robert H. (1993) "Comment", in: John Williamson, ed., *The Political Economy of Policy Reform*. Washington: Institute for International Economics, pp. 29–34.

Bates, Robert H. (1997) *Open-Economy Politics. The Political Economy of the World Coffee Trade*. Princeton; N. J.: Princeton University Press.

Béland, Daniel and Robert Henry Cox (2010), eds., *Ideas and Politics in Social Science Research*. Oxford: Oxford University Press.

Bennett, Andrew (2008) "Process Tracing: A Bayesian Perspective", in: Janet M. Box-Steffensmeier, Henry E. Brady, and David Collier, eds., *The Oxford Handbook of Political Methodology*. Oxford: Oxford University Press, pp. 702–721.

Berman, Sheri (1998) *The Social Democratic Moment: Ideas and Politics in the Making of Interwar Europe*. Cambridge, Mass.: Harvard University Press.

Best, Jacqueline (2004) "Hollowing out Keynesian norms: how the search for a technical fix undermined the Bretton Woods regime". *Review of International Studies* 30(3): 383–404.

Biglaiser, Glen (2002a) *Guardians of the Nation? Economists, Generals, and Economic Reform in Latin America*. Notre Dame: University of Notre Dame Press.

Biglaiser, Glen (2002b) "The Internationalization of Chicago's Economics in Latin America". *Economic Development and Culture Change* 50(2): 269–286.

Bird, Graham (2003) *International Finance and the Developing Economies*. Basingstoke: Palgrave.

Blyth, Mark M. (1997) '"Any More Bright Ideas?' The Ideational Turn of Comparative Political Economy". *Comparative Politics* 29(2): 229–250.

Blyth, Mark (2002), *Great Transformations: Economic Ideas and Institutional Change in the Twentieth Century*. Cambridge: Cambridge University Press.

Blyth, Mark (2003) "Structures Do Not Come with an Instruction Sheet: Interests, Ideas, and Progress in Political Science". *Perspectives on Politics* 1(4): 695–706.

Blyth, Mark (2009) "An Approach to Comparative Politics or a Subfield Within a Subfield? Political Economy", in: Mark Irving Lichbach and Alan S. Zuckerman, eds., *Comparative Politics. Rationality, Culture, and Structure*. 2nd ed., Cambridge: Cambridge University Press, pp. 193–219.

Blustein, Paul (2005) *And the Money Kept Rolling In (and Out): Wall Street, the IMF, and the Bankrupting of Argentina*. New York: PublicAffairs.

Boas, Taylor C. and Jordan Gans-Morse (2009) "Neoliberalism: From New Liberal Philosophy to Anti-Liberal Slogan". *Studies in Comparative International Development* 44(2): 137–161.

Boloña, Carlos (1996) "The Viability of Alberto Fujimori's Economic Strategy", in: Efraín Gonzales de Olarte, ed., *The Peruvian Economy and Structural Adjustment: Past, Present and Future*. Miami: University of Miami North-South Center Press, pp. 183–264.

Botero, Rodrigo (2005) "Una nota sobre la tecnocracia colombiana". *Coyuntura Económica* 35(2): 17–24.

Botero, Rodrigo (2011) Una Nota Crítica Acerca del Crecimiento Colombiano, transcript of presentation delivered at the LXVII Congress of the Colombian Industrialists Association (ANDI), Cartagena, August 11, 2011; available at: http://www.andi.com.co/Archivos/2011/Notificacion/Botero_Rodrigo_ANDI2011_20110822_070206.pdf (accessed December 23, 2011).

Boughton, James M. (2001) *Silent Revolution. The International Monetary Fund, 1979–1989*. Washington, D. C.: International Monetary Fund.

Brady, Henry E. and David Collier (2004), eds., *Rethinking Social Inquiry: Diverse Tools, Shared Standards*. Lanham: Rowman & Littlefield.

Broome, André (2010) *The Currency of Power. The IMF and Monetary Reform in Central Asia.* Basingstoke: Palgrave Macmillan.

Brooks, Sarah M. (2004) "Explaining Capital Account Liberalization in Latin America. A Transitional Cost Approach". *World Politics* 56(3): 389–430.

Brooks, Sarah M. and Marcus J. Kurtz (2007) "Capital, Trade, and the Political Economies of Reform". *American Journal of Political Science* 51(4): 703–720.

Brooks, Sarah M. and Marcus J. Kurtz (2012) "Paths to Financial Policy Diffusion: Statist Legacies in Latin America's Globalization". *International Organization* 66(1): 95–128.

Brune, Nancy (2006) Financial Liberalization and Governance in the Developing World. Ph.D. Book, Department of Political Science, Yale University.

Brune, Nancy and Alexandra Guisinger (2003) The Diffusion of Capital Account Liberalization in Developing Countries. Paper presented at the Annual Meeting of the American Political Science Association, August 28–31.

Brune, Nancy E. and Alexandra Guisinger (2007) Myth or Reality? The Diffusion of Financial Liberalization in Developing Countries. Mimeo.

Brune, Nancy E. and Alexandra Gibbons Guisinger (2009) Unpacking the Black Box: The Diffusion of Financial Liberalization Across Regional Integration Agreements (RIAs) in Developing Countries. Mimeo.

Campbell, John L. (2002) "Ideas, Politics, and Public Policy". *Annual Review of Sociology* 28: 21–38.

Capoccia, Giovanni and R. Daniel Kelemen (2007) "The Study of Critical Junctures: Theory, Narrative, and Counterfactuals in Historical Institutionalism". *World Politics* 59(3): 341–369.

Caporaso, James (2009) "Is there a quantitative-qualitative divide in comparative politics? The case of process tracing", in: Todd Landman and Neil Robinson, eds., *The SAGE Handbook of Comparative Politics*. London: SAGE, pp. 67–83.

Cárdenas, Mauricio (2009) *Introducción a la Economía Colombiana.* 2ª ed., Bogotá: Fedesarrollo and Alfaomega.

Cárdenas, Mauricio and Felipe Barrera (1997) "On the effectiveness of capital controls: the experience of Colombia during the 1990s". *Journal of Development Economics* 54(1): 27–57.

Cassidy, John (2009) *How Markets Fail: The Logic of Economic Calamities*. New York: Farrar, Straus and Giroux.

Centeno, Miguel A. and Patricio Silva (1998), eds., *The Politics of Expertise in Latin America.* Houndsmills: Macmillan.

Checkel, Jeffrey T. (1998) "The Constructivist Turn in International Relations Theory (A Review Essay)". *World Politics* 50(2): 324–348.

Checkel, Jeffrey T. (1999) "Norms, Institutions, and National Identity in Contemporary Europe". *International Studies Quarterly* 43(1): 84–114.

Chinn, Menzie D. and Hiro Ito (2008) "A New Measure of Financial Openness". *Journal of Comparative Policy Analysis* 10(3): 309–322.

Chwieroth, Jeffrey M. (2005) US Policy, IMF Financing Arrangements, and the Coercive Diffusion of Capital Account Liberalization to Emerging Markets. Robert Schuman Centre. EUI Working Paper RSCAS No. 2005/06.

Chwieroth, Jeffrey M. (2006) Cheerleading for Liberalization: The International Monetary Fund and Financial Globalization in Emerging Markets. Paper presented at the annual meeting of the American Political Science Association, Philadelphia, PA, Aug 31, 2006.

Chwieroth, Jeffrey (2007) "Neoliberal Economists and Capital Account Liberalization in Emerging Markets". *International Organization* 61(2): 443–463.

Chwieroth, Jeffrey M. (2010a) *Capital Ideas: The IMF and the Rise of Financial Liberalization*. Princeton: Princeton University Press.

Chwieroth, Jeffrey M. (2010b) "How Do Crises Lead to Change?: Liberalizing Capital Controls in the Early Years of New Order Indonesia". *World Politics* 62(3): 496–527.

Chwieroth, Jeffrey M. and Timothy J. Sinclair (2008) International Capital Mobility As a Social Fact: How You Stand Depends On How We See. Paper prepared for the Annual Meeting of the American Political Science Association, Boston, August 28–31.

Chwieroth, Jeffrey M., Alexander Hicks, and Diogo Pinheiro (2009) The New Institutionalism and Economic Globalization: The Case of Capital Account Liberalization in Latin America. Mimeo.

Clements, Benedict and Herman Kamil (2009) Are Capital Controls Effective in the 21st Century? The Recent Experience of Colombia. IMF Working Paper WP/09/30, Washington, D. C.: International Monetary Fund.

Coelho, Bruno and Kevin P. Gallagher (2010) Capital Controls and 21st Century Financial Crises: Evidence from Colombia and Thailand. PERI Working Paper No. 213, University of Massachusetts Amherst.

Cohen, Benjamin J. (1996) "Phoenix Risen: The Resurrection of Global Finance". *World Politics* 48(2): 268–296.

Cohen, Benjamin J. (2002) "International Finance", in: Walter Carlsnaes, Thomas Risse, and Beth A. Simmons, eds., *Handbook of International Relations*. London: SAGE, pp. 429–447.

Cohen, Alvin and Frank R. Gunter (1992) *The Colombian Economy. Issues of Trade and Development*. Boulder: Westview Press.

Colander, David (2007) *The Making of an Economist, Redux*. Princeton: Princeton University Press.

Conaghan, Catherine M. (1998) "Stars of the Crisis: The Ascent of Economists in Peruvian Public Life", in: Miguel Centeno and Patricio Silva, eds., *The Politics of Expertise in Latin America*, London: Macmillan, pp. 142–164.

Conaghan, Catherine M. (2005) *Fujimori's Peru: Deception in the Public Sphere*. Pittsburgh: University of Pittsburgh Press.

Conaghan, Catherine M. (2006) "The Immoral Economy of Fujimorismo", in: Julio F. Carrión, ed., *The Fujimori Legacy. The Rise of Electoral Authoritarianism in Peru*. University Park: The Pennsylvania State University Press 2006, pp. 102–125.

Concha, Álvaro and Arturo José Galindo (2009) An Assessment of Another Decade of Capital Controls in Colombia: 1998–2008. Washington, D. C.: Inter-American Development Bank.

Copelovitch, Mark S. (2010) "Master or Servant? Common Agency and the Political Economy of IMF Lending". *International Studies Quarterly* 54(1): 49–77.

Cortázar, Juan Carlos (2006) *La Reforma de la Administración Pública Peruana (1990–97)*. Lima: Instituto de Políticas Sociales.

Cortell, Andrew P. and James W. Davis, Jr. (1996) "How Do International Institutions Matter? The Domestic Impact of International Rules and Norms". *International Studies Quarterly* 40(4): 451–478.

Cortell, Andrew P. and James W. Davis, Jr. (2000) "Understanding the Domestic Impact of International Norms: A Research Agenda". *International Studies Review* 2(1): 65–87.

Cotler, Julio (1998a) *Los empresarios y las reformas económicas en el Perú*. Documento de trabajo no. 91, Lima: Instituto de Estudios Peruanos.

Cotler, Julio (1998b) *La articulación y los mecanismos de representación de las organizaciones empresariales*. Documento de trabajo no. 97, Lima: Instituto de Estudios Peruanos.

Cowan, Kevin and José de Gregorio (2007) "International Borrowing, Capital Controls, and the Exchange Rate: Lessons from Chile", in: Sebastian Edwards, ed., *Capital Controls and Capital Flows in Emerging Economies: Policies, Practices, and Consequences*. Chicago and London: University of Chicago Press, pp. 241–296.

Crystal, Jonathan (2003) "What Do Producers Want? On the Origins of Societal Policy Preferences". *European Journal of International Relations* 9(3): 407–439.
Crabtree, John (1992) *Peru under García. An Opportunity Lost*. Pittsburgh: University of Pittsburgh Press.
Currie, Lauchlin (1981) The *Role of Economic Advisers in Developing Countries*. Westport, Conn.: Greenwood Press.
Darden, Keith A. (2009) *Economic Liberalism and Its Rivals. The Formation of International Institutions among the Post Soviet States*. Cambridge: Cambridge University Press.
Dargent, Eduardo (2011) "Agents or Actors? Assessing the Autonomy of Economic Technocrats in Colombia and Peru". *Comparative Politics* 43(3): 313–332.
David, Antonio (2007) Are Price-Based Capital Account Regulations Effective in Developing Countries? World Bank Policy Research Paper Working Paper No. 4175, Washington, D.C.: World Bank.
Deeg, Richard and Mary A. O'Sullivan (2009) "The Political Economy of Global Financial Capital". *World Politics* 61(4): 731–63.
Denzau, Arthur T. and Douglass C. North (2000) "Shared Mental Models: Ideologies and Institutions", in: Arthur Lupia, Mathew D. McCubbins, and Samuel L. Popkin, eds., *Elements of Reason. Cognition, Choice, and the Bounds of Rationality*, Cambridge: Cambridge University Press, pp. 23–46.
Dezalay, Yves and Bryant G. Garth (2002) *The Internationalization of Palace Wars. Lawyers, Economists, and the Contest to Transform Latin American States*. Chicago and London: University of Chicago Press.
Díaz-Alejandro, Carlos (1985) "Good-be financial repression, hello financial crash". *Journal of Development Economics* 19(1-2): 1–24.
DiMaggio, Paul J. and Walter W. Powell (1983) "The Iron Cage Revisited: Institutional Isomorphism and Collective Rationality in Organizational Fields". *American Sociological Review* 48(2): 147–160.
Dobbin, Frank, (2004), ed., *The New Economic Sociology: A Reader*. Princeton: Princeton University Press.
Dollar, David and Jakob Svensson (2000) "What explains the success or failure of structural adjustment programmes?". *The Economic Journal* 110: E894–917.
Domínguez, Jorge I. (1997) "Technopols: Ideas and Leaders in Freeing Politics and Markets in Latin America in the 1990s", in: Jorge Domínguez, ed., *Technopols: Freeing Politics and Markets in Latin America in the 1990s*. University Park: Pennsylvania State University Press, pp. 1–48.
Dominguez, Kathryn M. E. and Linda L. Tesar (2007) "International Borrowing and Macroeconomic Performance in Argentina", in: Sebastian Edwards, ed., *Capital Controls and Capital Flows in Emerging Economies: Policies, Practices, and Consequences*. Chicago and London: University of Chicago Press, pp. 297–342.
Dosman, Edgar J. (2008) *The Life and Times of Raúl Prebisch, 1901–1986*. Montreal and Kingston: McGill-Queen's University Press.
Drake, Paul W. (2005) "The Hegemony of US Economic Doctrines in Latin America", in: Valpy FitzGerald and Rosemary Thorp, eds., *Economic Doctrines in Latin America. Origins, Embedding and Evolution*. Houndmills: Palgrave, pp. 72–96.
Dreher, Axel, Jan-Egbert Sturm, and James Raymond Vreeland (2009) "Global horse trading: IMF loans for votes in the United Nations Security Council". *European Economic Review* 53(7): 742–757.
Durand, Francisco (2002) "Business and the Crisis of Peruvian Democracy". *Business and Politics* 4(3): 319–341.
Durand, Francisco (2004) *El Poder Incierto: Trayectoria Económica y Política del Empresariado Peruano*. Lima: Fondo Editorial del Congreso del Perú.
Durand, Francisco (2010) *La Mano Invisible en el Estado: Crítica a los Neoliberales Criollos*. Lima: Fondo Editorial del Pedagógico San Marcos.

Eatwell, John and Lance Taylor (2001) *Global Finance at Risk: The Case for International Regulation.* New York: New Press.

Echeverry, Juan Carlos, Jaime Navas, Verónica Navas, and María Paula Gómez (2009) Oil in Colombia: History, Regulation and Macroeconomic Impact. Documentos CEDE 2009–10, Universidad de los Andes, Facultad de Economía, CEDE, Bogotá.

Edison, Hali J. and Francis E. Warnock (2003) "A simple measure of the intensity of capital controls". *Journal of Empirical Finance* 10(1/2): 81–103.

Edison, Hali J., Michael W. Klein, Luca Antonio Ricci, and Torsten Sløk (2004) "Capital Account Liberalization and Economic Performance: Survey and Synthesis". *IMF Staff Papers* 51(2): 220–256.

Edwards, Sebastian (2001) *The Economics and Politics of Transition to an Open Market Economy: Colombia.* Paris: Development Centre of the Organisation for Economic Co-operation and Development.

Edwards, Sebastian (2007) "Capital Controls, Sudden Stops, and Current Account Reversals", in: Sebastian Edwards, ed., *Capital Controls and Capital Flows in Emerging Economies.* Chicago and London: University of Chicago Press, pp. 73–119.

Eichengreen, Barry (1996) *Globalizing Capital. A History of the International Monetary System.* Princeton: Princeton University Press.

Eichengreen, Barry (2001) "Capital Account Liberalization: What Do Cross-Country Studies Tell Us?". *World Bank Economic Review* 15(3): 341–366.

Eichengreen, Barry (2008) *Globalizing Capital. A History of the International Monetary System.* 2nd ed., Princeton: Princeton University Press.

Eichengreen, Barry and Michael Mussa with Staff Team (1998) Capital Account Liberalization. Theoretical and Practical Aspects. Occasional Paper 172. Washington, D. C.: International Monetary Fund.

Epstein, Rachel A. (2006) "Cultivating Consensus and Creating Conflict. International Institutions and the (De)Politicization of Economic Policy in Postcommunist Europe". *Comparative Political Studies* 39(8): 1019–1042.

Estrada Álvarez, Jairo (2004) *Construcción del Modelo neoliberal en Colombia 1970–2004.* Bogotá: Ediciones Aurora.

Estrada Álvarez, Jairo (2005a), ed., *Intelectuales, tecnócratas y reformas neoliberales en América Latina,* Bogotá: Universidad Nacional de Colombia.

Estrada Álvarez, Jairo (2005b) "Élites intelectuales y producción de política económica en Colombia", in: Jairo Estrada Álvarez, ed., *Intelectuales, tecnócratas y reformas neoliberales en América Latina,* Bogotá: Universidad Nacional de Colombia 2005, pp. 259–320.

Evans, Peter B. (1979) *Dependent Development: The Alliance of Multinational, State and Local Capital in Brazil.* Princeton: Princeton University Press.

Fearon, James and Alexander Wendt (2002) "Rationalism *v.* Constructivism: A Skeptical View", in: Walter Carlsnaes, Thomas Risse, and Beth A. Simmons, eds., *Handbook of International Relations.* London: SAGE, pp. 52–72.

Feldstein, Martin and Charles Horioka (1980) "Domestic Saving and International Capital Flows". *Economic Journal* 90(358): 314–329.

Ferejohn, John (1991) "Rationality and Interpretation", in: Kirsten Monroe, ed., *The Economic Approach to Politics.* New York: HarperCollins, pp. 279–305.

Fernández Jilberto, Alex E. and Barbara Hogenboom (2007a) "Latin American conglomerates in the neoliberal era: the politics of economic concentration in Chile and Mexico", in: Alex E. Fernández Jilberto and Barbara Hogenboom, eds., *Big Business and Economic Development. Conglomerates and Economic Groups in Developing Countries and Transition Economies under Globalisation,* Abingdon and New York: Routledge, pp. 135–166.

Fernández Jilberto, Alex E. and Barbara Hogenboom (2007b) "The new expansion of conglomerates and economic groups: an introduction to global neoliberalisation and local power shifts", in: Alex E. Fernández Jilberto and Barbara Hogenboom, eds., *Big Business and Economic Development. Conglomerates and Economic Groups in Developing Countries and Transition Economies under Globalisation*, Abingdon and New York: Routledge, pp. 1–28.

Ffrench-Davis, Ricardo and Stephany Griffith-Jones (1995), eds., *Coping with Capital Surges: The Return of Finance to Latin America.* Boulder: Lynne Rienner.

Finnemore, Martha (1993) "International Organizations as Teachers of Norms: The United Nations Education, Scientific and Cultural Organization and Science Policy". *International Organization* 47(4): 565–597.

Finnemore, Martha (1996a) "Norms, Culture, and World Politics: Insights from Sociology's Institutionalism". *International Organization* 50(4): 325–347.

Finnemore, Martha (1996b) *National Interests in International Society*. Ithaca and London: Cornell University Press.

Finnemore, Martha and Kathryn Sikkink (1999), "International Norm Dynamics and Political Change", in: Peter J. Katzenstein, Robert O. Keohane, and Stephen Krasner, eds., *Exploration and Contestation in the Study of World Politics*. Cambridge, MA and London: MIT Press, pp. 247–277.

Fischer, Stanley (1997) Capital Account Liberalization and the Role of the IMF, Paper presented at the IMF's Seminar on Asia and the IMF, Hong Kong, 19 September. Washington, D. C.: International Monetary Fund.

FitzGerald, Valpy (2005) "The Conflict of Economic Doctrines in Latin America", in: Valpy FitzGerald and Rosemary Thorp, eds., *Economic Doctrines in Latin America. Origins, Embedding and Evolution*. Houndmills: Palgrave, pp. 97–114.

Flandreau, Marc, Carl-Ludwig Holtfrerich, and Harold James (2003) *International Financial History in the Twentieth Century: System and Anarchy*. Cambridge: Cambridge University Press.

Flórez Enciso, Luis Bernardo (2009) "Colombia: Economics, Economic Policy and Economists", in: Verónica Montecinos and John Markoff, eds., *Economists in the Americas*. Cheltenham: Edward Elgar, pp. 195–226.

Fourcade, Marion (2009) *Economist and Societies. Discipline and Profession in the United States, Britain and France, 1890s to 1990s*. Princeton and Oxford: Princeton University Press.

Fourcade-Gourinchas, Marion and Sarah L. Babb (2002) "The Rebirth of the Liberal Creed: Paths to Neoliberalism in Four Countries". *American Journal of Sociology* 108(3): 533–579.

Frankel, Jeffrey A. (1993) "Quantifying International Capital Mobility in the 1980s", in: Dilip K. Das, ed., *International Finance: Contemporary Issues*. London and New York: Routledge, pp. 27–53.

Frenkel, Roberto and Martín Rapetti (2007) Argentina's Monetary and Exchange Rate Policies After the Convertibility Regime Collapse. Washington, D. C.: Center for Economic and Policy Research.

Frenkel, Roberto and Martín Rapetti (2010) A Concise History of Exchange Rate Regimes in Latin America. Washington, D. C.: Center for Economic and Policy Research.

Frieden, Jeffry A. (1991) "Invested interests: the politics of national economic policies in a world of global finance". *International Organization* 45(4): 425–451.

Frieden, Jeffry A. (1999) "Actors and Preferences in International Relations", in: David Lake and Robert Powell, eds., *Strategic Choice and International Relations*. Princeton: Princeton University Press, pp. 39–76.

Frieden, Jeffry A. (2006) *Global Capitalism: Its Fall and Rise in the Twentieth Century*. New York: W. W. Norton.

Frieden, Jeffry A. and Ronald Rogowski (1996) "The Impact of the International Economy on National Policies: An Analytical Overview", in: Robert O. Keohane and Helen V. Milner, eds., *Internationalization and Domestic Politics*. Cambridge: Cambridge University Press, pp. 25–47.

Garay Salamanca, Luis Jorge, Alfredo Angulo Sanabria, and Claudia Cadena Silva (1994) *Cultura de Negociación. La Experiencia de la Deuda Externa*. Bogotá: FESCOL.

Garrett, Geoffrey and Peter Lange (1996) "Internationalization, Institutions, and Political Change", in: Robert O. Keohane and Helen Milner, eds., *Internationalization and Domestic Politics*. Cambridge: Cambridge University Press, pp. 48–78.

Gaviria, César (1990) Inauguration speech as Colombian president, Bogotá, August 7, published in: *El Espectador*, August 8.

Geddes, Barbara (2003) *Paradigms and Sand Castles. Theory Building and Research Design in Comparative Politics*. Ann Arbor: The University of Michigan Press.

George, Alexander L. and Andrew Bennett (2005) *Case Studies and Theory Development in the Social Sciences*. Cambridge, MA and London: MIT Press.

Gerring, John (2007) *Case Study Research: Principles and Practices*. Cambridge: Cambridge University Press.

Gerring, John (2008) "Case Selection for Case-Study Analysis: Qualitative and Quantitative Techniques", in: Janet M. Box-Steffensmeier, Henry E. Brady, and David Collier, eds., *The Oxford Handbook of Political Methodology*. Oxford: Oxford University Press, pp. 645–684.

Giacalone, Rita (1997) "Asociaciones empresariales, integración y Estado: Colombia y Venezuela". *Nueva Sociedad* 151: 155–167.

Gill, Stephen R. (1995) "Globalisation, Market Civilisation and Disciplinary Neoliberalism". *Millennium* 24(3): 399–423.

Goldfajn, Illan and André Minella (2007) "Capital Flows and Controls in Brazil: What Have We Learned?", in: Sebastian Edwards, ed., *Capital Controls and Capital Flows in Emerging Economies: Policies, Practices, and Consequences*. Chicago and London: University of Chicago Press, pp. 349–419.

Goldstein, Judith (1993) *Ideas, Interests, and US Trade Policy*, Ithaca and London: Cornell University Press.

Goldstein, Judith and Robert O. Keohane (1993) "Ideas and Foreign Policy: An Analytical Framework", in: Judith Goldstein and Robert O. Keohane, eds., *Ideas and Foreign Policy: Beliefs, Institutions and Political Change*. Ithaca and London: Cornell University Press, pp. 3–30.

Gómez-Mera, Laura (2011) "Markets, Politics, and Learning: Explaining Monetary Policy Innovations in Brazil". *Studies in Comparative International Development* 46(3): 243–269.

Gonzales de Olarte, Efraín (1998) *El Neoliberalismo a la Peruana: Economía Política del Ajuste Estructural, 1990–1997*. Lima: Instituto de Estudios Peruanos.

Gonzales de Olarte, Efraín and Lilian Samamé (1991) *El Péndulo Peruano*. Lima: Instituto de Estudios Peruanos and Consorcio de Investigación Económica.

Goodman, John B. and Louis W. Pauly (1993) "The Obsolescence of Capital Controls?: Economic Management in an Age of Global Markets". *World Politics* 46(1): 50–82.

Gottschalk, Ricardo (2000) Sequencing Trade and Capital Account Liberalization: The Experience of Brazil in the 1990s, Occasional Paper, UNCTAD/UNDP, UNCTAD/EDM/Misc. 132.

Gourevitch, Peter A. (1978) "The Second Image Reversed: International Sources of Domestic Politics". *International Organization* 32(4): 881–911.

Gourevitch, Peter A. (2005) "Economic Ideas, International Influences and Domestic Politics: A Comparative Perspective", in: Valpy FitzGerald and Rosemary Thorp, eds., *Economic Doctrines in Latin America. Origins, Embedding and Evolution*. Houndmills: Palgrave, pp. 23–47.

Grabel, Ilene (2003) "Averting Crisis? Assessing Measures to Manage Financial Integration in Emerging Economies". *Cambridge Journal of Economics* 27(3): 317–336.

Granovetter, Mark (1985) "Economic Action and Social Structure: The Problem of Embeddedness". *American Journal of Sociology* 91(3): 481–510.

Granovetter, Mark (2005) "The Impact of Social Structure on Economic Outcomes". *Journal of Economic Perspectives* 19(1): 33–50.

Grilli, Vittorio and Gian Maria Milesi-Ferretti (1995) "Economic Effects and Structural Determinants of Capital Controls". *IMF Staff Papers* 42(3): 517–551.

Grindle, Merilee S. (1977) "Power, Expertise and the 'Técnico': Suggestions from a Mexican Case Study". *The Journal of Politics* 39(2): 399–426.

Grindle, Merilee S. and John W. Thomas (1991) *Public Choices and Policy Changes: The Political Economy of Reform in Developing Countries.* Baltimore and London: The Johns Hopkins University Press.

Grosse, Robert (1992) "Colombia's Black Market in Foreign Exchange". *World Development* 20(8): 1193–1207.

Guitián, Manuel (1995) "Capital account liberalization: bringing policy in line with reality", in: Sebastian Edwards, ed., *Capital Controls, Exchange Rates and Monetary Policy in the World Economy.* Cambridge: Cambridge University Press, pp. 71–90.

Haas, Peter M. (1992) "Introduction: Epistemic Communities and International Policy Coordination". *International Organization* 46(1): 1–35.

Haas, Peter M. (2001) "Policy Knowledge: Epistemic Communities", in: Neil J. Smelser and Paul B. Baltes, eds., *International Encyclopedia of the Social & Behavioral Sciences.* Vol. 17, Amsterdam: Elsevier Science, pp. 11578–11586.

Haggard, Stephan (1986) "The Politics of Adjustment: Lessons from the IMF's Extended Fund Facility", in: Miles Kahler, ed., *The Politics of International Debt.* Ithaca and London: Cornell University Press, pp. 157–186.

Haggard, Stephan and Steven B. Webb (1993) "What Do We Know about the Political Economy of Economic Policy Reform?". *The World Bank Research Observer* 8(2): 143–168.

Haggard, Stephan and Steven B. Webb (1994), eds., *Voting for Reform: Democracy, Political Liberalization, and Economic Adjustment.* Oxford: Oxford University Press.

Haggard, Stephan and Robert R. Kaufman (1995) *The Political Economy of Democratic Transitions.* Princeton: Princeton University Press.

Haggard, Stephan and Sylvia Maxfield (1996) "The Political Economy of Financial Internationalization in the Developing World". *International Organization* 50(1): 35–68.

Haggard, Stephan and Mathew D. McCubbins (2001), eds., *Presidents, Parliaments, and Policy.* Cambridge: Cambridge University Press.

Hall, Peter A. (1989) "The Politics of Keynesian Ideas", in: Peter A. Hall, ed., *The Political Power of Economic Ideas: Keynesianism across Nations.* Princeton: Princeton University Press, pp. 361–389.

Hall, Peter A. (1993) "Policy Paradigms, Social Learning, and the State: The Case of Economic Policymaking in Britain". *Comparative Politics* 25(3): 275–296.

Hall, Peter A. (1997) "The Role of Interests, Institutions, and Ideas in the Comparative Political Economy of the Industrialized Nations", in: Mark Irving Lichbach and Alan S. Zuckerman, eds., *Comparative Politics. Rationality, Culture, and Structure.* Cambridge: Cambridge University Press, pp. 174–207.

Hall, Rodney Bruce (2003) "The Discursive Demolition of the Asian Development Model". *International Studies Quarterly* 47(1): 71–99.

Hartlyn, Jonathan (1985) "Producer Associations, the Political Regime, and Policy Processes in Contemporary Colombia". *Latin American Research Review* 20(3): 111–138.

Hartlyn, Jonathan (1988) *The Politics of Coalition Rule in Colombia.* Cambridge: Cambridge University Press.

Hay, Colin (2006) "Constructivist institutionalism", in: R.A.W. Rhodes, Sarah A. Binder, and Bert A. Rockman, eds., *The Oxford Handbook of Political Institutions*. Oxford: Oxford University Press, pp. 56–74.

Helmke, Gretchen and Steven Levitsky (2004) "Informal Institutions and Comparative Politics: A Research Agenda". *Perspectives on Politics* 2(4): 725–740.

Helmke, Gretchen and Steven Levitsky (2006a), eds., *Informal Institutions and Democracy: Lessons from Latin America*. Baltimore: The Johns Hopkins University Press.

Helmke, Gretchen and Steven Levitsky (2006b) "Introduction", in: Gretchen Helmke and Steven Levitsky, eds., *Informal Institutions and Democracy: Lessons from Latin America*. Baltimore: The Johns Hopkins University Press, pp. 1–30.

Helleiner, Eric (1994) *States and the Reemergence of Global Finance*. Ithaca and London: Cornell University Press.

Hira, Anil (1998) *Ideas and Economic Policy in Latin America. Regional, National and Organizational Case Studies*. Westport: Praeger.

Hiscox, Michael J. (2001) *International Trade and Political Conflict: Commerce, Coalitions, and Mobility*. Princeton: Princeton University Press.

Hnyilicza, Esteban (2001) *De la Megainflación a la Estabilidad Monetaria. Política Monetaria y Cambiaria Perú 1990–2000*, Banco Central de Reserva del Perú: Lima.

Hommes, Rudolf (2002) "La Apertura y las Reformas Económicas", in: Alberto Baquero Nariño, ed., *Modelos de Desarrollo Económico: Colombia 1960–2002*. Bogotá: Editorial Oveja Negra, pp. 253–294.

IEO [Independent Evaluation Office] (2005) *The IMF's Approach to Capital Account Liberalization*. Washington; DC: International Monetary Fund.

Ikenberry, G. John (1990) "The International Spread of Privatization Policies: Inducements, Learning, and 'Policy Bandwagoning'", in: Ezra N. Suleiman and John Waterbury, eds., *The Political Economy of Public Sector Reform*. Boulder, Co.: Westview Press, pp. 88–109.

IMF (1993) Peru – Staff Report for the 1992 Article IV Consultation and Economic Program for 1993–95, Washington, DC, January 28.

IMF (1994) Colombia – Staff Report for the 1994 Article IV Consultation, Washington, DC, December 20.

IMF (1995) The Acting Chairman's Summing Up at the Conclusion of the 1994 Article IV Consultation with Colombia, Executive Board Meeting 95/3, Washington, DC, January 11.

IMF (1998) Peru – Staff Report for the 1998 Article IV Consultations; and Extended Arrangement – Review, and Program for Third Year, Washington, DC, May 13.

IMF (2007) World Economic Outlook, October edition. Washington, D.C.: International Monetary Fund.

IMF (2009) Initial Lessons of the Crisis, February 6. Washington, D.C.: International Monetary Fund. http://www.imf.org/external/np/pp/eng/2009/020609.pdf (accessed December 3, 2009).

IMF (2010) Peru – Selected Issues. Complement to IMF Country Report No. 10/99. Washington, D.C.: International Monetary Fund.

Jacobsen, John Kurt (1995) "Much Ado About Ideas. The Cognitive Factor in Economic Policy". *World Politics* 47(1): 283–310.

Jacobsen, John Kurt (2003) "Dueling constructivisms: a post-mortem on the ideas debate in mainstream IR/IPE". *Review of International Studies* 29(1): 39–60.

James, Harold (1995) "The Historical Development of the Principle of Surveillance". *IMF Staff Papers* 42(4): 762–792.

Jaramillo, Juan C., Roberto Steiner, and Natalia Salazar (2001) "A Long-lasting Crawling Peg: Political Determinants of Exchange Rate Policy in Colombia", in: Jeffry Frieden and Ernesto Stein, eds.,

The Currency Game. Exchange Rate Politics in Latin America. Washington, D. C.: Inter-American Development Bank, pp. 199–248.

Johnston, R. B. and Natalia T. Tamirisa (1998) Why Do Countries Use Capital Controls?. IMF Working Paper 98/181. Washington, D. C.: International Monetary Fund.

Juárez, Carlos E. (1993) *Economía Política y Apertura Económica: Desarrollo Económico y Comercio Exterior, 1967–1991*. Monografías de Administración. Serie Empresa, Economía y Sociedad No. 36. Bogotá: Universidad de los Andes.

Junguito, Roberto (1986) *Memoria del Ministro de Hacienda 1984–1985*. Bogotá: Banco de la República.

Kahler, Miles (1992) "External Influence, Conditionality, and the Politics of Adjustment", in: Stephan Haggard and Robert R. Kaufman, eds., *The Politics of Economic Adjustment. International Constraints, Distributive Conflicts, and the State*. Princeton: Princeton University Press, pp. 89–136.

Kamas, Linda (2001) "Monetary and Exchange Rate Policy in Colombia: Effects on the Real Exchange Rate in the 1990s". *Journal of Development Studies* 38(2): 131–166.

Karcher, Sebastian and David A. Steinberg (2010) Assessing the Causes of Capital Account Liberalization: How Measurement Matters. Paper prepared for presentation at the 2010 Annual Meeting of the International Studies Association, New Orleans, February 17.

Kastner, Scott L. and Chad Rector (2003) "International Regimes, Domestic Veto-Players, and Capital Controls Policy Stability". *International Studies Quarterly* 47(1): 1–22.

Kastner, Scott L. and Chad Rector (2005) "Partisanship and the Path to Financial Openness". *Comparative Political Studies* 38(5): 484–506.

Katzenstein, Peter J. (1977) "Conclusion: Domestic Structures and Strategies of Foreign Economic Policy". *International Organization* 31(4): 879–920.

Katzenstein, Peter J. (1996), ed., *The Culture of National Security: Norms and Identity in World Politics*. New York: Columbia University Press.

Katzenstein, Peter J. (2010) "'Walls' between 'Those People'? Contrasting Perspectives on World Politics". *Perspectives on Politics* 8(1): 11–25.

Kelley, Judith (2004a) "International Actors on the Domestic Scene: Membership Conditionality and Socialization by International Institutions". *International Organization* 58(3): 425–457.

Kelley, Judith (2004b) *Ethnic Politics in Europe: The Power of Norms and Incentives*. Princeton: Princeton University Press.

Keynes, John Maynard (1973) *The Collected Writings of John Maynard Keynes, Vol. VII: The General Theory of Employment, Interest, and Money*. London: Macmillan.

Killick, Tony (1995) *IMF Programmes in Developing Countries: Design and Impact*. London and New York: Routledge.

Killick, Tony (1996) "Principals, Agents and the Limitations of BWI Conditionality". *The World Economy* 19(2): 211–229.

Killick, Tony with Ramani Gunatilaka and Ana Marr (1998) *Aid and the Political Economy of Policy Change*. London and New York: Routledge.

Kingdon, John W. (1995) *Agendas, Alternatives, and Public Choices*. 2nd ed., New York: HarperCollins.

Kingstone, Peter R. (2001) "Why Free Trade 'Losers' Support Free Trade. Industrialists and the Surprising Politics of Trade Reform in Brazil". *Comparative Political Studies* 34(9): 986–1010.

Kirshner, Jonathan (2000) "The Study of Money". *World Politics* 52(3): 407–436.

Klamer, Arjo and David Colander (1990) *The Making of an Economist*. Boulder, Co.: Westview Press.

Klarén, Peter F. (2000) *Peru: Society and Nationhood in the Andes*. Oxford: Oxford University Press.

Klein, Daniel B. and Charlotta Stern (2007) "Is There a Free-Market Economist in the House? The Policy Views of American Economic Association Members". *American Journal of Economics and Sociology* 66(2): 309–334.

Kofas, Jon V. (2002) *The Sword of Damocles. US Financial Hegemony in Colombia and Chile, 1950–1970.* Westport: Praeger.

Kogut, Bruce and J. Muir Macpherson (2008) "The Decision to Privatize: Economists and the Construction of Ideas and Policies", in: Beth A. Simmons, Frank Dobbin, and Geoffrey Garrett, eds., The *Global Diffusion of Markets and Democracy.* Cambridge: Cambridge University Press, pp. 104–140.

Kose, Ayhan M., Eswar S. Prasad, Kenneth S. Rogoff, and Shang-Jin Wei (2006) Financial Globalization: A Reappraisal. IMF Working Paper No. 06/189. Washington, D. C.: International Monetary Fund.

Kose, Ayhan M., Eswar S. Prasad, and Ashley D. Taylor (2009) Thresholds in the Process of International Financial Integration, NBER Working Paper 14916. Cambridge, MA: National Bureau of Economic Research.

Krasner, Stephen D. (1993) "Westphalia and All That", in: Judith Goldstein and Robert O. Keohane, eds., *Ideas and Foreign Policy: Beliefs, Institutions, and Political Change.* Ithaca and London: Cornell University Press, pp. 235–264.

Kratochwil, Friedrich and John Gerard Ruggie (1986) "A State of the Art on an Art of the State". *International Organization* 40(4): 753–775.

Krugman, Paul R. and Maurice Obstfeld (2009) *International Economics. Theory & Policy.* 8th ed., Boston: Addison-Wesley.

Kurtz, Marcus J. and Sarah M. Brooks (2008) "Embedding Neoliberal Reform in Latin America". *World Politics* 60(2): 231–280.

Labán, Raúl and Felipe Larraín (2000) "Can a Liberalization of Capital Outflows Increase Net Capital Inflows?", in: Felipe Larraín, ed., *Capital Flows, Capital Controls, and Currency Crises: Latin America in the 1990s.* Ann Arbor: University of Michigan Press, pp. 19–37.

Lake, David A. (2004) "International Political Economy: A Maturing Interdiscipline", in: Barry R. Weingast and Donald Wittman, eds., *The Oxford Handbook of Political Economy*, Oxford: Oxford University Press, pp. 757–776.

Lal, Deepak (2001) "The Development and Spread of Economic Norms and Incentives", in: Richard N. Rosecrance, ed., *The New Great Power Coalition*, Lanham: MD: Rowman & Littlefield, pp. 237–259.

Lane, Philip R. and Gian Maria Milesi-Ferretti (2007) "The external wealth of nations mark II: Revised and extended estimates of foreign assets and liabilities, 1970–2004". *Journal of International Economics* 73(2): 223–250.

Larraín, Felipe (2000) "Capital Flows, Capital Controls, and Currency Crises in Latin America", in: Felipe Larraín, ed., *Capital Flows, Capital Controls, and Currency Crises: Latin America in the 1990s.* Ann Arbor: University of Michigan Press, pp. 1–18.

Latinobarómetro (2009) *Informe 2009.* Santiago de Chile: Corporación Latinobarómetro.

Leal Buitrago and Andrés Dávila Ladrón de Guevara (2009) *Clientelismo: el sistema político y su expresión regional.* 3a ed., Bogotá: Universidad de los Andes.

Leblang, David A. (1997) "Domestic and Systematic Determinants of Capital Controls in the Developed and Developing World". *International Studies Quarterly* 41(3): 435–454

Leblang, David A. (1999) "Domestic Political Institutions and Exchange Rate Commitments in the Developing World". *International Studies Quarterly* 43(4): 599–620.

Ledesma, Patricia (2001) The Peruvian Experience with Financial Liberalization, 1990–1999. Paper presented at the 2001 meeting of the Latin American Studies Association, Washington D. C., September 6–8.

Leiteritz, Ralf J. (2005) "Explaining organizational outcomes: the International Monetary Fund and capital account liberalization". *Journal of International Relations and Development* 8(1): 1–26.

Leiteritz, Ralf and Manuela Moschella (2010) "The International Monetary Fund and Capital Account Liberalization: A Case of Failed Norm Institutionalization", in: Susan Park and Antje Vetterlein, eds., *Owning Development: Creating Policy Norms in the IMF and the World Bank.* Cambridge: Cambridge University Press, pp. 163–180.

Li, Quan and Dale Smith (2002) "The Dilemma of Financial Liberalization: State Autonomy and Societal Demands". *Journal of Politics* 64(3): 764–790.

Lora, Eduardo (2005) "Dos pasos adelante y uno atrás: 35 años de reformas estructurales en Colombia". *Coyuntura Económica* 35(2): 41–48.

Losada, Rodrigo (2000) *Los Gremios Empresariales en Colombia en los Inicios del Siglo XXI.* Bogotá: Pontifica Universidad Javeriana.

Love, Joseph L. (2005) "The Rise and Fall of Structuralism", in: Valpy FitzGerald and Rosemary Thorp, eds., *Economic Doctrines in Latin America. Origins, Embedding and Evolution.* Houndmills: Palgrave, pp. 157–181.

Lukauskas, Arvid and Susan Minushkin (2000) "Explaining Styles of Financial Market Opening in Chile, Mexico, South Korea, and Turkey". *International Studies Quarterly* 44(4): 695–723.

MacKenzie, Donald, Fabian Muniesa, and Lucia Siu (2007), eds., *Do Economists Make Markets? On the Performativity of Economics.* Princeton: Princeton University Press.

Madrid, Raúl L. (2005) "Ideas, Economic Pressures, and Pension Privatization". *Latin American Politics and Society* 47(2): 23–50.

Magud, Nicolas and Carmen M. Reinhart (2007) "Capital Controls: An Evaluation", in: Sebastian Edwards, ed., *Capital Controls and Capital Flows in Emerging Economies: Policies, Practices, and Consequences.* Chicago and London: University of Chicago Press, pp. 645–674.

Mahon, James E., Jr. (1996) *Mobile Capital and Latin American Development.* University Park: Pennsylvania State University Press.

Mahoney, James, Kendra Koivu, and Erin Kimball (2009) "The Logic of Historical Explanation in the Social Sciences". *Comparative Political Studies* 42(1): 114–146.

Manzetti, Luigi (1999) *Privatization South American Style.* Oxford: Oxford University Press.

March, James G. and Johan P. Olsen (1989) *Rediscovering Institutions: The Organizational Basis of Politics.* New York: The Free Press.

March, James G. and Johan P. Olsen (1999) "The Institutional Dynamics of International Political Orders", in: Peter J. Katzenstein, Robert O. Keohane, and Stephen D. Krasner, eds., *Exploration and Contestation in the Study of World Politics.* Cambridge; MA and London: MIT Press, pp. 303–329.

March, James G. and Johan P. Olsen (2006) "Elaborating the 'New Institutionalism'", in: R.A.W. Rhodes, Sarah A. Binder, and Bert A. Rockman, eds., *The Oxford Handbook of Political Institiitions.* Oxford: Oxford University Press, pp. 3–20.

Markoff, John and Verónica Montecinos (1993) "The Ubiquitous Rise of Economists". *Journal of Public Policy* 13(1): 37–68.

Mauceri, Philip (1997) "Return of the Caudillo: Autocratic Democracy in Peru". *Third World Quarterly* 18(5): 889–911.

McNamara, Kathleen R. (1998) *The Currency of Ideas: Monetary Policy in the European Union.* Ithaca and London: Cornell University Press.

Meisel, Adolfo (1996) *Why No Hyperinflation in Colombia? On the Determinants of Stable Economic Policies.* Borradores Semanales de Economía No. 54, Bogotá: Banco de la República.

Meseguer, Covadonga (2009) *Learning, Policy Making, and Market Reforms.* Cambridge: Cambridge University Press.

Meyer, John W. and Brian Rowan (1977) "Institutionalized Organizations: Formal Structure as Myth and Ceremony". *American Journal of Sociology* 83(2): 340–363.

Meyer, John W., John Boli, George M. Thomas, and Francisco O. Ramirez (1997) "World Society and the Nation-State". *American Journal of Sociology* 103(1): 144–181.

Milner, Helen V. (2002) "International Trade", in: Walter Carlsnaes, Thomas Risse, and Beth A. Simmons, eds., *Handbook of International Relations*. London: SAGE, pp. 448–461.

Miniane, Jacques (2004) "A New Set of Measures on Capital Account Restrictions', *IMF Staff Papers* 51(2): 276–308.

Mirowski, Philip and Dieter Plehwe (2009), eds., *The Road from Mont Pèlerin. The Making of the Neoliberal Thought Collective*. Cambridge, MA: Harvard University Press.

Mishkin, Frederic S. (2006) *The Next Great Globalization: How Disadvantaged Nations can Harness their Financial Systems to Get Rich*. Princeton: Princeton University Press.

Mishkin, Frederic S. (2009) "Why We Shouldn't Turn Our Backs on Financial Globalization". *IMF Staff Papers* 56(1): 139–170.

Montecinos, Verónica (1997) "Economists in Political and Policy Elites in Latin America", in: A.W. Coats, ed., *The Post-1945 Internationalization of Economics*. Durham: Duke University Press, pp. 279–300.

Montecinos, Verónica and John Markoff (2010), eds., *Economists in the Americas*. Cheltenham: Edward Elgar.

Montenegro, Armando (1990) "La Reforma del Estatuto Cambiario", in: Florangela Gomez Ordoñez, ed., *Apertura económica y sistema financiero*. Compilación de los documentos presentados en el XII simposio sobre mercado de capitales, Bogotá: Asociación Bancaria de Colombia, pp. 352–380.

Morón, Eduardo and Cynthia Sanborn (2006) *The Pitfalls of Policymaking in Peru: Actors, Institutions and Rules of the Game*. Research Network Working Paper R-511. Washington: Inter-American Development Bank.

Morris, Felipe (2000) "La reforma del sistema financiero", in: Roberto Abusada, Fritz Du Bois, Eduardo Morón, and José Valderrama, eds., *La reforma incompleta: rescatando los noventa*. Vol. 1, Lima: Instituto Peruano de Economía, pp. 313–342.

Moschella, Manuela (2009) "When Ideas Fail to Influence Policy Outcomes: Orderly Liberalization and the International Monetary Fund". *Review of International Political Economy* 16(5): 854–882.

Moschella, Manuela (2010) *Governing Risk. The IMF and Global Financial Crises*. Basingstoke: Palgrave Macmillan.

Moschella, Manuela (2012) "Seeing Like the IMF on Capital Account Liberalisation". *New Political Economy* 17(1): 59–76.

Mosley, Layna (2003) *Global Capital and National Governments*. Cambridge: Cambridge University Press.

Mukherjee, Bumba and David Andrew Singer (2010) "International Institutions and Domestic Compensation: The IMF and the Politics of Capital Account Liberalization". *American Journal of Political Science* 54(1): 45–60.

Nelson, Joan M. (1990) "Introduction: The Politics of Economic Adjustment in Developing Nations", in: Joan M. Nelson, ed., *Economic Crisis and Policy Choice. The Politics of Adjustment in the Third World*. Princeton: Princeton University Press, pp. 3–32.

Nelson, Joan M. (1996) "Promoting Policy Reforms: The Twilight of Conditionality?" *World Development* 24(9): 1551–1559.

Nelson, Richard R., T. Paul Schultz, and Robert L. Slighton (1971) *Structural Change in a Developing Economy. Colombia's Problems and Prospects*. Princeton: Princeton University Press.

North, Douglas (1990) *Institutions, Institutional Change and Economic Performance*. Cambridge: Cambridge University Press.

Nye Jr., Joseph S. (2004) *Soft Power. The Means to Success in World Politics*. New York: PublicAffairs.

Obstfeld, Maurice (1998) "The Global Capital Market: Benefactor or Menace?". *Journal of Economic Perspectives* 12(4): 9–30.
Obstfeld, Maurice (2009) "International Finance and Growth in Developing Countries: What Have We Learned?". *IMF Staff Papers* 56(1): 63–111.
Ocampo, José Antonio and Camilo E. Tovar (2003) "La experiencia colombiana con los encajes a los flujos de capital". *Revista de la CEPAL* 81: 7–32.
Ocampo, José Antonio, Shari Spiegel, and Joseph E. Stiglitz (2008) "Introduction: Capital Market Liberalization and Development", in: José Antonio Ocampo and Joseph E. Stiglitz, eds., *Capital Market Liberalization and Development*. Oxford: Oxford University Press, pp. 1–48.
Odell, John S. (2002) "Bounded Rationality and the World Political Economy", in: David M. Andrews, C. Randall Henning, and Louis W. Pauly, eds., *Governing the World's Money*. Ithaca and London: Cornell University Press, pp. 168–193.
Offe, Claus and Helmut Wiesenthal (1980) "Two Logics of Collective Action: Theoretical Notes on Social Class and Organizational Form". *Political Power and Social Theory* 1(1): 67–115.
Ortega, Francisco J. (1987) "El Estatuto de Comercio Exterior y cambios internacionales", in: *Colombia. 20 años del régimen de cambios y de comercio exterior: Simposio*. Bogotá: Banco de la República, pp. 12–20.
Ortiz de Zevallos, Felipe (1989) *The Peruvian Puzzle*. New York: Priority Press.
Ostry, Jonathan D., Atish R. Gosh, Karl Habermeier, Marcos Chamon, Mahvash S. Qureshi, and Dennis B. S. Reinhardt (2010) Capital Inflows: The Role of Controls. IMF Staff Position Note SPN/10/04, February 19, Washington, D. C.; International Monetary Fund.
Palacios, Marco (1980) *Coffee in Colombia, 1850–1970. An Economic, Social and Political History*. Cambridge: Cambridge University Press.
Palacios, Marco (2005) "Knowledge is Power: The Case of Colombian Economists", in: Valpy FitzGerald and Rosemary Thorp, eds., *Economic Doctrines in Latin America. Origins, Embedding and Evolution*. Houndmills: Palgrave, pp. 182–216.
Palacios, Marco (2006) *Between Legitimacy and Violence: A History of Colombia, 1875–2002*. Durham: Duke University Press.
Palma, José Gabriel (2009) "Why did the Latin American critical tradition in the social sciences become practically extinct?", in: Mark Blyth, ed., *Routledge Handbook of International Political Economy (IPE). IPE as a Global Conversation*. Abingdon and New York: Routledge, pp. 243–265.
Park, Susan and Antje Vetterlein (2010), eds., *Owning Development: Creating Policy Norms in the IMF and the World Bank*. Cambridge: Cambridge University Press.
Parsons, Craig (2003) *A Certain Idea of Europe*. Ithaca and London: Cornell University Press.
Pascó-Font, Alberto and Piero Ghezzi (2001) "Exchanges Rates and Interest Groups in Peru, 1950–96", in: Jeffry Frieden and Ernesto Stein, eds., *The Currency Game. Exchange Rate Politics in Latin America*. Washington, D. C.: Inter-American Development Bank, pp. 249–277.
Pastor, Manuel A. and Carol Wise (1992) "Peruvian Economic Policy in the 1980s". *Latin American Research Review* 27(2): 83–117.
Payer, Cheryl (1969) *The Debt Trap: The International Monetary Fund and the Third World*. New York: Monthly Review Press.
Pepinsky, Thomas B. (2009) Openness without Liberalization: Why Bankers in Emerging Markets Support Financial Internationalization. Paper prepared for presentation at the Annual Conference of the International Political Economy Society, College Station TX, November 13–14.
Pepinsky, Thomas B. (2012) "Do Currency Crises Cause Capital Account Liberalization?". *International Studies Quarterly*.
Polanyi, Karl (1944) *The Great Transformation: The Political and Economic Origins of Our Time*. Boston: Beacon Press.

Pop-Eleches, Grigore (2009) *From Economic Crisis to Reform. IMF Programs in Latin America and Eastern Europe*. Princeton: Princeton University Press.

Prasad, Eswar S., Kenneth S. Rogoff, Shang-Jin Wei, and M. Ayhan Kose (2003) Effects of Financial Globalization on Developing Countries: Some Empirical Evidence, IMF Occasional Paper No. 220. Washington, D. C.: International Monetary Fund.

Prasad, Eswar S., Raghuram Rajan, and Arvind Subramanian (2007) "Foreign Capital and Economic Growth". *Brookings Papers on Economic Activity* (1): 153–209.

Quinn, Dennis (1997) "The Correlates of Change in International Financial Regulation". *American Political Science Review* 91(3): 531–551.

Quinn, Dennis P. (2003) "Capital Account Liberalization and Financial Globalization, 1890–1999: A Synoptic View". *International Journal of Finance and Economics* 8(3): 189–204.

Quinn, Dennis P. and Clara Inclán (1997) "The Origins of Financial Openness: A Study of Current and Capital Account Liberalization". *American Journal of Political Science* 41(3): 771–813.

Quinn, Dennis P. and A. Maria Toyoda (2008) "Global ideology and voter sentiment as determinants of international financial liberalization", in: Beth A. Simmons, Frank Dobbin, and Geoffrey Garrett, eds., *The Global Diffusion of Markets and Democracy*. Cambridge: Cambridge University Press, pp. 173–219.

Quispe, Zenón (2000) "Monetary Policy in a Dollarised Economy: the Case of Peru", in: Lavan Mahadeva and Gabriel Sterne, eds., *Monetary Policy Frameworks in a Global Context*, London and New York: Routledge, pp. 330–353.

Reinhart, Carmen M. and Kenneth S. Rogoff (2004) "The Modern History of Exchange Rate Arrangements: A Reinterpretation". *Quarterly Journal of Economics* 119(1): 1–48.

Reisen, Helmut and Bernhard Fischer (1993) *Financial Opening: Policy Issues and Experiences in Developing Countries*. Paris: OECD Development Centre.

Remmer, Karen L. (1986) "The Politics of Economic Stabilization: IMF Standby Programs in Latin America, 1954–1984". *Comparative Politics* 19(1): 1–24.

Remmer, Karen L. (1998) "The Politics of Neoliberal Economic Reform in South America, 1980–1994". *Studies in Comparative International Development* 33(2): 3–29.

Rennhack, Robert and Masahiro Nozaki (2006) *Financial Dollarization in Latin America*. IMF Working Paper 06/7. Washington, D. C.: International Monetary Fund.

Restrepo, Juan Camilo (1991) "Las reformas al estatuto cambiario y la apertura", en: Hernán Beltz Peralta and Eduardo Lora, eds., *Apertura y modernización: las reformas de los noventa*. 2ª ed., Bogotá: Tercer Mundo and Fedesarrollo, pp. 83–111.

Rettberg, Angelika (2003) "Entre el Cielo y el Suelo: Una Mirada Crítica a los Gremios Colombianos", in: Ann C. Mason and Luis Javier Orjuela, eds., *La Crisis Política Colombiana. Más que un Conflicto Armado y un Proceso de Paz*. Bogotá: Universidad de los Andes 2003, pp. 253–267.

Rettberg, Angelika (2006) "Tras la Tormenta Viene.... Otra Tormenta: Empresarios, Reestructuración y Conflicto Armado en Colombia", en: Francisco Leal Buitrago, ed., *En la Encrucijada. Colombia en el Siglo XXI*. Bogotá: Norma 2006, pp. 207–232.

Revéiz, Edgar (1997) *El Estado como Mercado: La Gobernabilidad Económica y Política en Colombia antes y después de 1991*. Bogotá: Fonade, Carlos Valencia Editores.

Rincón, Hernán and Leonardo Villar (2003) "Capital flows and foreign exchange regimes in the Colombian Economy", in: Albert Berry, ed., *Critical Issues in Financial Reform: A View from the South*. Transaction Publishers: New Brunswick, N. J. and London.

Risse, Thomas, Stephen C. Ropp, and Kathryn Sikkink (1999), eds., *The Power of Human Rights: International Norms and Domestic Change*. Cambridge: Cambridge University Press.

Rodríguez, Octavio (2006) *El estructuralismo latinoamericano*. México, D. F.: Siglo XXI.

Rodríguez, Martha, José Valderrama, and Julio Velarde (2000) "El programa de estabilización", in: Roberto Abusada, Fritz Du Bois, Eduardo Morón, and José Valderrama, eds., *La Reforma Incompleta: Rescatando los Noventa.* Lima: Universidad del Pacífico and Instituto Peruano de Economía, pp. 91–119.

Rodrik, Dani (1996) "Understanding Economic Policy Reform". *Journal of Economic Literature* 34(1): 9–41.

Rodrik, Dani (1997) *Has Globalization Gone Too Far?.* Washington, DC: Institute for International Economics.

Rodrik, Dani (1998) "Who Needs Capital Account Convertibility?", in: Stanley Fischer et al., *Should the IMF pursue capital account convertibility*? Princeton Essays in International Finance No. 207, Princeton, NJ: International Finance Section, Department of Economics, Princeton University, pp. 55–65.

Rodrik, Dani and Arvind Subramanian (2009) "Why Did Financial Globalization Disappoint?". *IMF Staff Papers* 56(1): 112–138.

Rossini, Renzo G. and Carlos E. Paredes (1991) "Foreign Trade Policy", in: Carlos E. Paredes and Jeffrey D. Sachs, eds., *Peru's Path to Recovery: A Plan for Economic Stabilization and Growth.* Washington, D. C.: Brookings Institution, pp. 275–298.

Rueschemeyer, Dietrich (2006) "Why and How Ideas Matter", in: Robert E. Goodin and Charles Tilly, eds., *The Oxford Handbook of Contextual Political Analysis.* Oxford: Oxford University Press, pp. 227–251.

Ruggie, John Gerard (1983) "International Regimes, Transactions, and Change: Embedded Liberalism in the Postwar Economic Order", in: Stephen D. Krasner, ed., *International Regimes.* Ithaca and London: Cornell University Press, pp. 195–231.

Safford, Frank (1976) *The Ideal of the Practical: Colombia's Struggle to Form a Technical Elite.* Austin: University of Texas Press.

Safford, Frank and Marco Palacios (2001) *Colombia: Fragmented Land, Divided Society.* Oxford: Oxford University Press.

Savastano, Miguel A. (1996) *Dollarization in Latin America: Recent Evidence and Some Policy Issues.* IMF Working Paper 96/4. Washington, D. C.: International Monetary Fund.

Schamis, Hector E. (1999) "Distributional Coalitions and the Politics of Economic Reform in Latin America". *World Politics* 51(2): 236–268.

Schimmelfenning, Frank (2003) "Internationale Sozialisation: Von einem 'erschöpften' zu einem produktiven Forschungsprogramm?", in: Gunther Hellmann, Klaus Dieter Wolf, and Michael Zürn, eds., *Die neuen Internationalen Beziehungen. Forschungsstand und Perspektiven in Deutschland.* Nomos: Baden-Baden, pp. 401–427.

Schindler, Martin (2009) "Measuring Financial Integration: A New Data Set". *IMF Staff Papers* 56(1): 222–238.

Schmidt, Vivien A. (2008) "Discursive Institutionalism: The Explanatory Power of Ideas and Discourse". *Annual Review of Political Science* 11: 303–326.

Schmidt, Vivien A. (2010) "Taking ideas and discourse seriously: explaining change through discursive institutionalism as the fourth 'new institutionalism'". *European Political Science Review* 2(1): 1–25.

Schneider, Ben Ross (2004) *Business Politics and the State in Twentieth-Century Latin America.* Cambridge: Cambridge University Press.

Schneider, Ben Ross (2010) "Business Politics in Latin America: Patterns of Fragmentation and Centralization", in: David Coen, Wyn Grant, and Graham Wilson, eds., *The Oxford Handbook of Business and Government.* Oxford: Oxford University Press, pp. 307–329.

Schonhardt-Bailey, Cheryl (2006) *From the Corn Laws to Free Trade. Interests, Ideas, and Institutions in Historical Perspective*. Cambridge, MA and London: MIT Press.

Scott, James C. (1998) *Seeing Like a State: How Certain Schemes to Improve the Human Condition Have Failed*. New Haven and London: Yale University Press.

Seabrooke, Leonard (2006) *The Social Sources of Financial Power: Domestic Legitimacy and International Financial Orders*. Ithaca: Cornell University Press.

Searle, John R. (1995) *The Construction of Social Reality*. New York: Free Press.

Sheahan, John (1994) "Peru's Return Toward an Open Economy: Macroeconomic Complications and Structural Questions". *World Development* 22(6): 911–923.

Sheahan, John (2006) "Redirection of Peruvian Economic Strategy in the 1990s: Gains, Losses, and Clues for the Future", in: Julio Carrión, ed., *The Fujimori Legacy: The Rise of Electoral Authoritarianism in Peru*, pp. 178–200.

Shepsle, Kenneth A. (2006) "Rational Choice Institutionalism", in: R.A.W. Rhodes, Sarah A. Binder, and Bert A. Rockman, eds., *The Oxford Handbook of Political Institutions*. Oxford: Oxford University Press, pp. 23–38.

Sikkink, Kathryn (1991), *Ideas and Institutions. Developmentalism in Brazil and Argentina*. Ithaca and London: Cornell University Press.

Sil, Rudra and Peter J. Katzenstein (2010a) "Analytic Eclecticism in the Study of World Politics". *Perspectives on Politics* 8(2): 411–431.

Sil, Rudra and Peter J. Katzenstein (2010b) *Beyond Paradigms: Analytic Eclecticism in the Study of World Politics*. London: Palgrave Macmillan.

Sil, Rudra and Peter J. Katzenstein (2010c) "Analytic Eclecticism: Not Perfect, but Indispensable". *Qualitative & Multi-Method Research: Newsletter of the American Political Science Association Organized Section for Qualitative and Multi-Method Research* 8(2): 19–24.

Silva, Eduardo (1998) *The State and Capital in Chile: Business Elites, Technocrats, and Market Economics*. Boulder: Westview Press.

Silva, Patricio (1991) "Technocrats and Politics in Chile: From the Chicago Boys to the CIEPLAN Monks". *Journal of Latin American Studies* 23(2): 385–410.

Silva, Patricio (2008) *In the Name of Reason. Technocrats and Politics in Chile*. University Park: Pennsylvania State University Press.

Simmons, Beth A. and Zachary Elkins (2004) "The Globalization of Liberalization: Policy Diffusion in the International Political Economy". *American Political Science Review* 98(1): 171–189.

Simmons, Beth A., Frank Dobbin, and Geoffrey Garrett (2008) "Introduction: the diffusion of liberalization", in: Beth A. Simmons, Frank Dobbin, and Geoffrey Garrett, eds., *The Global Diffusion of Markets and Democracy*. Cambridge: Cambridge University Press, pp. 1–63.

Smelser, Neil J. and Richard Swedberg (2005), eds., *The Handbook of Economic Sociology*, 2nd ed., Princeton: Princeton University Press.

Stallings, Barbara (1990) "Politics and Economic Crisis: A Comparative Study of Chile, Peru, and Colombia", in: Joan M. Nelson, ed., *Economic Crisis and Policy Choice. The Politics of Adjustment in the Third World*. Princeton: Princeton University Press, pp. 113–167.

Stallings, Barbara (1992) "International Influence on Economic Policy: Debt, Stabilization, and Structural Reform", in: Stephan Haggard and Robert R. Kaufman, eds., *The Politics of Economic Adjustment. International Constraints, Distributive Conflicts, and the State*. Princeton: Princeton University Press, pp. 41–88.

Stiglitz, Joseph E. (2000) "Capital Market Liberalization, Economic Growth, and Instability". *World Development* 28(6): 1075–1086.

Stiglitz, Joseph E. (2002) *Globalization and Its Discontents*. New York and London: W.W. Norton 2002.

Stiglitz, Joseph E. (2004) "Capital-market Liberalization, Globalization, and the IMF". *Oxford Review of Economic Policy* 20(1): 57–71.

Stokes, Susan C. (1997) "Democratic Accountability and Policy Change: Economic Policy in Fujimori's Peru". *Comparative Politics* 29(2): 209–226.

Stone, Diane (2004) "Transfer agents and global networks in the 'transnationalization' of policy". *Journal of European Public Policy* 11(3): 545–566.

Stone, Randall W. (2002) *Lending Credibility. The International Monetary Fund and the Post-Communist Transition*. Princeton: Princeton University Press.

Stone, Randall W. (2008) "The Scope of IMF Conditionality". *International Organization* 62(4): 589–620.

Strange, Susan (1996) *The Retreat of the State: The Diffusion of Power in the World Economy*. Cambridge: Cambridge University Press.

Summers, Lawrence H. (1998) Remarks before the International Monetary Fund, US Treasury Press Release RR-2286, Washington D.C.

Summers, Lawrence (2000) "Introductory Remarks". *The Brookings-Wharton Papers on Financial Services* 2000: 1–9.

Tanaka, Martín (2003) "The Political Constraints on Market Reforms in Peru", in: Carol Wise and Riordan Roett, eds., *Post-Stabilization Politics in Latin America. Competition, Transition, Collapse*. Washington, D.C.: Brookings Institution, pp. 221–248.

Tarrow, Sidney (2010) "The Strategy of Paired Comparison: Toward of Theory of Practice". *Comparative Political Studies* 43(2): 230–259.

Teichman, Judith A. (2001) *The Politics of Freeing Markets in Latin America: Chile, Argentina, and Mexico*. Chapel Hill: University of North Carolina Press.

Teichman, Judith (2004) "The World Bank and Policy Reform in Mexico and Argentina". *Latin American Politics and Society* 46(1): 39–74.

Thorp, Rosemary (1991) *Economic Management and Economic Development in Peru and Colombia*. Houndmills: Macmillan.

Thorp, Rosemary and Francisco Durand (1997) "A Historical View of Business-State Relations: Colombia, Peru, and Venezuela Compared", in: Sylvia Maxfield and Ben Ross-Schneider, eds., *Business and the State in Developing Countries*. Ithaca and London: Cornell University Press, pp. 216–236.

Treisman, Daniel (2004) "Stabilization Tactics in Latin America: Menem, Cardoso, and the Politics of Low Inflation". *Comparative Politics* 36(4): 399–419.

Urrutia, Miguel (1983) *Gremios, Política Económica y Democracia*. Bogotá: Fedesarrollo.

Urrutia, Miguel (1991) "On the Absence of Economic Populism in Colombia", in: Rüdiger Dornbusch and Sebastian Edwards, eds., *The Macroeconomics of Populism in Latin America*. Chicago and London: University of Chicago Press, pp. 369–386.

Urrutia, Miguel (1994) "Colombia", in: John Williamson, ed., *The Political Economy of Policy Reform*. Washington, DC: Institute for International Economics, pp. 285–315.

Urrutia, Miguel (2002) *Una Visión Alternativa: La Política Monetaria y Cambiaria en la Última Década*. Borradores de Economía No. 207. Bogotá: Banco de la República.

Valdés, Juan Gabriel (1995) *Pinochet's Economists: The Chicago School of Economics in Chile*. Cambridge: Cambridge University Press.

Van Evera, Stephen (1997) *Guide to Methods for Students of Political Science*. Ithaca and London: Cornell University Press.

Villar, Leonardo, David M. Salamanca, and Andrés Murcia Pabón (2005) "Crédito, represión financiera y flujos de capitales en Colombia, 1974–2003". *Desarrollo y Sociedad* 55: 167–209.

Vreeland, James Raymond (2003) *The IMF and Economic Development*. Cambridge: Cambridge University Press.

Vreeland, James R. (2006) "IMF program compliance: Aggregate index versus policy specific research strategies". *Review of International Organizations* 1(4): 359–378.

Wade, Robert (2001a) "The US role in the long Asian crisis of 1990–2000" in: Arvid J. Lukauskas and Francisco L. Rivera-Batiz, eds., *The Political Economy of the East Asian Crisis and Its Aftermath: Tigers in Distress*. Northampton, MA and Cheltenham: Edward Elgar, pp. 195–226.

Wade, Robert (2001b) "Capital and Revenge: The IMF and Ethiopia". *Challenge* 44(5): 67–75.

Walter, Andrew (2005) "Understanding Financial Globalization in International Political Economy", in: Nicola Phillips, ed., *Globalizing International Political Economy*. Basingstoke: Palgrave, pp. 141–164.

Waltz, Kenneth N. (1959), *Man, the State, and War: A theoretical analysis*. New York: Columbia University Press.

Webb, Richard (1994) "Peru", in: John Williamson, ed., *The Political Economy of Policy Reforms*. Washington, D. C.: Institute for International Economics, pp. 355–375.

Wedel, Janine R. (2009) *Shadow Elite: How the World's New Power Brokers Undermine Democracy, Government, and the Free Market*. New York: Basic Books.

Wendt, Alexander (1994) "Collective Identity Formation and the International State". *American Political Science Review* 88(2): 384–396.

Wendt, Alexander (1998) "On Constitution and Causation in International Relations". *Review of International Studies* 24(5): 101–118.

Wendt, Alexander (1999) *Social Theory of International Politics*. Cambridge: Cambridge University Press.

Weyland, Kurt (2002a) *The Politics of Market Reform in Fragile Democracies: Argentina, Brazil, Peru, and Venezuela*. Princeton: Princeton University Press.

Weyland, Kurt (2002b) "Limitations of Rational-Choice Institutionalism for the Study of Latin American Politics". *Studies in Comparative International Development* 37(1): 57–85.

Weyland, Kurt (2007) *Bounded Rationality and Policy Diffusion: Social Sector Reform in Latin America*. Princeton: Princeton University Press.

Weyland, Kurt (2008) "Toward of New Theory of Institutional Change". *World Politics* 60(2): 281–314.

Widmaier, Wesley W. (2004) "The Social Construction of the 'Impossible Trinity': The Intersubjective Bases of Monetary Cooperation". *International Studies Quarterly* 48(2): 433–453.

Widmaier, Wesley W., Mark Blyth, and Leonard Seabrooke (2007) "Exogenous Shocks or Endogenous Constructions? The Meanings of Wars and Crises". *International Studies Quarterly* 51(4): 747–759.

Williams, Marc Eric (2002) "Market Reforms, Technocrats, and Institutional Innovation". *World Development* 30(3): 395–412.

Williamson, John (1990), ed., *Latin American adjustment: has much has happened?*. Washington: Institute for International Economics.

Williamson, John (2003) "Appendix: Our Agenda and the Washington Consensus", in: Pedro-Pablo Kuczynski and John Williamson, eds., *After the Washington Consensus. Restarting Growth and Reform in Latin America*. Washington, D. C.: Institute for International Economics, pp. 323–331.

Williamson, John and Stephan Haggard (1994) "The Political Conditions for Economic Reform", in: John Williamson, ed., *The Political Economy of Policy Reform*. Washington, DC: Institute for International Economics, pp. 527–596.

Williamson, John and Molly Mahar (1998) A Survey of Financial Liberalization, Essays in International Finance, Department of Economics, Princeton University, No. 211.

Wise, Carol (2003) *Reinventing the State. Economic Strategy and Institutional Change in Peru*. Ann Arbor: University of Michigan Press.

Woods, Ngaire (2005) "The Bretton Woods Institutions and the Transmission of Neo-liberal Ideas in Mexico", in: Valpy FitzGerald and Rosemary Thorp, eds., *Economic Doctrines in Latin America. Origins, Embedding and Evolution.* Houndmills: Palgrave, pp. 217–244.

Woods, Ngaire (2006) *The Globalizers. The IMF, the World Bank, and Their Borrowers.* Ithaca and London: Cornell University Press.

Yee, Albert S. (1996) "The Causal Effect of Ideas on Policies". *International Organization* 50(1): 69–108.

www.ingramcontent.com/pod-product-compliance
Lightning Source LLC
Chambersburg PA
CBHW061214240926
51846CB00006B/1222
9783531185286